Harnessing
Globalization
A Review of East Asian Case Histories

HARNESSING GLOBALIZATION
A REVIEW OF EAST ASIAN CASE HISTORIES

HENRY Y WAN, JR
Cornell University, USA

 **World Scientific**

NEW JERSEY · LONDON · SINGAPORE · BEIJING · SHANGHAI · HONG KONG · TAIPEI · CHENNAI

Published by

World Scientific Publishing Co. Pte. Ltd.

5 Toh Tuck Link, Singapore 596224

USA office: 27 Warren Street, Suite 401-402, Hackensack, NJ 07601

UK office: 57 Shelton Street, Covent Garden, London WC2H 9HE

Library of Congress Cataloging-in-Publication Data
Wan, Henry Y.
  Harnessing globalization : a review of East Asian case histories / Henry Y. Wan.
    p. cm.
  Includes bibliographical references.
  ISBN-13 978-981-256-709-3 (alk. paper)
  ISBN-10 981-256-709-7 (alk. paper)

                                                                    2006045786

British Library Cataloguing-in-Publication Data
A catalogue record for this book is available from the British Library.

First published 2006 (Hardcover)
Reprinted 2016 (in paperback edition)
ISBN 978-981-3203-24-2

Printed in Singapore

For Simone

Contents

Preface

Globalization continues to be a vortex of vigorous debate in chancelleries, academia and mass meetings. There is no denying, however, that those East Asian economies which enjoyed the most stunning advances would never have done so in isolation.

This compact volume tries to review the highlights of the East Asian episodes: how globalization is harnessed. Interaction with the technologically advanced societies forms the shared theme. Through trade investment and the movement of people comes the movement of ideas, including technology and information. Japan emerged as the world's second largest economy by this channel. Korea, Taiwan, Hong Kong and Singapore proved that the Japanese record is no fluke. Now by similar means, China has become the workshop of the world. Intra-East Asian transaction bloomed. The early mover transforms the late comer and becomes transformed in return. It has been so between Japan and the rest of East Asia, China included. It is so between all the rest of East Asia, Japan included, and China. Together, the progress made has been larger in East Asia than in West Europe, in the 60 years after World War II.

The story seems well known, but actually not quite. Often times the statistics are presented without the analysis, so that the mechanism remains obscure. Or, theories are advanced, without fully accounting for some crucial facts, which are well known to observers but not in a statistical form which can be formally tested. Or, as a matter of intellectual exchange, the profession rightfully encourages the presentation of stimulating contrarian views, notwithstanding that they might not cover the whole truth. In particular, for East Asian growth, technology acquisition is often a by-product of other transactions such as export trade on the subcontract basis, and adequate analytic treatment is scarce. For these reasons, I have focused my professional attention on this area for the last decade and a half, using conventional tools when possible, parting company with conventional wisdom if necessary and striking out for the less trodden paths as the situation demands.

This volume is part of a larger research program. It includes fifteen papers, selected not only because they cover highlights of the East Asian story, but also because they offer a cogent narrative when taken together. In contrast to material from a monograph, these papers appeared originally as articles for journals and collected volumes for conference proceedings. By nature, they are more densely written, and section by section, the content has passed through more intense attention under peer review process, and benefited more from comments and criticisms by conference participants.

The matching brief notes specially prepared for this volume then round up the picture and supply the context as well as the updated development. On the other hand, in the East Asian saga, where the product cycle first went from Japan to the four "Newly Industrialized Economies" of Korea, Taiwan, Hong Kong and Singapore, and next from these four to Mainland China, an extensive scrutiny of those four economies would also present matters from additional angles. In that regard, readers are encouraged to consult my monograph, *Economic Development in a Globalized Environment, East Asian Evidences* (Kluwer 2004 and Springer 2005, in paperback).

Most of the material I present here originated from two undergraduate courses I taught at Cornell, with some having benefited from the term reports presented by participants in the courses. Later they often were presented in conferences and received critical comments from fellow participants. As a staff at Cornell and a corresponding researcher at the Institute of Economics, Academia Sinica, I also enjoyed stimulating discussions with colleagues in both places. Furthermore, many chapters here are joint projects, and my co-authors have gracefully allowed me to publish them in this volume. As my fellow graduate student and then as my spouse for the last 40 years, Simone Clemhout has been offering me encouragement and comments. While I claim sole propriety to all the imperfections of this volume, I owe all of the above my heart-felt thanks. To my Cornell secretary, Paulette Carlisle, I appreciate her effort in typing many of the essays at one stage or another. To Juliet Lee at World Scientific Publishing and Imperial College Press, I am grateful for her professional support.

Henry Y. Wan, Jr.
March 2006

PART I

Harnessing Globalization — How has East Asia Done it

The Pre-Conditions: East Asia Missed Out in Launching the Industrial Revolution

Review of "A Note on Knowledge Capital and the Needham Paradox"[*]

The puzzle This is my attempt to resolve the popular puzzle: Why did the Industrial Revolution happen only in Britain during the 18th Century, and not much earlier in China of the Sung dynasty, notwithstanding the brilliance of the Chinese technology? The same question has been asked independently by other researchers, especially Lin, J. Y. (1995). The explanation of Lin is that technical progress went on by experience in ancient China, but by systematic experiment (cum science) in Europe. In the end, Europe outdistanced China in technology. My explanation is in a sense complementary to Lin's experience-versus-experiment view, but with a somewhat different emphasis: institutions.

To pinpoint the relevant institutional issues, my approach differs from the rest of literature in two ways. First, the focus is not so much why China missed out the launching of *the* Industrialization, perhaps in a bilateral Sino-British comparison. Instead, one asks the broader question: What favorable conditions single out Britain among all others (China included) as the site for *the* Industrial Revolution? Second, turning reality on its head, one poses the counter-factual question: If the historical James Watt (a prime mover of *the* Industrial Revolution) were in China, at birth, as well as at various other stages of his life, could he have invented his steam engine or gotten it accepted?

The role of institutions It is maintained here that, other things being equal, the Industrial Revolution is the result of the accumulation of technical development. The Watt steam engine was an improvement on a sequence of its predecessors. The net rate of accumulation is the difference between the mean rate of new inventions in excess of the rate of loss. The former increases with the current stock of knowledge, and the latter is proportional to it. The presence of such *institutions* as universities of the Western European type provides a favorable matrix for invention. It also reduces the chance for loss. Watt was a repairman receiving much assistance from the teaching staff at the University of Glasgow.

---

[*]The article is reprinted from the *International Economic Journal*, Vol. 2, No. 1, pp. 101–108, 1988, published by Routledge (part of the Taylor & Francis Group).

University archives preserve the received wisdom from classical times. Further, the patent law of Britain in Watt's time stimulates inventors to pursue their inventive activity. It takes good institutions for a society to accumulate enough knowledge to break out into continued progress, instead of to stumble back into a pre-Industrial Revolution stable equilibrium. Watt would be most welcome in China when he brought along his engine, already invented. But under the Chinese institutions then in place, he could not invent his engine in China. As it was, Watt quit invention to be a surveyor, until the renewal of his patent brought along venture capital.

Relationship to different explanations My discussion is complementary to some explanations of others, especially the "experience-versus-experiments" explanation by Lin. Chinese learning-by-doing yields experience at negligible cost. But more lasting European gains require costly, systematic experiments which only the institutionalized protection of intellectual property rights (IPR) can summon forth. Sources for the Article state that Watt's backer, Boulton, financed Watt to perfect his invention only when the latter's patent got renewed by the Parliament. The explanation here is in terms of "Britain against the world". But in its application to the case of "Britain against China", the comparison of situations *with* and *without* the IPR protection dovetails well with the "experiments-versus-experience" explanation. It is a lesson still relevant today.

A related recent study is by Mokyr (2000) about how the Netherlands missed out on launching the Industrial Revolution, which also deals with institutional matters. The closeness of natural philosophers, engineers and entrepreneurs in Britain (and its absence in the Netherlands) was viewed as the key. Certainly in Confucian China, such closeness was unthinkable. This was mentioned in my original Article, even though not in a crystalized form.

ACADEMIA ECONOMIC PAPERS

23 : 2 (August 1995), 1–24

A NOTE ON KNOWLEDGE CAPITAL AND THE NEEDHAM PARADOX

Henry Y. Wan, Jr.*

ABSTRACT

Sung China led the West in science and technology, but Industrial Revolution came to Britain, centuries later. Historians and economists offer various explanations, but no consensus. This issue is relevant to endogenous growth theory, concerning the process of producing and using knowledge through R. & D.

We compare the experiences of Britain, China, France and Japan, asking what enabled Watt to introduce his steam engine and whether he could succeed in China. Evidences highlight the environment for R. & D. Universities in post-Renaissance Europe gave European inventors better insights and efficacy than East Asians. Thus, Japan, though free from nomadic occupation or harmful imperial examinations suffered by China, did not industrialize ahead of Britain. Intellectual property rights also matter. The British patent system of 1624 promoted product development and its eventual spread; French inventions could not be developed for market; much Chinese trade secret was lost throughout history.

Watt's engine would drain Chinese mines well like the British mines. Land/labor ratio and wage level did not block Chinese from inventing.

---

* Research Fellow, The Institute of Economics, Academia Sinica.

1.   INTRODUCTION

It is my honor to contribute an essay for the 80th birthday of Professor M. H. Hsing. As an assistant at the NTWU in the 50s, I sat in Professor Hsing's lectures on national income accounting and the input-output systems. When I returned to Taipei 10 years later, I observed with admiration when Professor Hsing set the tune of research for the Institute of Economics, Academia Sinica as its founding director. With my interest turning to the East Asian growth, I relied upon the early national income series for Hong Kong, developed under Professor Hsing's personal leadership. On my visits to Professor Hsing in Taiwan, each time I became awed with his persistent interest with basic conceptual issues in economics. Everything he does is focused at the fundamentals. Those of us familiar with the heritage of Simon Kuznets can readily discern a similar spirit in Professor Hsing's teaching and work.

In economics today, we all specialize. My usual work does not involve the fundamental questions. Yet, we all give thoughts to some of those challenging issues, like the Needham Paradox. It is altogether proper to write on such a topic to honor Professor Hsing.

After documenting the achievements of Chinese science and technology, and their impact on the West, Joseph Needham (1981) questioned why did not Industrial Revolution come to China first.

This is a subject in Chinese economic history, a field I have never worked in. Yet it is also a question concerning technology change and economic growth, over which I have studied for at least 30 years. I do not claim that I can offer definitive explanations, yet it should not be inappropriate for me to raise questions. After all, economic historians do not write economic history for economic historians only. Nor has the discussion of issues in economic history ever been limited to full time economic historians. This short essay is written in that spirit.

In the ensuing section, I shall present the advantage of framing the question in terms of endogenous growth. Next comes a brief review of the extant arguments over the Needham Paradox. Following that is a growth-theoretic appraisal of the discovery of steam engine of James Watt. We then return to the context of Chinese economic history, raising issues as we go along. Finally we offer tentative comments concerning the direction of the theory of endogenous growth.

2.   A CASE FOR A GROWTH THEORETIC APPROACH

At the heart of the Needham Paradox is the event of Industrial Revolution: why did it not come to China first. As Hughes (1970) noted, by convention, historical Industrial Revolution arrived in the "seventy British years" of 1760-1830, spearheaded by the steam engine of James Watt and followed with an explosive expansion of industrial knowledge. Watt has a *homo economicus* incarnate, working purposefully on engine design, not for curiosity but for profit.

As of today, there is no consensus about why not there any "Chinese Watt" before Watt. A new approach with new concepts seems to be justified for the old problem. In the theory of endogenous growth [Shell (1966), Romer (1986) and Lucas (1988)], knowledge is the growth engine, accumulated by purposeful actions and providing spill-over benefits. In such a perspective, would-be "Chinese Watt's" must have been thwarted for lacking the critical capability, or dissuaded from innovative intentions, or both. If 18th century British institutions were adequate, then inadequacies on the Chinese scene might be discovered by comparison. Thus, the growth-theoretic approach offers an agenda for research, if not ready made explanations.

The theory of endogenous growth is micro-based, specifying sequences of purposeful decisions taken by individuals with given means, wants, technology, information and beliefs, under particular rules of game. This suits well the well documented episode of Watt and his engines.

Addressing the Needham Paradox would be useful also for the theory of endogenous growth. At this moment, this theory of endogenous growth is long in analytic development but short in empirical applications. History shows that confronting facts is the best opportunity to improve theory, in economics no less than in natural science.

An inherent difficulty in testing endogenous growth theory is the coexistence of innovation and imitation in the cross-country, data base. Fast growth means either a rapid accumulation of knowledge capital, or the efficient use of others' knowledge. Disentangling these two is not easy. By Lau and Wan (1993), the sustained rapid growth in East Asia is mainly the result of knowledge spill-over, and not knowledge capital formation. At the time of Industrial Revolution, firms in Belgium could learn whatever was invented in Britain in 10 days [See Pollard (1985)]. Then as now, international information spill-over was rapid. The growth differential between Korea and the Philippines [Lucas (1993)] may lie in their difference in using foreign technology. Since no economy is an "island", the chance is scarce for testing the relative efficacy for knowledge accumulation. The Needham Paradox may present one of such rare occasions. To be sure, Needham himself documented the spill-overs from China to Europe. Yet, such interactions tend to be modest in those centuries when China was being overtaken by Europe.

We next review the literature on the Needham Paradox before applying our own approach.

3.   THE EXPLANATIONS OFFERED FOR THE NEEDHAM PARADOX

Many explanations have been offered for the Needham Paradox, Few, if any, is accepted as adequate in the literature by consensus. For example:

(1) Needham (1981) laid to rest that the traditional Chinese outlook *on time and chance* was detrimental to progress.

(2) Elvin (1973) disputed the *'low level equilibrium trap'* view of inadequacies in capital and market size.

(3) Elvin, ibid, further doubted that *government oppression* was a decisive factor.

(4) Finally, Elvin, successfully documented the fact that Chinese *firms* were not all *too short-lived* and *small-in-size* to sustain the Industrial Revolution.

(5)   Lin (1992) criticized Elvin's explanation of the *high level equilibrium trap* [modified by Chao (1986) and Tang (1979)], where a high labor density on land implies a subsistence wage rate and no incentive for (labor-saving) innovations. Lin showed that the labor-land ratio has fluctuated over time, so that Elgin could not be right, at all times.

(6)   Lin, ibid, claimed that the *non-scientific orientation* of the Chinese imperial examination caused the technological slowing down, when technology has become science-based.

(7)   Eberhard (1977) mentioned that *nomadic conquest* may also be a cause of technological stagnation.

Lin's explanation is ingenious itself but not entirely compelling. Chinese imperial examination may well be harmful to technological growth. But presumably Industrial Revolution would not arrive to China first, in any case. There appears to be other barriers. Medieval Japan had no imperial examination, but enjoyed access to most, if not all, Chinese inventions. All Chinese versions of T'ien Kung Kai Wu, the great technological encyclopedia by Sung Ying Hsing in 1637 were destroyed. Our present knowledge came from a Japanese reprint [Mokyr (1990a, 222-3)]. If imperial examination is the only obstacle to Industrial Revolution for any economy sharing the Chinese knowledge capital, then surely Industrial Revolution should originate in Japan, not Great Britain!

The above argument also applies to Eberhard's explanation of nomadic conquest. Kublai Khan's fleets were sunk by the Sacred Typhoon (the *original* Kamikaze). If the un-vanquished Japan did not have the Industrial Revolution first, some other factor must be at work.

A cross cultural perspective raises further questions to other explanations about why a society fails to industrialize. The unity of China is perceived as a disadvantage to Mokyr (1990a, 231), seconding Needham; the disunity of India is held as a barrier by Landes (1969, 39), invoking Marx. If Industrial Revolution came to Great Britain, a component of the 'non-unified' West Europe, why not to any part of the 'non unified' South Asia?

Overall, history is replete with societies experiencing intermittent swings of technological progress: bursts of creativity alternating with slowed advance, if not virtual stagnation. This process is to some extent stochastic, but over all subject to certain regularities.

Randomness applies especially to societies with limited technical capability for systematic search. The failure to re-invent the wheel in pre-Columbian Americas can scarcely be explained by simple economic rationale. Transparent glass seems to be absent in ancient China, but available in other cultures. People in some society may simply fail to perceive certain possibilities. Yet, for a society like ancient China to miss Industrial Revolution, some systemic dysfunction must be afoot.

The pattern of progress followed by slow-downs may be understood with concepts now made familiar with the theory of endogenous growth. Knowledge, the growth engine, is accumulated by serendipidity (like penicillin), out of intellectual curiosity (i.e., 'basic research'), or else, due to purposes of economic or non-economic motives (The Manhattan Project and the Apollo Program illustrate the last case). The theory of endogenous growth focuses upon the 'external' and 'internal' effects of knowledge and the formation of 'knowledge capital' for economic gain, by individuals with forethought. Since knowledge has external effect, a society with a larger initial stock of knowledge is better positioned to accumulate more, given that individuals have the same access to past accumulated information. Since knowledge has internal effect, then individuals have the motive to accumulate more knowledge. The strength of such motive depends upon the institutionally decided incentives.

Chance element notwithstanding, a society solves easier technical problems before confronting the more difficult ones. Given (a) the initial stock of knowledge, (b) the 'sample path' of information accumulation from non-economically motivated causes, and (c) the institutional set-up, a society may reach a plateau, or punctuated equilibrium. This episode will be ended by some external shock, or structural transition.

Examples for such stasis are legion. The Classic period of Europe ended in the Dark Ages, the Golden Age of Islamic technology ran its course by 1200, ancient

Chinese creativity peaked about 1450 and the Japanese precocity reached its plateau 150 years later [according to Mokyr (1990b)]. Similar patterns happened in the Americas before the arrival of the *conquistador*.

The punctuated equilibrium may end by either an encounter with a superior technical society, or by an internal transformation. What happened in West Europe during the Industrial Revolution is by a transformation episode. What happened to the other societies as they became 'discovered' by Europe is by an external-shock.

4.   THE STEAM ENGINE OF WATT

4.1   A Brief Summary of Facts

When placed in the above framework, the failure of ancient China to launch an Industrial Revolution is not an exception but a rule. In contrast, the success of West Europe to revive its Greco-Roman heritage and initiate the Industrial Revolution is a special case deserving careful scrutiny. Having identified the key elements of West European success, we will then be in a better position to identify what held ancient China back.

Since Toynbee (1884), scholars identify Industrial Revolution with the British discoveries in 1760-1830, and the steam engines of James Watt became the archetypal inventions in that period. It is natural to concentrate on steam engine the machine and James Watt the man, as a window into that period [For facts, see Dickinson (1967) and discussions in Scherer (1984)]. The current economic theory is micro-based, specifying the sequence of purposeful decisions by individuals with given wealth, technology, preference, information and probabilistic beliefs, under particular institutional 'rules-of-the-game'. The wealth of well-preserved collection of Watt's papers and data on his engines give us the means to follow through such an approach.

The steam engine traces its roots to the Alexandrine gadgets in Hero's Pneumatica (first century A.D.). Opening and closing temple doors with heated air and water, that device must have struck wonder and awe in the hearts of the attending crowd.

Practical applications became possible only with the understanding of the nature of the atmosphere and the vacuum. Mokyr, ibid. would trace ideas used by Watt to the research of Torricelli, the assistant of Galileo (who held a chair at Padua for 18 years) and Papin (the student of Huygens, for 15 years a member of *bibliotheque du roi* of Louis XIV), as well as the experiment of von Guericke, mayor of Magdeburg, who was trained at Leyden.

The practical steam engines were developed, for the special purpose of draining mines, by Savery, and then by Newcomen. Despite of their low thermo-effciency, they were used until displaced by a more efficient model. Thus, the Newcomen engine displaced the Savery engine, and the Watt engine displaced the Newcomen engine. By Industrial Revolution, products were invented mainly with an economic rationale.

The discoveries by Watt and his contemporaries allowed the use of the steam engine for milling and for transportation. In the former application, steam power competed against water power and both technologies made great advances in that period.

The development of steam power owes much to Hornblower, Bull and Trevithick, all contemporaries of Watt, and the first two were successfully, opposed by Watt in court on patent right. Trevithick, once the assistant to Bull, was responsible for the development of steam-powered locomotives, and hence, railroad transport.

The life history of Watt is fascinating to economists. Here we have a well-documented case of an inventor at work.

It was on the advices of his acquaintances at the University of Glasgow that Watt went to London as an apprentice for the trade of mathematical instrument maker. He returned to open a shop inside the college. After his experiments with Papin's engine in 1761 and 1762 got nowhere, his interest was reawakened when repairing a Newcomen steam engine owned by the college. From reverse engineering to improvement engineering was still no simple step for Watt. He learned latent heat from Professor Joseph Black who discovered it the year before. He had frequent discussions with John Robison, a graduate at Glasgow and later a professor at

Edinburgh, when developing his separate condenser. It was also through Black, Watt met his first sponsor and partner, Dr. Roebuck of Birmingham. Through the latter's connection, he met Dr. Boulton who became his partner on the bankruptcy of Roebuck.

It was not easy to turn Watt's inventive ideas into profit. The idea of a separate condenser came in 1765. But his lack of experience in full size machines, poor material and inferior workmanship thwarted him. Being in debt, he entered into partnership with Roebuck, ceding 2/3 of ownership. Even after a patent was awarded in 1769, Watt was so discouraged by the lack of success to spend five years as a surveyor. This slowed down his experiments and Roebuck was bankrupt in the depression of 1772-3. Boulton took over the latter's share and Watt resumed work. Now supplied by Wilkinson, who patented his high quality cylinders in 1773, Watt got his first engine working in 1774. First commercially installed machine came in 1776 and their firm turned profitable only in 1780. To Boulton's relief, their patent was then extended to 1800.

To make their efforts pay, Boulton and Watt had to charge customers by a new practice: a share of the cost their engines saved. Soon as their engine became a success, various infringements of their patents came. Both Bull and Hornblower worked for Boulton and Watt. Now each brought out improved engines of his own, incorporating the separate condenser. Boulton and Watt then took them to court and won heavy damage awards in 1799, after seven years of litigation. Other offenders were forced to pay arrears. By 1800, the Parliament refused to extend again the patent of Boulton and Watts. Watt retired.

The uncertainties and costliness of invention faced by Watt is quite typical, now as well as then. See, e.g., Rosenberg (1994) and Scherer and Ross (1990).

4.2   A Comparison with France

As noted by Mokyr, ibid, the steam engine of Watt is the culmination of an international joint effort. Yet, the British prowess in commercializing their inventions cannot be doubted during the Industrial Revolution. Thus, in power technology,

Papin of France suggested an unworkable steam engine in 1690. It was Savery in Great Britain who got his patent in 1698. Cugnot of France built a steam carriage in 1769. It was Trevithick of Great Britain who invented the steam-driven locomotive in 1804. A Swiss in 1766 remarked that 'for a thing to be perfect, it must be invented in France and worked out in England' [see Rostow (1978)]. It is further noted in Rostow (1975), that in the late 18th century, the British granted three times as many patents as the French. Apparently, the British environment was then more favorable for product development. Why this is so is less than certain, yet some incidents relating to the steam engine of Watt are thought provoking.

In 1777, Perier of France came to England and tried to buy Watt's engine from Wilkinson instead of Boulton and Watt. Wilkinson declined. Next, Comte d'Heronville approached Boulton and Watt to buy an engine. The order was accepted on condition that this nobleman would use his influence to obtain an *arret de conseil*. This was granted in 1788, though d'Heronville never applied the technology.

In that period, the patent system or its equivalent, existed in both Great Britain and France. Although not impressed with the quality of assessment at the British Parliament, Watt followed the law, applied for his own patents, and testified against the extension of Hornblower's. When believing that his rights were violated, he retained lawyer to litigate and was relieved when some judge favored his case more forcefully than his own lawyer. When dealing with the French *ancien regime*, he traded favor with an aristocrat, asking him to lobby with his influence! If this represents fairly how justice was perceived to work under the two governments, it is no surprise that when Watt focused on engine efficiency, the talented and energetic Perier would try 'rent-seeking', dealing with Wilkinson and not Watt. With fewer marketable products, the French applied for fewer patents. What a tale of two nations!

We study pre-Revolution France because it is 'mid way' between post-Sung China and Great Britain in the Industrial Revolution. The French could design science-based products but not develop it for the market. By Scherer and Ross, ibid, it is a case of technical success but not commercialization nor financial successes. In contrast, no exciting innovation came from the post-Sung China, a land surely being twice-disadvantaged.

4.3   Some General Principles

What appear striking in the episode of Watt's steam engine are:

1. The role European universities (and similar institutions) played. Without the post-renaissance universities, there probably would not be any steam engine of the 18th century Europe, nor would Watt work as an inventor.

2. The dual function of the patent system; it provided the incentive for inventors to concentrate on their work, but it also compelled them to make public technical information, which facilitates emulation once the patent has expired. Clearly, without this system Watt would never complete his experimentation. As it was, he quit to spend five years as a surveyor, for the lack of success in his experiments. In fact, Wilkinson also developed his professional expertise under the same British patent system. By Mokyr, ibid, without Wilkinson, Watt's ideas would never be implemented just like those designs by Da Vinci.

On both scores, institution certainly matters [cf. North (1990)].

5.   THE CHINESE CASE ONCE MORE

5.1   A Comparison of Institutions

To isolate the reasons why Industrial Revolution did not come to China first, we shall study the institutional differences between West Europe and China, in two particular aspects.

First, between the Renaissance and the Industrial Revolution, universities in West Europe served to generate, preserve and transmit scientific knowledge. Institutions like the French *biblioteque du roi* fulfilled a similar purpose. Among the social clites, from the merchant princes of the Medicis to royalties like Catherine the Great would patronize scientific knowledge no less than fine art and literature. Ironically, the ostentatious passion of much of the leisure class becomes a future source of strength and prosperity of an elitist society.

Disinterested scientific curiosity was simply lacking in ancient China, probably due to the stern Confucian outlook. It was viewed as unseemly for either the ruling class or the scholars to waste time and thought on the trivial pursuits of collecting rare plants and stones (the fatal passion of the Sung Emperor, who lost his throne to the Jurchen conquerors!). Apart from the small esoteric group specializing in astronomy (related no doubt to the ancient duties of the Chinese priest-kings), studying nature was hardly a becoming passion. It would be far better to debate the fine points of religious philosophy, subjects supposedly relevant for the art of governance. To prepare for statesmanship, the Confucian Analects advised scholars to 'learn many names of birds, beasts, plants and trees' from the Book of Odes, but not experimentation!

Second, the patent system in West Europe [especially the British Statute of Monopolies of 1624; see North and Thomas (1973)] seems to be the key to the British success in the steam engine. The system strikes a fine balance between providing incentives for the innovator and facilitate the task of eventual imitation. Applicants for a patent are compelled to supply details of their invention and argue their merits in documents placed in the public domain. When the temporary monopoly expires, speedy emulation is expected. Thus, the generation and transmission of technical knowledge are both assured. The system embodies even more subtlety than it is immediately apparent. Recognizing 'information asymmetry' between the State which is the less informed and the inventor who is the more knowledgeable, the State avoids the sponsoring of white elephant projects. Instead, by granting a temporary monopoly, the inventor is forced to do one's best, like Watt, to produce engines 'good and cheap'.

Gadgets may embody innovative principles and promise spin-off gains. But it is efficient products which provide immediate benefit and secure for themselves assured survival by wide use.

Nothing like the patent system existed in ancient China, even though its sagacious cynicism would delight greatly the Legalist masters, like the Machiavellian Han-Fei Tzu. Alas, the imperially-sanctioned philosophy in ancient China was not Legalism but Confucianism, in fact, the Confucianism of the Mencius branch (which believes in the perfectibility of the human nature) rather than the Hsing-Tzu branch (which recognizes that all human beings are capable of evil-doing). Confucius criticized his disciple who prospered through trading and Mencius regarded monopoly as despicable. It is understandable, but no less unfortunate that the ancient Chinese did not accept the temporary monopoly under the patent system as a 'necessary evil'. With no protection for intellectual property rights, trade secrets usually were passed father to son, or the son-less father-in-law to son-in-law, on rare occasions (unlike the Japanese reliance on adopted sons). Many actually got lost [Examples are Su Sung's water clock and the shock-absorbing imperial carriage – made in Tang China but used untill the Sung Dynasty – defying all attempts for replication. Cf. Sun (1993) for details of the latter.]. Rarely would manuals be dictated by *illiterate* masters for the record, like Mu Ching [Needham (1981, 22)].

5.2   China after the Golden Age

Elvin (1975) reviewed the traditional Chinese technology, after the Sung Golden Age.

Specifically:

1. Documents show that by the end of the 13th century, both China and West Europe had water-powered textile machines capable to substitute human labor for simultaneous complex tasks (Elvin, ibid., 85).

2. Despite the destructive nomad conquests, the growth of technology did resume, but at a slow pace (Elvin, ibid., 86).

3. Chinese recognized that technical inventions were needed, including the labor-saving type, for operations like draining mines – operations motivated the early steam engines of Europe. They were ready to adopt Western discoveries (though not philosophy) when possible. On this point, Elvin conceded that it is hard to

explain the lack of Chinese progress in the hydraulic field, in terms of his own theory of 'high level equilibrium trap' (Elvin, ibid.,107).

4. A contemporary French visitor reported that there was keen competition in the market, yet the Chinese seemed to be unable to afford anything but the bare necessities. In other words, the Chinese were apparently not in a position to undertake the risky task of product development (Elvin, ibid., 108).

These are consistent with our discussions above. Would-be Chinese inventors lacked both the scientific support equivalent to the European universities and the protection of patent right which encourages them to take the gamble. Moreover, without the product development to make them cost-effective, technically advanced Chinese inventions failed to become 'unforgettable' by their wide use [e.g. the spinning jenny noted in Mokyr (1990a, 221)]. Such marginalized curios soon got lost because of the lack of a male issue in the inventor's house, or due to the frequent uprisings, civil wars and invasions. An example is the water clock of Su Sung [Mokyr ibid., 220]. With a high rate of depreciation' and a modest pace of accumulation, it is only natural that the ancient China knowledge capital failed to reach the critical mass for Industrial Revolution.

All these seem to be the consequences of that Confucian outlook, shared by the East Asian societies of China, Japan, Korea and Vietnam. During the period, East Asia was ahead in science and technology and Europe stagnated in its Dark Age. Yet, no East Asian state had either the scientific curiosity or the patent system. That perhaps explains why the Industrial Revolution did not come to them first. This is so, even though no East Asian state ever regarded any scientific discovery as taboo, in contrast to Rome's prosecution of Galileo.

In the literature, apparently no one has asked why the Industrial Revolution did not happen in Japan in the first place, ahead of Great Britain. Yet, in discussing the initial difficulties of Japan in setting up an electric equipment industry, Uchida (1991) cited the lack of a scientific tradition as one of the primary sources of problems.

In passing, one might compare the cases of China, Japan, etc. with the Islamic world, another society which had contributed to Western technology but failed to have an Industrial Revolution ahead of Europe. Readers of Seyyed Nasr (1968) would note that under the Aristotelian influence, Islamic societies did have a scientific curriculum which was an advantage over East Asia. But like Medieval Rome, the Islamic orthodoxy – even to this day – would not sanction certain discoveries of modern astronomy [See also Landes, ibid on the Islamic world in his cross culture comparison.]. The situation parallels Stalin's preference for the 'Lysenko biology' over views of the rest of the scientific world. As we have seen, this is a handicap East Asian societies have never suffered. It perhaps also explains how European science and technology went into the Dark Age and then emerged out of it [cf. Landes, op. cit., 30].

5.3   Counter-factual Exercises

Our assessment of the situation may well be in error. The least we shall try is to channel the issues into a list of counter-factual questions, on which researchers may disagree.

Consider there were a Watt in China, one may then ask:

1. Would Watt's engine be welcome in post-Sung China? By Elvin, contemporary Chinese complained about the difficulties of draining mines with human efforts, whether wage was low in general. Thus, Watt's engines could drain the Chinese mines like they did the Cornish mines.

2. Would Watt be welcome as an inventor? Elvin documented that Chinese inventors would be honored as gods after death. Even for Mongol conquerors, craftsmen were spared when all citizens perish for their failed defense of a fallen city.

3. Would posterity know how Watt's engine work? Not sure. The only son surviving Watt never got married.

4. Could a Watt in China get his hands on a previous engine to improve on? Doubtful. Watt reverse engineered a Newcomen engine belonging to the University of Glasgow. No comparable institutions in post-Sung China would collect such devices for instruction.

5. Would something like the Newcomen's engine arise in China in the first place? Doubtful. Such engines are based upon the concept of the vacuum, discovered by people around Galileo and Huygens, the leaders of the Renaissance. China had nothing then comparable to the Renaissance.

6. Would Watt have access to people like Black and Robison in the college? Hardly. Watt, a craftsman could have access to his academic consultants in the university atmosphere in 18th century Britain. We know nothing of a similar Chinese institution. In China, master craftsmen were illiterate and scholars are not particularly interested in science, let alone engineering.

7. Would Watt be supported in China then to improve his engine? Perhaps not. Watt's first successful engine was backed by Boulton. Boulton believed that his investment could be recouped only if Watt's patent got extended. A Chinese inventor enjoyed no protection over their intellectual property right.

8. Would Watt succeed if he did his development work in China? Not sure. After a decade's failures, Watt's effort was saved by the shop of Wilkinson, who just patented a process to make a cylinder smooth. Or else, Watt's ideas would have joined the 5,000 pages of unimplemented designs of Da Vinci [Mokyr, ibid, 103-4]. China had nothing like a patent law to encourage Wilkinson and Watt.

9. Would Watt have persisted in invention? Probably not. He considered and accepted a job as a surveyor for five years. Without a patent system, he had nothing to stop people like Perier, Bull and Hornblower.

We have bypassed textile machines which have figured in the Needham Paradox, through the careful study of Chao (1986) on ancient Chinese textile technology. We do not underrate the important role of textiles in the history of industrializalion, nor insights which may be gained along that line of inquiry. However, (1) Watt improved steam engines for mining and they spread directly to locomotives and steamships. This happened without first displacing water power in textile mills, and (2) post-Sung China needed engines to drain mines, whether Chinese labor was cheap or not. Thus, we may learn much by asking why ancient China produced no Watt. Whether a state with locomotives, steamships and steam-powered electric generators, but no machine-powered textile machines is authentically an industrialized country is another story.

We also note that researchers on Indian economic history seem to pay a great deal of attention to the history of their textile industry and then conclude that India failed to industrialize because of the colonization of Britain. That question, important may it be, should not exclude a prior question: why did not Industrial Revolution come to India first (an Indian version of the Needham Paradox). Had Industrial Revolution came to India first, there should never be any colonization. Thus, the list of counter-factual questions asked above may also clarify some interesting issues for the Indian economic history as well.

5.4   Knowledge Dynamics

To summarize concisely our tentative views on the Needham Paradox, we recapitulate in symbolic terms.

Let,

k(t) and K(t) be the stocks of the individual and social average levels of knowledge capital in period t, respectively,

y(t) be the output in t,

a be the accretion of knowledge, each period, by serendipidity,

b(t) be the increase of knowledge capital due to 'basic research', out of pure curiosity,

n(t) be the increase of knowledge capital, for non-economic reasons (e.g., for defense),

v(t) be the economically motivated knowledge accumulation,

D be the periodic rate of knowledge depreciation, $0 < D < 1$,

i be institutional factors,

then, we shall postulate that,

$y(t) = f(K(t))$, the production function,

$b(t) = g(t; i)$, showing the dependence of basic research on institutions,

$v(t) = h(k(t), K(t), i)$, showing the inventive zeal depends what level of knowledge an individual has, and what the society average is, as well as institutional factors, h increasing in k, K,

$D = j(i)$, showing the depreciation rate is institutionally dependent,

and,

$k(t) = K(t)$, showing that at the equilibrium, the representative person has the same level as the society.

Our model predicts that for a largely self-contained society (e.g., China or Europe),

$$K(t + 1) = (1 - j(i))K(t) + a + g(t; i) + n(t) + h(k(t), K(t), i)$$

so that, it follows that any (punctuated) equilibrium value of knowledge, K^*, is characterized by:

$$K^* = [a + g(t; i) + n(t) + h(K^*(t), K^*(t), i)/j(i)$$

Although knowledge is not quantifiable, the above formalism suggests:

1. Contrary to the usual perception, in general, an economy may have a tendency to gravitate toward stagnation, and in particular, it is not a surprise that for post-Sung China, nothing exciting was invented.

2. Any institutional reform that halves the 'depreciation rate' will *more* than double the steady state stock of knowledge, *ceteris paribus* (more, since h increases with K^*).

3. With some form of the h function, K may grow without a bound, under some institutions. One may define Industrial Revolution as initiating an unbounded growth path for K.

4. The steady state level of knowledge can be increased through the spill-over from basic research, or the enhancement of R. & D., or the reduction of 'depreciation'. All three channels are affected by institutional factors.

The moral of the above inquiry is quite clear for public policy. Basic research and institutions of higher learning should be supported in an untrammeled manner, and intellectual property right must be protected with enlightened legislation.

5.5   Network Causality

We believe that the success or failure of a society to attain an Industrial Revolution is related to a network of causal factors, many of which are relevant, even though none of them need be necessary or sufficient. An analogy may serve our purpose here. To cook food, one needs either (1) both (a) 1) charcoal *or* 2) firewood *and* (b) 1) a match *or* 2) a lighter, or (2) a micro-wave oven.

In this note, what we suggest is to recast of the debates on the Needham Paradox along some fresh lines. For example,

(1) The size of China may be relevant. Thus, in the Age of Discovery, trade could be a sizable source of national income to an European state, but not to Ming China. Thus, trade incentive could not stimulate China for innovation.

(2) Both (a) the world view of the elites and (b) the safeguard for intellectual property rights may be relevant. Thus, because of (a), scientific studies were patronized in post-Renaissance Europe, but not in the post-Sung China under the *fundamentalist* Confucian ethos. Because of (b), Chinese craftsmen, unlike their British counterparts, could neither be induced for major product development nor compelled to place their trade secret in the public domain.

Note that (2) is related to the Confucian ethos and not just the Confucian curriculum for the imperial examination. Japan shared the former but not the latter.

The argument in (1) is not absolute. The Netherlands could be too small, so that one suffers brain drain (e. g. Huygens) and the domestic market may be too small to make the patent provision attractive enough. [Boulton, for example, was not interested to licence Watt's engine for part of the British market.]

This is an essay on economics. We shall not speculate here how did the philosophy of Confucious (a modest, cautious and humanistic thinker) became transformed into an *established philosophy* of the Han state (in 136 BC) to the exclusion of the studies on statecraft by Han-Fei Tzu, the pacificist-technocratic heritage of Mo Tzu, and the deductive dialectics of Chuang Tzu and Hui Shi, as in the joy-of-fish debate. (In turn, in a similar trial aud error process, Chinese inventors may be less able than Europeans in pattern recognition, due to this neglect of logics training, as suggested by Tang, ibid.) Suffice to say here is that, not all economically-relevant events are decided by the economic imperative.

6.   REFLECTIONS ON ENDOGENOUS GROWTH THEORY

We have applied concepts from the theory of endogenous growth to the Needham Paradox. This undertaking also lead us to believe that for the future development of the theory of endogenous growth, certain issues should be raised:

(1)   The 'consumption' of a society assumes many forms.   Part of the national expenditure share may take the form of 'basic research', supported by the society with little thought about its future economic value.   Other components may be motivated by increasing the security or prestige of the State, like the Manhattan Project and the Apollo Program.   A significant proportion of the economically relevant 'knowledge capital' can be generated by such spending.

(2)   In similar manner, the external effect of a particular stock of 'knowledge capital' – say, measured by consumption foregone – cannot be separated from such institutional factors like the operation of the university system, or the interactions between religious fundamentalism and scientific research.

To place our research in a balanced perspective, the above mentioned factors cannot be neglected when matching theory against facts.

(3)   If the theory of endogenous growth is to be anchored on micro-foundations, then institutions like the patent system must be allowed a role to play in the formulation, in one form or another.   After all, this can be decisive on the volume of knowledge capital formation.

(4)   As the episode of Watt's steam engine indicates, his invention rested on a knife-edge, even under the protection of the British patent system.   But how

effective is a patent system – as our Franco-British comparison highlighted – may well depend on matters *de facto* rather than *de jure*. Such factors may be hard to quantify, but one cannot simply ignore the matter altogether.

It is not our intention to insist that everything under the sun must be included to clutter a simple economic model. At the same time, in discussing real life issues, it will be desirable to place the analytic model in perspective.

7.   NOTE OF ACKNOWLEDGEMENT

My interest in history-based economic studies dates back from my initial economics training under Professor S. J. Yang in the late 40s. This is revived by a recent seminar at Cornell by Professor Douglass North [North (undated)]. Their imprint on my thought is obvious. My colleagues George Boyer, Thomas Lyons, Peter McClelland Bruce Reynolds and Bruce Smith have all provided me important sources for this note. I myself is solely responsible for all the deficiencies.

REFERENCES

Chao (1977), The Development of Cotton Textile Industry in China, Harvard University, Cambridge, MA.

—— (1986), Man and Land in Chinese History: An Economic Analysis, Stanford University Press, Stanford, CA.

Dickinson, H. W. (1967), James Watt, Craftsman and Engineer, Kelley Publishers, N.Y., NY.

Eberhand, Wolfram (1977), A History of China, University of California Press, Berkeley, CA.

Elvin, Mark (1973), Pattern of the Chinese Post, Stanford University Press, Stanford, CA.

—— (1975), Skills and Resources in Late Traditional China in Dwight H. Perkins ed., China's Modern Economy in Historical Perspective, Stanford University Press, Stanford, CA.

Hughes, Jonathan (1970), Industrialization and Economic History, NY.

Landes, David (1969), Unbound Prometheus, Cambridge University Press, New York, NY.

Lau, Manlui and Henry Wan, Jr. (1993), The Mechanism of Catching-Up. *European Economic Review.*

Lin, Justin, Y. F. (1992), The Needham Puzzle: Why the Industrial Revolution Did Not Originate in China, Working Paper No. 650, Department of Economies, U. C. L.A.

Lucas, Robert Jr. (1988), The Mechanism of Economic Development, Journal of Monetary Economics.

—— (1993), To Make a Miracle, Econometrica.

Mokyr, Joel (1990a), The Lever of Riches, Technological Creativity and Economic Progress, Oxford University Press, N. Y., NY.

—— (1990b), Twenty-Five Centuries of Technical Change, A Historical Survey, Harwood Academic Press, N. Y., NY.

Nasr, Seyyed (1968), Science and Civilization in Islam, Harvard University Press, Cambridge, MA.

Needham, Joseph (1981), Science in Traditional China, A Comparative Perspective, The Chinese University Press, Hong Kong.

North, Douglass and Robert Thomas (1973), The Rise of the West World, Cambridge University Press, N. Y., NY.

—— (1990), Institutions, Institutional Change and Economic Performance, Cambridge University Press, N. Y., NY.

—— (undated), The Paradox of the West, mimeo.

Pollard, Sydney (1985), Industrialization and the European Economy, in Joel Mokyr, ed., The Economics of the Industrial Revolution, Rowman and Allanheld, Totowa, NJ.

Romer, Paul (1986), Increasing Returns and Long Run Growth, *Journal of Political Economy,* 94.

Rosenberg, Nathan (1994), Exploring the Black Box, Cambridge Press, N. Y., NY.

Rostow, W. W. (1975), How it All Began, McGraw Hill, N. Y., NY.

—— (1978), No Random Walk, A Comment, *Economic History Review,* 31.

Scherer, Frederic (1984), Innovation and Growth: Schumpeterian Perspectives, M. I. T. Press, Cambridge, MA.

—— and David Ross (1990), Industrial Market Structure and Economic Performance, Houghton Miflin, Boston, MA.

Shell, Karl (1968), Toward a Theory of Inventive Activity and Capital Accumulation, *American Economic Review*, 56.

Sun, Ji (1993), Zhong Guo Gu Yu Fu Lum Cun "Essays on Ancient Chinese Chariots and Clothing", Wen Wu Chu Ban She, Beijing. P. R. C., (Chinese)

Tang, Anthony (1979), China's Agricultural Legacy, Economic Development and Cultural Change, 28.

Toynbee, A. (1884), Lectures on the Industrial Revolution Ashton, NY.

Uchida, Hoshima (1991), The Transfer of Electrical Technology from the U. S. and Europe to Japan, 1869–1914, in David Jeremy ed. International Technology Transfer: Europe, Japan, and U. S. A., 1700–1914, Aldershot, England.

摘　　要

　　宋代科技領先西方,而工業革命,日後肇始英國。經濟與歷史學者,各有解釋迄無定論。此問題對於新成長論中知識之累積,甚可啓發。

　　本文比較中、日、英、法史實,及瓦特蒸汽機之特例,發現兩點:

1. 文藝復興後之大學制度,使歐洲發明家之知見深於東亞發明家。論者常云,中國受害於蒙元、科舉。日本則未受此等影響,仍不能先於英國而有工業革命,原因乃在科學不如歐洲。

2. 智慧產權重要,英國 1624 年之專利制,既獎勵研發,又保證成果以後社會共享。當時法國發明多而早,但不能市場化,中國則固有技術,常有失傳現象。

　　宋代以後,中國礦井需要抽水與英國相同,人稠、工資低,並非阻撓中國發明之充足條件。

The Second Chance After WWII:
The Record of East Asia Among the Late-Comers

Review of "On the Mechanism of Catching Up", coauthored with Man-lui Lau*

The leader This Article describes the catching-up relationship between the South and the North, which can also be applied to the relationship between the rest of the world and America. America is the world's undisputed leader in wealth, technology and per capita income ever since World War II. To wit, in the series of the relative per capita real GDP in Penn World Table version 6.1, there are 5,847 entries over the 51 years, 1950–2000, for all economies. Among the 5,796 pairwise comparisons between America and any other economy, America is ahead in 5,755 entries (about 99.25%) with the exceptions of Switzerland ahead in 24 out of the 51 years and Luxembourg ahead in 17 out of the 51.

American supremacy in 1948 was the preoccupation in *A Review of Current Trends in U.S. Foreign Policy,* by George Kennan, the author of the successful containment strategy that won the Cold War:

"... we have about 50% of the world's wealth but only 6.3% of its population. This disparity is particularly great as between ourselves and the peoples of Asia. In this situation, we cannot fail to be the object of envy and resentment. Our real task in the coming period is to devise a pattern of relationships which will permit us to maintain this position of disparity without positive detriment to our national security."

Re-entered Japan While Kennan does not always represent American government policy, the use of Japan to supply much of the need of military operations in the Korean War was presumably only in part for cost saving, but also to keep the Japanese fully employed, instead of going communist, out of economic desperation.

Among all other economies, Japan has been one of the most successful in catching up with American per capita income. Much of this has been

---

*The article is reprinted from the *European Economic Review*, Vol. 38, Nos. 3 and 4, pp. 952–963, 1993, published by Elsevier Science Publishers.

accomplished through what might be called dependent innovation, exemplified in the following table:

Industry	Initial American technology	Japanese innovation against Europe
Camera	Optical sensor	Viewfinder
Watches	Micro-electronics	Digital watch
Machine tools	Micro-computer	CNC machine tools
Automobile	Quality control	Toyota quality control system

Whatever is the success of Japanese firms over its rivals in Europe as well as in America, itself, it is underpinned by some American basic technology. In proceeding in this manner, any chance of overtaking the technology leader is at best remote.

The issue of leadership One naturally questions whether the American leadership can last forever, or at any rate for how long. Suffice to say, the change of leadership is possible in logic, and happened once between Britain and America. But that was the only change in the two and half centuries after the Industrial Revolution, and the change was preceded by a tripartite interlude between Britain, America and Germany over the inter-World War period, and finalized through the massive migration of science and technology elite from Central Europe to America. It is therefore safe to say that there is no indication in sight for any more imminent change, as of today. Nor is there much use yet to speculate such a happening.

As a formal model, this Article describes a mode of interdependent growth, not recognized in most, if not all, of the growth literature.

ELSEVIER

European Economic Review 38 (1993) 952–963

EUROPEAN
ECONOMIC
REVIEW

On the mechanism of catching up

Man-lui Lau [a], Henry Wan, Jr. [b]*

[a] *University of San Francisco, San Francisco CA, USA*
[b] *Cornell University, Ithaca, NY 14853, USA*

Abstract

We draw upon the experiences of Japan and the Asian NIEs, the economies with the longest records of sustained rapid growth. This study then explains the observed patterns of growth with a control theoretical model. With imitation costly, and the benefit of imitative effort rising with technical capability but declining with the reduction of technology backlog, the poorest economies would allow the income gap to open further, but middle income economies would temporarily grow faster than the developed economies, through a first stage of trend acceleration and then a stage of deceleration. Evidence suggests that trade is one of the necessary but insufficient conditions for such a catching up process.

Key words: Catching up; Endogenous growth; Technology transfer
JEL classification: O19; O33; O41

1. Introduction

Economists have found patterns of growth, varying over time and all economies. To organize facts with theory, the theory of endogenous growth focuses on the knowledge capital – a durable public input created at private risk (Shell, 1966). Attention is attracted to the increasing returns which can arise from the external effect of knowledge capital (Romer, 1986). But by Ethier (1982) and Lucas (1988), national economies are arbitrary units for knowledge spill-overs: as part of the trading world, Lilliputian Singapore has no less advantage than an insular India. Explaining observations remains a challenge.

According to the endogenous growth view, we identify the growth of per

---

* Corresponding author.
Thanks for comments from S. Clemhout, G. Grossman, T. Mitra, X. Sala-i-Martin, K. Shell, C. Sims, T.N. Srinivasan, E. Thorbecke, P. Wang and A. Young as well as assistance from P. Carlisle.

capita output as an 'output-augmenting' increase in knowledge capital. We then follow Mowery and Rosenberg (1989) in recognizing that technology transfer is costly. For any transfer to be operational, one must acquire complementary facilities and skill. The benefit from efforts in borrowing technology varies across countries, depending on the technical capability and the opportunity for borrowing. By such an analysis, the high growth of Japan and the NIEs (i.e., Korea, Taiwan, Hongkong and Singapore) is possible for technology followers, in their middle phase of development, and under circumstances favorable to international exchange.

We present below stylized facts and related evidences, then a control theoretic explanation, followed by comments on the source of growth.

2. Seven stylized facts

Here are the stylized facts, the first four and the last are from Lucas (1988).

A. Growth rates vary more among the poor economies than among the rich.
B. Mid income economies grow fastest, then, the advanced economies, the poorest are the slowest.
C. There is no convergence of growth rates in the long run.
D. Economies grow fastest only after 'trend acceleration', in the terms of Klein and Ohkawa (1968).
E. Economies growing fast will slow down eventually.
F. Both 'acceleration' and 'deceleration' depend on the phase of development of an economy, and not the worldwide economic climate.
G. Economies growing the fastest have increased exports of new goods not exported by them before.

Leaving G for the last section, we note that for A, Lau and Wan (1991) have compared the distributions of mean growth of per capita real GNP for 18 developed economies and 76 less developed economies, averaged over 1965–87 (data from *World Development Report 1989* and *Taiwan Statistical Databook 1990*). The null hypothesis of 'both samples sharing the same variance' is rejected at the 1% significance level.

For B, we use data from *World Table 1991* and *Taiwan Statistical Databook 1990* for 120 market economies over 1981–87, and regress G_{81-87}, the seven-year mean growth rate of per capita real GNP, against Q_{84}, the per capita real GNP of the year 1984 (which is the middle year over the seven-year period):

$$G_{81-87} = -866.296 + 0.5419Q_{84} - 0.0000297(Q_{84})^2,$$
$$(-2.0163)(0.1633) \quad (-2.8954)$$

$$R^2 = 0.0789, \quad n = 120, \quad F = 5.01,$$

where the numbers in parentheses are t-values.

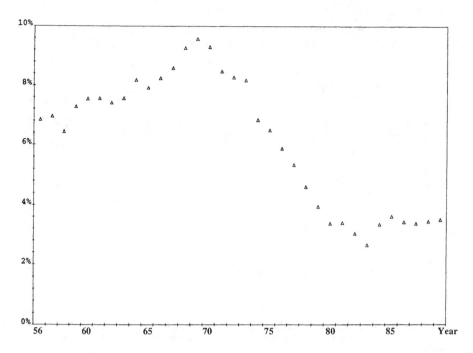

Fig. 1. Japan: Per capita growth rate (10-year moving average).

The negative sign of the quadratic coefficient is significant at the $\frac{1}{2}\%$ level.

We check the broad correspondence of stylized facts C, D, E and F with the statistical record, using data of Japan, the NIEs, and the ASEAN-3 (sometime called the Next NIEs) of Indonesia, Thailand and Malaysia. For comparison, Indian statistics are also included.

Fig. 1 shows the series of 10-year average growth of Japanese per capita real GDP. It first rises, then peaks in the early 70s, and finally falls. Series from most of the NIEs show a similar pattern. To verify that this is not the result of some 'climate effect' alone, we plot in Fig. 2a the difference in the real growth of per capita GDP between 'economy i' and Japan, where i = Singapore, Hongkong, Taiwan, Korea, Malaysia, Thailand, Indonesia, and India. The NIEs 'outgrew' Japan first, then the Next NIEs, with India following closely. This yields the pattern in Fig. 2b.

3. A simple model

Let x and y be the per capita outputs of a particular developing economy and 'the developed world'. The latter is the source of technology. For the former, ratio $z = x/y \in (0, 1)$ measures its *technical capability*. $1 - z$ plays a dual

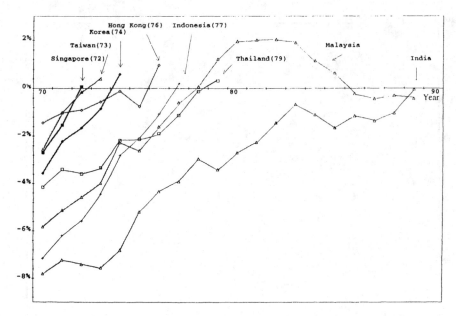

Fig. 2a. Growth rate of per capita GDP in excess of Japanese growth (10-year moving average).
Note: The year in the parentheses of country *i* was the year when country *i* outgrew Japan for
the first time.

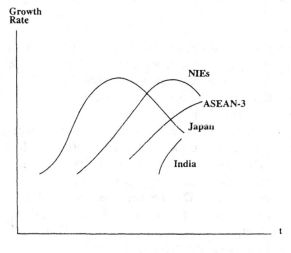

Fig. 2b

role: both the *technological gap* which it may narrow down and the
technology backlog of Gerschenkron (1962) which denotes the opportunities
for imitation. Let c be the per capita consumption of the developing
economy and $s = 1 - (c/x)$ be the portion of output forgone to narrow the
technology gap, by the dynamic equation

$$dz/dt = g(s,z), \quad \delta g/\delta s > 0, \quad g(s,\cdot) \quad \text{is quasi-concave in } z. \tag{1}$$

We choose the simplest function forms in our assumptions.

Assumption 1.

$$g(s,z) = b(s)f(z), \tag{2}$$

where

$$b(s) = b_0(\cdot)(s - s_0), \quad 0 < s_0 < 1; \quad f(z) = z^a(1-z), \quad a > 1. \tag{3}$$

The separable form in (2) facilitates interpretations of our results. The form of $b(s)$ in (3) implies that there is some opportunity cost just to prevent the gap from widening. The form for $f(z)$ extends the Mansfield–Baumol formula (where $a = 1$) to $a > 1$ to allow for trend acceleration. $b_0(\cdot)$ is assumed to be a constant b^* in this section.

Assumption 2. The developing economy evolves to maximize

$$\int_0^\infty e^{-rt} \log c \, dt = \int_0^\infty e^{-rt}[\log(1-s) + \log z] \, dt + \int_0^\infty e^{-rt} \log y \, dt, \quad r > 0, \tag{4}$$

where r is the time preference rate.

With the logarithmic payoff, terms involving the endogenous variables z and s in (4) are additively separable from the exogenous variable y. This makes the optimal behavior of the developing economy independent of the y-path.

For possible reference, note that f is strictly quasi-concave, with a maximum at $z^* = a/(a+1)$ and $f(0) = 0 = f(1)$; f' is strictly concave with a maximum at $z_* = (a-1)/(a+1)$ and $f'(0) = 0$; $f(z)/z$ reaches a maximum $m = f(z_0)/z_0 = (a-1)^{a-1}/a^a$ at $z_0 = (a-1)/a$ where $z_* < z_0 < z^*$.

To avoid the trivial situation that the technological gap always widen and to simplify graphic display, we next adopt

Assumption 3.

$$r < m. \tag{5}$$

Assumption 4.

$$dy/dt = hy \quad \text{for} \quad h > 0. \tag{6}$$

No single developing economy is likely to have appreciable influence on the evolution of the developed world, but collectively they can be, as in Krugman (1979) or Grossman and Helpman (1992). We simply assume that h in (6) pertains to some world equilibrium path when all these are taken into consideration (in some over-all model).

For a developing economy, denote the current value costate variable as p and the current value Hamiltonian as

$$H = \log(1-s) + \log z + pb^*(s-s_0)f(z). \tag{7}$$

The maximum principle and the costate equation become, respectively,

$$0 = \delta H/\delta s = -(1-s)^{-1} + pb^*f(z), \tag{8}$$

$$dp/dt = rp - \delta H/\delta z = rp - [z^{-1} + pb^*(s-s_0)f'(z)]. \tag{9}$$

To simplify, set $q = 1/p$, $e(z) = zf'(z)/f(z) = a - z(1-z)^{-1}$ and we get:

$$dz/dt = b^*(1-s_0)f(z) - q, \tag{10}$$

$$dq/dt = [e(z)dz/dt + (q-rz)]q/z = [q-g(z)][1-e(z)]q/z, \tag{11}$$

where $g(z)$ stands for $[r - b^*(1-s_0)f'(z)]z/[1-e(z)]$.

Lemma 1 (Characterization of equilibrium).   Given $dz/dt = 0$, then $dq/dt = 0$ if and only if $q = rz$.

Proof.   By (11).

Lemma 2. $f(z)/z$ reaches its maximum m at z_0.

Proof.   Direct computation.

Lemma 3 (Solution of equilibrium).   There are three equilibria $z = 0$, z_1, and z_2: $0 < z_1 < z^* < z_2$.

Proof.   By Assumption 3, phase line $q = b^*(1-s_0)f(z)$ (for $dz/dt = 0$) meets the ray: $q = rz$ at $z = 0$, also at z_1 and z_2, the roots of $z^{a-1}(1-z) = r/b^*(1-s_0)$. Apply then Lemma 1.

Lemma 4 (Stability of equilibrium).   We have stable equilibria at 0 and z_2, unstable equilibrium at z_1.

Proof.   At both z_1 and z_2, the optimal trajectory $q = k(z)$ has slope $(dq/dt)/(dz/dt) = r \cdot e(z)$. At $z = 0$, note that any solution of (10)–(11) must cross the ray $q = rz$ at the angle $r \cdot e(z)$. This angle decreases with z. So, $k(z)$ cannot cross that ray at any $z < z_1$. Thus, $\lim_{z \downarrow 0} k'(z) \in [0, r]$.

Next, for the phase diagram analysis in Fig. 3a, $k'(z) \geqslant b^*(1-s_0)f'(z) > g'(z)$ at 0, $k'(z) < b^*(1-s_0)f'(z) < g'(z)$ at z_1 and $k'(z) > g'(z) > b^*(1-s_0)f'(z)$ at z_2. The stability results follows.

One can read off $dz/dt = b^*(1-s_0)f(z) - k(z)$ from Fig. 3a and deduce the

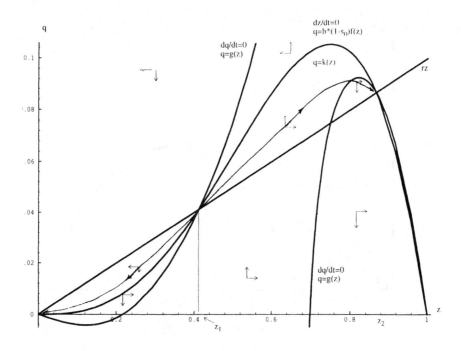

Fig. 3a

behavior of the expression, $(dz/dt)/z$, in Fig. 3b, as z varies. Now, $(dz/dt)/z = (dx/dt)/x - (dy/dt)/y$ is the excess of the growth rate of the developing economy over that of the developed economy, i.e., h.[1] Fig. 3c compares the time paths of the growth rate of three typical economies.

Thus we have deduced graphically the following:

Proposition.   Under Assumptions 1–4,

---

[1] Let

$$dz/dt = b^*(1 - s_0) f(z) - k(z)$$
$$= w(z),$$

say, then

$$w(z_1) = 0 = w(z_2), \quad w(z) > 0, \quad \text{for} \quad z_1 < 0 < z_2,$$
$$(d/dt)[(dz/dt)/z] = (d/dt)\{[b^*(1 - s_0) f(z) - k(z)]/z\}$$
$$= \{(d/dz)[w(z)/z]\}(dz/dt)$$
$$= \{[(dw/dz) - w/z]/z\}(dz/dt)$$
$$= [(dw/dz) - w/z][(dz/dt)/z],$$

where the second term is positive between z_1 and z_2, and the first is continuous and positive at z_1 and negative at z_2 so that at some interval of time (T_1, T_2), where $z(T_1) > z_1$ is near z_1, the expression is positive and at some other interval of time (T_3, ∞), where $z(T_3) < z_2$, the expression is negative because of the continuity of the expression as a function of t.

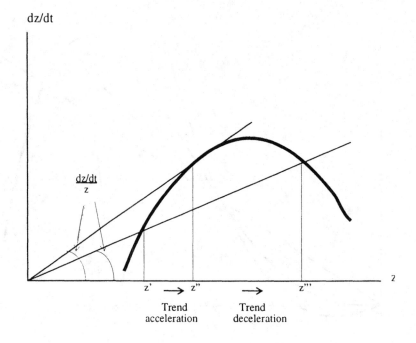

Fig. 3b

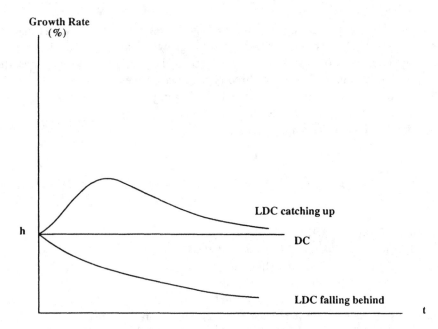

Fig. 3c

(a) *Not all economies converge in growth with each other.*

(b) *Economies with an initial technical capability $z(0) \geq z_1$ will converge in growth with the advanced economies. The difference in per capita output grows exponentially, if the developing economy engages only in imitation (and not innovation).*

(c) *With an initial technical capability $z(0) \in (z_1, z_2)$, there is a 'high growth' period, preceded(followed) by a phase of 'trend acceleration' ('trend deceleration').*

(d) *With an initial technical capability $z(0) \in (0, z_1)$, the technology gap widens forever.*

These theoretical findings are consistent with Stylized Facts A–F of the last section as well as Barro and Sala-i-Martin (1992) on 'convergence clubs'. Other novel implications also follow: (i) Efficiency in technology transfer (perhaps through international interactions) can improve growth, (ii) Differences in growth over an extended period can arise solely from the difference in timing of the high growth phase, (iii) The high growth period, though transient, marks the end of poverty. Its early arrival is therefore desirable.

Our model is in the tradition of Krugman as well as Grossman and Helpman (1992): the North always innovates, the South forever imitates, with no provision for Japan to metamorphose. Presumably an extension can be done along the lines of Wan (1993).

4. Concluding remarks

So far r and b^* are taken as given. Convergence in growth happens if and only if $z(0) > z_1(r, b^*)$. One can show that $\delta z_1/\delta r < 0 < \delta z_1/\delta b^*$. By allowing economies to differ in (r, b^*) one may also explain how one economy can overtake another in technical capability. Our analysis so far may also be viewed as a preparation for studying the differences of b^* (or $b_0(\cdot)$) across countries.

$b_0(\cdot)$ depends upon policies and institutions. Yet, *which* factor has *what* effect is not easy to verify empirically. Many factors can be necessary but not sufficient for sustained rapid growth. Sustained rapid growth itself can be a lengthy but transient phase.

For illustration, we study the question: *whether* in the post-WWII East Asia, being export-oriented is instrumental to sustained rapid growth. Two questions are addressed with scatter diagrams. (i) In *what* sense do some East Asian economies exemplify sustained rapid growth? and (ii) *what* role does export-orientation play for these economies? The approach is more suggestive than analytic, but sheds light for future research.

For (i), we use data from *World Table 1991* and *Taiwan Statistical*

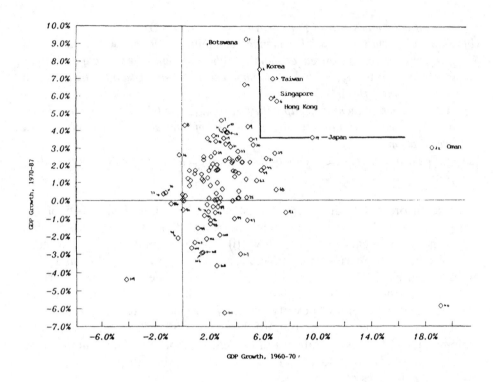

Fig. 4

Databook 1990 and plot in Fig. 4 the mean real growth rates of per capita output for the group of 112 market economies over 1970–87 against those for 1960–70. *Only* the five East Asian economies ('the East Asian Five' from now on) – Japan and the NIEs – have mean growth rates at least 0.91 standard deviations above the group average for 1970–87 *and* at least 0.87 standard deviations above the group average for 1960–70. In that sense, these five exemplify sustained rapid growth. In contrast, Omani oil and Botswanaian diamonds provide a growth which is *fast* but not *sustained*.

For (ii), we note that 'large economies export proportionately less'. For 1965, we find that the ratio $Z = \text{Export}/\text{GDP}$ is negatively correlated to GDP. To control this effect, we compute R^{65}, the residual for the above regression for 112 economies. Next we compute for the same economies, $D^{(22)}$, the difference between the mean growth rate of export and the mean growth rate of GDP, over the period 1965–87. When $D^{(22)}$ is plotted against R^{65} in Fig. 5, the East Asian Five is 'Pareto-nondominated' by any of the other 107 economies. Specifically, index the East Asian Five by i and the others by j, then there is no (i,j) with both $R_i^{65} < R_j^{65}$ and $D_i^{(22)} < D_j^{(22)}$.

Thus, each of these five (which exhibits sustained rapid growth), either was already highly export-oriented (i.e., Hong Kong and Singapore), or increase

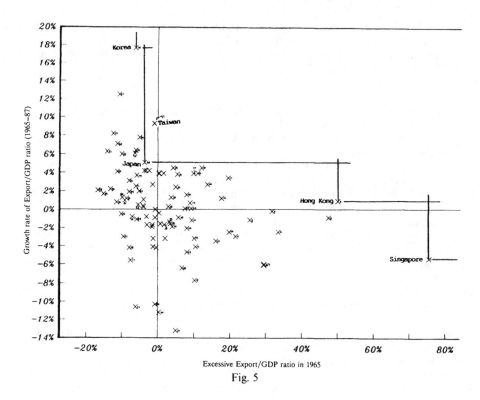

Fig. 5

their export orientation in the period of high growth (i.e., Japan, Korea and Taiwan). In a Kuhn–Tucker sense, export matters for sustained rapid growth, East Asian fashion. But more export helps only if complementary conditions are met.

The following case studies and statistical evidences have provided clues about how export enhances growth for the NIEs both directly and indirectly. (i) By Kojima (1978), the NIEs are favorite export platforms of foreign investors. (ii) By Watanabe (1980), foreign investments bring useful technology with spillovers. (iii) By Morawetz (1981), with developed professionalism, the NIEs have outperformed Latin Americans in export markets. (iv) By Lau (1986), the changing comparative advantage proceeds hand in hand with the intersectoral shift of NIEs' labor inputs. (v) By Young (1993), the shifting labor mix is a major source of the NIEs' growth. These, taken together, are consistent with Stylized Fact G.

References

Barro, Robert and Xavier Sala-i-Martin, 1992, Convergence, Journal of Political Economy 100, 223–251.

Ethier, Wilfred, 1982, National and international return to scale in the modern theory of international trade, American Economic Review 72, 389–405.

Gerschenkron, Alexander, 1962, Economic backwardness in historical perspective (Harvard University Press, Cambridge, MA).

Grossman, Gene M. and Elhanan Helpman, 1992, Innovation and growth in the global economy (MIT Press, Cambridge, MA).

Klein, Lawrence and Kazushi Ohkawa ed., 1968, Economic growth: The Japanese experience since the Meiji era (Irwin, Homewood, IL).

Kojima, Kiyoshi, 1978, Direct foreign investment: A Japanese model, Multinational Business Operations (Croom Helm, London).

Krugman, Paul, 1979, A model of innovation, technology transfer and the world distribution of income, Journal of Political Economy 87, 253–266.

Lau, Man-lui, 1986, The importance of manufacturing up in the development of the Far Eastern Four: Hong Kong, Singapore, South Korea and Taiwan, Doctoral Thesis (Cornell University, Ithaca, NY).

Lau, Man-lui and Henry Wan, Jr., 1991, The theory of growth and technology transfer: Experience from East Asian economies, The Seoul Journal of Economics 4, 109–122.

Lucas, Robert E., Jr., 1988, On the mechanism of economic development, Journal of Monetary Economics 23, 3–42.

Morawetz, David, 1981, Why the emperor's new clothes are not made in Colombia: A case study of Latin American and East Asian manufacturing export (Oxford University Press, Oxford).

Mowery, David C. and Nathan Rosenberg, 1989, Technology and the pursuit of economic growth (Cambridge University Press, Cambridge).

Romer, Paul, 1986, Increasing returns and long run growth, Journal of Political Economy 94, 1002–1037.

Shell, Karl, 1966, Toward a theory of inventive activity and capital accumulation, American Economic Review 56, 64–68.

Wan, Henry Y., Jr., 1993, Trade, development and inventions, in: Horst Herberg and Ngo Van Long, eds., Trade, welfare and economic policies (Michigan University Press, Ann Arbor, MI).

Watanabe, Susumu, 1980, Multinational enterprises and the employment oriented appropriate technologies in developing countries, ILO working papers, Multinational Enterprise Program, No. 14 (ILO, Geneva)

Young, Alwyn, 1994, Lesson from East Asian NIEs: A contrarian view, European Economic Review, this issue.

Japan Pioneered Industrialization via Institutional Development: The Post-WWII Transformation of Corporate Governance

Review of "Nipponized Confucian Ethos or Incentive-Compatible Institutional Design: Notes on Morishima, 'Why has Japan Succeeded?' "*

Institution matters In retrospect, what made the Japanese economy successful in the early decades after World War II is the effective development and utilization of its labor force (which is the focus of this Note), plus the effective mobilization of domestic saving to support the development effort. All these were realized, not so much because of the constant prodding of the fallible MITI (see Komiya, 1988; and Miwa, 1996), but due to the setting up of the *keiretsu* system, through the effort of the Ministry of Finance and the Bank of Japan. The uniqueness of such a system requires some digression. See Morishima (2000) and also Miyajima (1999).

The brief intermezzo Before World War II, large Japanese corporations were owned by founders' families and formed networks of branches to dominate the economy. In wartime, the government sent out officials to supervise the production of ammunition on credit. The repudiation of such liabilities after the Japanese surrender made most large firms bankrupt. To prevent the revival of Japanese militarism, the business groups were split up, the top corporate officers were removed and banned for life from business leadership, and the stockholdings of the founding families were seized and distributed to employees or citizens at large. Dominated by the inexperienced small stockholders who were ready to sell their holdings for capital gain, the companies delayed re-investment to pay dividends, the economy was near collapse, and many Japanese believed that the American corporations would swarm in, taking over what was left.

The rise of the phoenix When the Korean War broke out, America scrapped any plan to de-industrialize Japan but used it to supply its war needs, so that the population would not go communist out of desperation. The Japanese

---

*The article is reprinted from the *International Economic Journal*, Vol. 2, No. 1, pp. 101–108, 1988, published by Routledge (part of the Taylor & Francis Group).

government officials then swapped stockholdings among firms within the former business groups and promoted the third rank corporate officials to head the firms and vote as boards of directors of each other. When deprived of alternatives, households deposited savings in banks. The banks were forbidden to buy large share of corporate stocks, so they could only finance corporations with loans at low interest rates stipulated by the government, and provide oversight over corporations in the capacity of "main banks". Under term limits, top corporate officials retired at an early age, and then worked to manage subcontracting firms, so they were interested in corporate expansion and not high dividends.

The strength and the weakness In those years, the highly leveraged Japanese corporations financed by low interest bank loans would outspend their rivals in capital expenditure and enabled the Japanese economy to rise like a phoenix from World War II.

The system eventually deteriorated for several reasons: the main banks mired in irregularities during the financial bubbles (Morishima, 2000). The lack of free-standing small firms of the spin-off type, due to the crowding out by large firms, makes the economy less responsive than the American economy in a technological environment of frequent and rapid change.

INTERNATIONAL ECONOMIC JOURNAL
Volume 2, Number 1, Spring 1988

NIPPONIZED CONFUCIAN ETHOS OR INCENTIVE-COMPATIBLE INSTITUTIONAL DESIGN: NOTES ON MORISHIMA, "WHY HAS JAPAN SUCCEEDED?"

HENRY WAN, JR.*

Cornell University

In his well-cited book, Morishima offered a cultural explanation of the Japanese economic success. Thus, first, the Nipponized confucianism breeds political loyalty and, second, this bushido ethos spawns the discipline and efficiency in the modern Japanese labor. However, the facts he cited have not convinced us on either points. Political loyalty is not more conspicuous in Japanese history than in the political life of other societies. Loyalty in the Japanese workplace seems to have evolved in corporations which practice modern principles of scientific management long after the passing of the bushido institution. [800]

1. INTRODUCTION

The recent rise of the Japanese economic power has far reaching significances beyond its immediate importance. It shows that a non-Western society, by economic means can gain prosperity and a prominent status in world affairs, where her former effort via armed conflicts only ended in grief. It also shows that market mechanism is much more efficacious than both central planning, and the system of state enterprises Japan tried and abandoned one hundred years ago.

How much of such experience is replicable elsewhere is interesting to all LDCs, the home of 4/5 of the present mankind. The crucial question is what contributes to the Japanese success. Two contending hypotheses may be considered. First, there is the culture-historical view, and second, there is the 'economic system' explanation. If the performance of Japan is intrinsically rooted in her history and culture, clearly her success is a lesson of quite limited value to other societies, at least in the short run. This is not what we perceive as the case.

We believe that the performance of the Japanese economy is largely due to her labor-related institutions. Features of these institutions conform to the discussions in current economic theory. The evolution of such institutions reflects the economic forces as well as some historical events. To be sure, cultural and social heritages play their part. The fact that such heritages are allowed to play their

---

* I would like to thank Professor Morishima for kindly answering me in private correspondence. I still fail to share his view that Confucianism influenced the Japanese public only after the Meiji era. I readily agree that Japanese history is not my specialty. But I exclude sources other than Morishima by choice and not entirely due to ignorance. I find his survey of Japanese history credible, thus I focus upon his interpretations.

part, rather than obliterated by time and external shocks, is ultimately a consequence of the economic forces.

A scrutiny of the Japanese economy from the labour economics viewpoint is appropriate, since the driving force of that economy is her human resources. It also provides a laboratory case to illustrate various theories in labour economics at work. A fine source for beginners about the Japanese economy is the study, "Why Has Japan Succeeded?" by Morishima (1982). We rely on this volume heavily.

We review in the next three sections some key aspects of the Japanese labor market: the selection scheme, the reward system and the expected working relationships. After an overview of these facts, we come to the interpretations. Suffice to say here that we by no means agree with the central theme of Morishima, that Confucianism, selectively "Nipponized" under Regent Shotoku Taishi, has bred the political ethos of loyalty, and such ethos, when transformed into the economic context, makes the Japanese labour force the marvel of the present world. Finally, we offer further comments to corroborate our own interpretations.

2. THE RECRUITMENT MECHANISM

The screening process for a modern day Japanese is uni-dimensional and well understood. The life-long success of a person is decided by securing a job in a firm within the modern sector through passing an entrance examination. To get such a job, one must come from a top university. To be admitted to a top university, one must be from a top high school. The chain goes on, so that children receive pre-school instructions in order to enter a top kindergarten. At each step, test scores, and nothing else, decide the issue [see Morishima(1982: 192)]. There is only one chance to be recruited by a desirable firm: in that year one graduates from a university (ibid.: 174). Such relentless pressure on students and their families assures a maximum rate of human capital formation. Since the selection is not by birth, or race, or creed, such a meritocracy assures high intergenerational mobility but also reduces inter-class hostility (ibid.: 180-183).

Moreover, there is a 'tunneling effect'. Those who succeed must be disciplined and hard-working, a sorting and behavior-modifying process which conditions the properties of the Japanese labor force. Further, the best of the Japanese universities are precisely those traditionally emphasizing engineering and technology (ibid.: 135-136).

Such a system is actually the product of recent evolution. Before the Meiji Revolution of 1868, the society was stratified by birth, with minimal intergenerational mobility (ibid.: 11). The employment process was 'traditional', through the service of 'labor bosses' until the 1890s (ibid.: 105). The dualistic labor market developed only at the end of the first world war, with the rise of the 'heavy and chemical' industries (ibid.: 109).

3. THE LIFE-TIME TENURE AND ADVANCE BY SENIORITY

The dualistic Japanese labor market is dominated by the large firms which constitute the 'modern sector'. Large firms offer highly-paid and permanent employment to regular employees in exchange for the abandoning of any labour mobility, altogether.

From the viewpoint of incentive contracts, such a system must guard against the urge *to quit*, or the urge *to shirk* on the part of the employee. Specifically, the compensation scheme must be such to take account of both the *individual rationality* and the *incentive compatibility* constraints.

Quitting is prevented by denying to employees viable alternatives. The employee cannot hope to start business on their own, with their acquired expertise on the job. One does not dream of competing against a giant firm, with its capital, clientele and connections. The employee cannot hope to be employed by a rival firm. In a sequential equilibrium among the large, oligopsonistic firms, a self-enforcing 'no-raiding' understanding is in force, to the mutual benefit of all employers (*ibid.*: 106). This is in contrast to the mutual 'poaching' of skilled workers as practiced in the 1890s (*ibid.*: 105). Even then, an employee may leave, seeking employment with a firm in the 'traditional' sector of small and medium sized firms. Here, the deterrence is a high and rapidly rising 'seniority wage system' (*ibid.*: 105-106). Firms in the traditional sector do not seem to have the motivation of raiding large firms for employees. Once a worker is in the small/medium business sector, a different moral standard applies. He can and does enjoy the personal freedom of moving from one firm to another (*ibid.*: 118-119), so he may not be worth that much as an object for raiding, after all. For all the ethos of the Japanese Confucianism which focuses upon loyalty (*ibid.*: 4-6), in the end, the feelings of loyalty still has to be *purchased* [italics mine] with economic incentives. This not only includes a steep wage progression curve, but also an implicit contract offering job security. To maintain a stable employment level for itself, in the face of fluctuating market conditions, the large firms will surround themselves with the buffer of small and medium-sized firms as sub-contractors [called Type C firms in Morishima (*ibid.*: 102)]. This is of course in accordance to the 'peak-load' model of the industrial organization literature. These affiliated firms act like feudal vassals to the large firms. Yet, their emergence is quite recent, having no relationship with the pre-1868 feudalism.

We now turn to the question of monitoring in the employment relationship. On the surface, individual competition in Japan ends with the entrance examination into a large firm. From then on, the fierce competition is on a team basis, between employee groups in the same company and among various companies (*ibid.*: 115-116). The fruits of the competition are distributed in sizable bonus payments. Competition by team introduces a 'tournament scheme' in coalition form. This system of 'competition by team' may victimize individuals of ability who are surrounded by incompetent colleagues (*ibid.*: 119-120). In reality, the astute observer will readily discern where lurks the disciplinary mechanism. The ultimate check is of course, that the 'ship of the firm' may capsize, with 'all hands lost' (!) but would colleagues sit on their hands while an incompetent run amok? Table 7 of Morishima (*ibid.*: 179) suggests otherwise. While all Japanese employees enjoy the prestige, security and high reward of jobs in large companies, within a sample studied, 47% of those blue-collar workers and 27% of those white collar workers who started in large companies were found to end up *elsewhere* (!).

As a matter of fact, 'if at any time subsequently the life-time employment decided here for any reason ends in disaster, then the worker has no alternative but to look for a new employer on the second, mercenary market' (*ibid.*: 118). But one of such a 'disaster' is inherently provided for employees in the large firms, and this is not just for out-right incompetents, either. It is the transfer to the management of a subcontractor, a fate likened to that of a commander sent to the front line: there is the possibility to return to a high position if one distinguishes oneself, but-there is also a high probability of death in battle (*ibid.*: 102). Symmetrically, 'virtuous', 'devoted' workers are rewarded by 'good posts in the future and high bonuses' (*ibid.*: 117). But who does the monitoring then? The top management? Evidence suggest otherwise. The top manager consults his subordinates on various matters. For all their comradeship with each other, the time will come for Japanese employees, with decades of closest observation about each other, to come down to the collective judgement of who should remain and who must be transferred out. Their bonus depends on it, and so does their job security. The keenest peer monitoring is what keeps Japanese employees on their toes.

After they have received a modest pension, Japanese employees retire early, only to move to second jobs, with reduced pay. Hence, employees who have past their peak are offered financial security, but not the power of making major decisions.

The strength of the enduring relationship between large Japanese firms and their regular employees is the willingness of the firms to invest in the human capital of their employees. Elaborate training programs are provided for the latter, since they have managed to internalize the externalities of training the employees. The test of pudding is the high productivity of their senior personnel.

4. THE ALL-INCLUSIVE INVOLVEMENT OF EMPLOYEES

It is well known that Japanese employees of large firms only socialize within the firm (*ibid.*: 120). Non-conformers are penalized by 'complete isolation', through peer pressure (*ibid.*: 117). They sometimes also invest their life-time savings in the same firm (*ibid.*: 114). This may sound innocuous to the casual observer. But it is a fact crucial to the survivability of a firm under stressful conditions. Risk sharing between the employer and the employee becomes a natural outcome: the employee has no place to turn, if the firm goes bankrupt. Hence, volunteered wage concessions to save a firm in distress can be easily counted upon from the workers. After all, what alternative do they have?

The fact that large firms take the top-cut of new workers, the fact that they offer higher pay, better benefits and more job security, act together to provide high social status for their employees (*ibid.*: 118). The demand of large firms that employees do not change jobs for higher pay, also become enshrined as a 'virtue' and self-enforced by peer group judgement.

5. OVERVIEW: THE FACTS

Th₂ dualistic labor market is apparently the source of strength for the Japanese economy. This dualism did not evolve in a vacuum. It was a conscious choice of the Japanese State in the forced march toward modernization, as it faced its perceived peril of foreign domination (*ibid.*: 97-98). A replay of the same drama happened under the National Income Doubling Plan of 1960 when the Ministry of International Trade and Industry picked the designated 'winners' for favored treatment (*ibid.*: 188-189). It is this national consciousness which permits the government to favor particular sectors over the rest. Perceiving that economic growth as the only feasible way to regain national strength, after losing the first nuclear war in human history, it is no wonder that the Japanese only allow their union movement to develop in a fashion which makes costly strikes out of the question.

It is possible to attribute such national consciousness rather than profit motive as the source of the Japanese success (whether Western firms consciously maximize profits is also an open question). Whether it is Confuscian influence, or Shintoism, or any other heritage which contributes to this sense of nationhood lies beyond our analysis.

On the other hand, a skeptical comparison with the European ethos is not entirely out of place. In Chivalric Japan, a knight (samurai) either follows his lord (daimyo), or becomes a knight errant (ronin), a station of ambiguity and misfortune. The code of knighthood (bushido) as an institution ends with the Tokugawa period, with the rights of the clan lords abolished by 1871 (*ibid.*: 75). Workers for the State enterprises were heavily drawn from samurai families which are supposed to be disciplined (*ibid.*: 90). Yet discontentment from the same samurai class also frequently started revolts (*ibid.*: 93). At any rate, despite the Imperial Rescripts of 1890, aimed at impressing Confucian loyalty on all people (through compulsory education), by the time of 1890, "a spirit of loyalty was still a very *rare commodity*, and to that extent a company had to make special *payment* with a view to procuring it" (*ibid.*: 105, italics mine). The means of buying such purchaseable loyalty, i.e., the typical 'Japanese' wage difference only emerged around 1920 (*ibid.*: 109), a full half a century after the end of the old samurai system.

It is true even in Mid-Tokugawa days. Large scale shops arose, demanded loyalties from 'shop-boys' by appropriating the samurai ethics as the merchants' moral code (*ibid.*: 50). Yet these shops themselves did not form the basis of Meiji industry (*ibid.*: 92). The state enterprises in the Meiji period were further 'privatized' about 1880 (*ibid.*: 93-94).

It is hence quite debatable whether it is 'culture' or 'nurture' that allows firms in the Japanese modern-sector to arrogate to themselves the latter-day daimyo status and impose the samurai-like obligations on their current employee.

It behooves us to conjecture, that given an adequate incentive package, the ICI or the British Leland may buy off their 20 century employees to play Sir Percival or Sir Galahad. One may then marvel that the once-and-forever Arthurian spirit is again en fleur, . . . perhaps.

6. OVERVIEW: THE INTERPRETATION

The views of Morishima have not received undivided support in Japan. This involves issues we shall not delve into. We take for granted his facts, but ask "what do we make of them".

Two points are important. First, did Shotoku Taishi succeed to impart in Japanese politics, an 'unusual' sense of loyalty which is based upon Japanese Confucianism? Second, does the 'unusual' behavioral code among the modern Japanese labor force flow from such 'unusual' political ethos in historical Japan?

We have presented our doubts in the last section concerning the second question. Our view is that the Japanese Confucianism has provided the convenient vocabulary of 'loyalty' (Chu). This concept is given an interpretation by parties in power to suit their purpose. The success in receiving 'loyal' service depends upon an entire reward system. Had Confucianism not arrived in Japan, the Japanese would be perfectly capable to invent an equivalent nomenclature, or to borrow from elsewhere some suitable concept, say, the Chivalric tradition of Western Europe.

Returning to the first question, the Seventeen Article Constitution of Shotoku might have called for loyalty to a totally neutral emperor (*ibid.*: 22-28), but left unsaid how the actual power of the state should be exercised. Such a principle of loyalty verges on the vacuous. It did not prevent revolutionaries to overthrow the allied clan (Soga) of Shotoku soon after his death (*ibid.*: 28-30). It did not prevent numerous civil wars (*ibid.*: 32, 45 and 55). It did not prevent repeated Ikko and peasant uprisings (*ibid.*: 42, 76-77), the alleged regicide of Emperor Komei (*ibid.*: 71), the rebellion of Satsuma (*ibid.*: 75), and finally the February 26 coup d'etat (*ibid.*: 154). Contestants no doubt profess 'loyalty', perhaps to some 'higher principle'. But, we believe this is hardly relevant. 'Politics by the sword' of this type does not necessarily set up standards of 'discipline' and 'harmony' for the employees of modern Japanese firms.

Thus, either the Japanese Confucianism did not impart the sense of loyalty to actual Japanese politics, or that brand of 'loyalty' in Japanese politics has little to do with the sort of discipline and dedication, so valuable in the modern Japanese labor force. The 'feeling of loyalty' in modern Japanese firms is *pur-*

chased, period. It is 'purchased' with judiciously designed reward systems which are rightfully the pride of modern Japanese management. Above all, it can and should be emulated elsewhere, be it the developed America or the developing world of the LDCs.

At any rate, the Japanese is a gifted, adaptable people. Japanese ethos and institutions can change radically, if the needs arise. This includes their marriage and family (*ibid.*: 20-21). Whatever ethos or institution that survives for thirteen and a half centuries must have its survival value. This certainly should apply to the Japanese Confucian ethos, even if it matters.

7. FURTHER COMMENTARY

Going beyond the 'internal evidence' in Morishima's book, we note that the high efficiency of Japanese labor has also been commonly attributed to the superior Japanese management practices, and not just the working ethos of the Japanese labor force. Some of these practices were developed in America and improved upon in Japan, as recent as the post World-War II era. One example is the concept of 'quality control' which was introduced from America in the 1950s, and merged with the 'small team' principle, at the Japanese Productivity Center, to become the widely adopted system of the 'quality control circle'. Another example is the 'zero defect' principle which has its origin in the American missiles industry. Neither has any roots in the Confucian traditions. When recently these practices were introduced back by Japanese-managed factories into the non-Confucian America, the efficiency of American workers has approached their Japanese counterparts.

Moving further afield from Japan, but focussing upon the issue of how much a particular cultural background matters, one may note that the same Cantonese worker force works at both Shen-tseng, PRC, and the New Territory, Hong Kong, across the border. Many in the factories at the latter location came over the border, just a few years back. The highly-paid workers south of the border produce for the much more profitable world market, while their low-wage bretheren produce only for domestic consumption in the PRC. The fact that foreign factory owners south of the border do not move north to enjoy favors in PRC and reduce labor cost implies that people with similar culture-historical background can work with different efficiency levels. The fact that efficiency levels can differ widely suggests that the implementable management practices may differ on two sides of the border.

It would be quite wrong to say that Confucian culture has no effect upon the Japanese as workers. What is in question is how to isolate the minimum sufficient condition in a culture which helps development. Apparently, both the Protestant ethic and the Confucian ethos (at least the Japanese version) possess such conditions.

This work of Morishima has received broad attention. Up to August 1987, 40 citations and book reviews have appeared in English language journals alone, including references by Chakravarty (1987a and b), Sen (1983, 1986), and Yoo (1985) beside reviews by Dore (1983), Sinha (1983), Taira (1984) and Yonekawa (1984). The most lasting contribution of this thought-provoking book is perhaps to urge economists to reconsider the role culture plays in economic development, in Japan and elsewhere.

REFERENCES

Chakravarty, S, "Marxist Economics and Contemporary Development Economies," *Cambridge Journal of Economics*, March 1987(a), 3-22.

_____, "The State of Development Economics," *The Manchester School of Economics and Social Studies*, June 1987(b), 125-143.

Dore, Ronald, "Book Notes," *Economic Journal*, June 1983, 465.

Morishima, M., *Why Has Japan 'Succeeded'?*, Cambridge: Cambridge University Press, 1982.

Sinha, R,. "Review," *Economica*, November 1983, 488.

Sen, A. K., "The Profit Motive," *Lloyd Bank Review*, January 1983, 1-20.

_____, "Prediction and Economic Theory," *Proceedings of the Royal Society of London*, Series A 407, 1986, 3-21.

Taira, K. "Review," *History of Political Economy*, Spring 1984, 151-153.

Yonekawa, Shinichi, "Review," *Business History*, July 1984, 239-241.

Yoo, J. H., "Does Korea Trace Japanese Footsteps? A Macro-economic Appraisal," *Kyklos*, Volume 85, Fasc. 4, 1985, 578-598.

East Asian Development: Japan as the Growth Pole

Review of "Comments on Chakravarty's 'Marxist economics and contemporary development economics'"*

Two principal points This note takes issue with Chakravarty on two related aspects. The common thread is that the East Asian growth is not basically exploitative. First, wage rate rose in East Asia as economies became opened to world trade. This lengthening of working hours reflects the enriched opportunities, not the intensified exploitation. In the labor market, what has shifted to the right was the derived demand schedule, and not the supply schedule. Farmers go for multiple crops to earn extra income from exporting. They choose to work longer hours by their own volition. Second, the extension of the supply chain for America from Japan through the East Asian Newly Industrialized Economies (Korea, Taiwan, Hong Kong and Singapore) and beyond has brought prosperity along the network. Japan has played the multiple roles, from being the role model, the middleman, the supplier of products by skilled labor, the financier, and so on. Yet, this process has brought for Japan economic reward, but not monopoly power. In fact, for Korea, government policy makes sure that in the long run, the economy would compete against Japan, not depend on the later, in industry after industry. For Taiwan, the Japanese used the economy as an export platform for plastic shoes, but then American buyers came to introduce the leather shoe production, easing the Japanese out.

Further extensions This discussion may be amplified to show the historical perspective.

First, the rise of wage in response to export expansion reflects labor shortage. This happened first for Japan. As a result of the Korean War, at one time 70% of Japanese export was military (Ruttan, 2001). Because of the international politics after the Korean armistice, the economy was transformed again under American assistance, to export civilian goods for the American market.

Second, there are two sides of the same coin. On one side, there is the local labor shortage as reflected in long working hours. On the other, there is the

---

*The article is reprinted from the *Cambridge Journal of Economics*, Vol. 14, No. 2, pp. 233–239, 1990, published by Oxford University Press.

extension of America's supply chain as reflected in the migration of industries in search of labor at lower cost (Kojima, 1978).

Third, what happened to Japan, namely, the rising labor cost and emigrating industries, eventually happened to the Newly Industrialized Economies. For various inputs in producing disk drives, Singapore led in comparative costs. As the top supplier of footwear for OECD countries, Mainland China succeeded Taiwan (as shown graphically on p. 336 and p. 348, Wan, 2004).

Fourth, the existence of such smoothly operating "internal" division of labor in East Asia is unmatched in West Europe. This may explain why East Asian economies are more successful than Western European economies in their catching up process versus America (as shown graphically on p. 58, Wan, 2004).

Fifth, such diffusion of economic activities is not entirely benign. For Hong Kong, the income ratio of the richest fifth to the poorest fifth reached 20 in 2001, but was only 11 ten years earlier (see p. 251,Wan, 2004).

Last but not the least, trade expansion of Mainland China may bring in a somewhat new situation, due to its large population and the relative ease of labor migration inside China than across borders. See Article 9 and also Article 11.

Cambridge Journal of Economics 1990, **14**, 233–239

Comments on Chakravarty's 'Marxist economics and contemporary developing economies'

Henry Wan, Jr*

I

In his Suzy Paine Lecture,[1] Professor Chakravarty offered one of the most profound analyses of the transformation of the East Asian Five (Japan and the 'Gang of Four': South Korea, Taiwan, Hong Kong and Singapore). These five are often held as exemplary models to the four-fifths of the mankind in the LDCs. In exploring a non-neoclassical approach (here, Marxian) to the East Asian experience, Chakravarty expressed reservations on three key questions:

1. Is it reasonable to study the East Asian Five as a unit, with Japan as the engine of growth?

2. How can we explain the determination and implications of the terms of employment (including the long working week) in the East Asian Five? Chakravarty cited Marx, 'there is . . therefore . . right against right. . . Between equal rights, force decides', and suggested this may possibly be relevant to the East Asian Five.

3. How should we assess the role of the MNCs as a source of technological dynamism? Chakravarty viewed technical change as an issue left incomplete by Marx, and considered the related debates about the role of direct foreign investment to be inconclusive.

The purpose of this note is to stimulate discussion by supplying facts on these three points and by drawing tentative inferences of our own.

II

Chakravarty is undoubtedly right about Japan's role as an engine of growth. Two questions follow: first, what is the nature of this growth-engine role, and second, what is its implication for appraising the 'gang of four'?

First, vis-à-vis the 'gang of four', post-war Japan is neither their 'neo-colonial' political master, nor the largest market for their exports. It plays the growth engine role through four channels:

Manuscript received 4 March 1988.

*Cornell University. I acknowledge the helpful and generous comments of Professor Chakravarty as well as discussions by David Berrian. Any remaining errors are, of course, my own.

[1] *Cambridge Journal of Economics*, vol. 11, no. 1, March 1987.

0309–166X/90/020233 + 07 $03.00/0

(1) *By serving as a role model*. This includes both the conscious emulation of Japan by the South Korea of President Park, and the subtle but no less profound influence of Japan on most Chinese societies (e.g. Taiwan, Hong Kong and Singapore) *via* their primary and middle school systems. These emulate their Japanese counterparts, originally set up by the Imperial Rescript on Education in the Meiji Era. Such a universal education system instills the ethic of disciplined hard work into the female labour force in the textile, clothing, footwear and electronics sectors.

(2) *By intensifying international competition*, mainly in the American market. This forces competitive cost cutting between Japanese and American firms. As a matter of survival, both sides resort to 'offshore production' in the 'gang of four' countries, where labour costs are relatively low while workers are well-motivated and educated, Japanese style.

(3) *By the transfer of technology through joint ventures*. Prosperity in Japan drives up Japanese wage rates. Under government assistance, many plants emigrate to the 'gang of four' countries to 'mine' labour. They take along technology, experience and brand names, but often little capital. To manage local labour efficiently, save capital, and reduce risk, they often seek out local partners in joint ventures. The Japanese may have a slight preference for East Asian partners: 'transaction costs' are reduced by the 'common knowledge' given by cultural and historical affinity.

(4) *By supplying industrial inputs at competitive terms*. As the 'gang of four' begin to industrialise, Japan seizes a new niche in the international division of labour, retaining the production of specialised steel, advanced synthetic fibre, computer chips, dye stuff for clothing, etc. These products are capital-intensive, technologically advanced or subject to scale economies. Cheaper than the equivalent US or European products and initially more reliable than local supplies in the 'gang of four', they are sold to various down-stream firms throughout East Asia, whether they are Japanese-owned, locally owned, or American-owned. They help to pay Japan's fuel and raw materials bill.

Close as its relationship is to the 'gang of four', post-WWII Japan has never enjoyed absolute economic dominance over the 'gang of four', both because of the presence of rivals in the market (especially America) and because of the small size of its investments. Japanese influence is based on technical expertise, market *savoir faire* and the cost-competitiveness of Japanese products. The Japanese role is pervasive, profitable but never indispensable, and often fragile, as the 'gang of four' mature, eroding the Japanese advantages. This is not quite what one expects in the classical 'dependence relationship'.

At one time, when the People's Republic of China (PRC) threatened to blacklist Japanese firms trading with Taiwan and South Korea, invoking the Chou Principle, those Japanese firms which withdrew found themselves quickly replaced by American and European firms (which were less impressed by the PRC trade). At a pinch, Taiwan and South Korea can always switch from Japanese to the higher-priced American and European sources, by absorbing the cost differential in the wage share. Given the tempo of their real wage growth, such a shift would be costly but quite manageable.

Second, one corollary of the 'Japan-as-growth-engine' thesis is that, with Japan playing this role, there are other, equally viable approaches to sustained rapid growth, pursued by various members of the 'gang of four'. In particular, export-led, labour-intensive industrialisation does not have to be in the 'South Korean' mode. If we are dissatisfied with some aspects of South Korean development, we might consider the rather different paths taken by the other three among the 'gang of four'. Take the following.

(1) While Korea is developing under strong state guidance, Hong Kong pursues the purest laissez faire;

(2) South Korea sustains the heavy burden of servicing external debt, while Taiwan is embarrassed by its massive foreign reserves, Hong Kong and Singapore maintain essentially balanced current accounts;

(3) South Korea has been ready to keep labour costs low by authoritarian measures (until the summer of 1987); Hong Kong has never tampered with personal freedom for economic benefits;

(4) South Korea (along with Taiwan) was politically dominated by Japan between 1895 and 1945; Hong Kong and Singapore were occupied by Japan for only three and a half years, during World War II.

In fact, among these four economies, South Korea has consistently, over a 30-year period, had the lowest per capita GNP and the highest average inflation rate. Among these three countries, the policy regime pursued in Hong Kong is perhaps as different as it could be from that of South Korea. It is usually believed that Hong Kong is too atypical to be emulated by LDCs, either because of its size, its lack of rural underemployment or the importance of its service sectors. The truth is much more complex.

In the first place, Hong Kong may not be so atypical, after all. Firstly, at 5·5 million, Hong Kong is actually more populous than Denmark, Norway, Finland and Ireland in Europe, Uruguay and Paraguay in South America, Lebanon, Jordan and Israel in the Middle East, Chad, Libya, Liberia, Sierra Leone, Togo, Cameroon in Africa and any Central American republics apart from Guatemala. Secondly, in 1950, Hong Kong was burdened with two million refugees, a situation much worse than massive rural under-employment, where physical subsistence is rarely in question. Finally, 46% of currently employed labour in Hong Kong is in either manufacturing or construction, in contrast to 28% for the UK and 27% for the US.

How much Hong Kong has benefited from its proximity to the People's Republic of China (PRC) deserves further scrutiny. Its industrialisation started first as the UN banned trade with China (but that was during the 'Korean boom'). Its growth seems to have been relatively immune to Chinese upheavals (e.g. the 'Great Leap Forward', the 'Cultural Revolution').

In addition, differences in population size may not matter much, up to a point. With 20 million people, Taiwan is almost four times as populous as Hong Kong. Its policy reform in the 1950s (which ushered in the sustained rapid growth) was a conscious and selective effort to emulate Hong Kong, in exchange rate liberalisation, in setting up export processing zones, etc. The emulation was successful.

Finally, the socio-economic indices of Hong Kong compare favourably with those of South Korea in almost all aspects: life expectancy, percentage of protein intake in all calories, the ownership of cars, radio, television, etc. Furthermore, despite there being no government protection, local business is not heavily dominated by 'non-Chinese' aliens (query: are Shanghainese aliens?). This poses a curious contrast with Canada and Australia, whose industries are so heavily dominated by UK and US investors. The development of Hong Kong is a relatively neglected success story, which deserves further analysis.

In the search for causal explanations for East Asian growth, the diversity of pattern eliminates many possibilities, although not all similarities are relevant. Culturally, North Korea is closer to South Korea than to Japan, and PRC is closer to Singapore, Hong Kong and Taiwan than to Japan, and the two Koreas. Cultural affinity alone does not explain the shared growth experience of the East Asian Five.

III

Chakravarty cites the Marxian proposition that a long working week reduces the unit wage cost (which may be force-determined or market-determined) and raises capitalists' profits and that this profit finances capital formation, in the form of capital assets. He asks whether the long working week in the East Asian Five reflects such a scenario.

We are not sure. In Hong Kong and Taiwan, (i) workers vote with their feet; annual labour turnover exceeds 100% in some export sectors; (ii) wages have risen rapidly for decades, forcing wave after wave of labour-intensive firms and industries to emigrate or to go bankrupt; (iii) many small and middle sized firms raid each other for labour with non-price inducements (e.g., an air conditioned working place, or music in lunch rooms); and finally, (iv) firms negotiate with workers individually for paid overtime work. What makes the long working week persist in such a sellers' market for labour does not seem to be accounted for by the usual Marxian explanation.

In South Korea (before the summer of 1987) and in Singapore, firms are larger and the state participates in wage-setting: overtly in Singapore and covertly in South Korea. But in the latter the authoritarian state is controlled by no class and the anxious rulers applied their 'deciding force' for their own survival (politically, as well as physically—recall Rangoon). Their anxiety is traceable to Marx: not to Marxian economics, but to Marxism in Peking or Pyongyang. Wages will be kept low, if unemployment threatens, and the government perceives that 'low employment at a high wage' is more threatening than 'high employment at a low wage'. Here, the 'political economy' approach, and not the neoclassic paradigm, is apparently called for.

Once full employment is assured, denying labour the fruits of growth has its own perils. After the Korean summer of 1987, it now seems that the influence of an authoritarian state can be easily overestimated. Strikes may be forbidden, as they are in South Korea, Taiwan and Singapore. But forbidden strikes did happen and did succeed, in the South Korea of 1979 and again in the summer of 1987. The guns of the security force might be turned against the ruler (as in 1979) or thrown down before a rising populace (as in the summer of 1987). It is never certain whether enlisted men will fire on civilians. In the end, authoritarian rulers still rule by the will to acquiesce of the people: whether the people tolerate a long working week better than low pay is a matter of taste as well as of custom. But Marx would probably regard customs (like the state itself) as superstructures of the underlying economic forces.

Presumably, in all economies where real wages are allowed to rise markedly and consistently for decades, owing either to market force or to pressure from workers, the long working week persists only by the implicit choice of the working people.

One is tempted to offer a 'dual' premise: apart from historical factors, a legislated short working week survives in less affluent economies because it shares the burden of unemployment more equitably and not because it reflects the leisure-preference of the people. In fact, before migrating to the cities, those workers who owned land probably toiled long hours on their own farms.

IV

We now come to the heart of the development issues: what causes the rapid and persistent rise of real wages in the East Asian Five, three or four decades in a row and, more important, what causes the growth of labour productivity which permits the wage increases? The stock answer is, capital formation and technology. For our purpose, there seems to be a simpler answer.

At present, persistent, rapid growth prevails in both South Korea with its heavy foreign borrowing and Taiwan with its massive, accumulated foreign reserves. Thus, for such outward-looking economies, domestic investment is 'de-linked' from domestic savings. In making contemporary comparisons among such economies, the only key factor is technology change.

Technical progress in the Far East Five is largely decided by the absorption of the 'technological backlog' (i.e., inward technology transfers), not the modest local R and D spending. Thus, for the last 15 years, growth has slowed down in Japan but not in the 'gang of four': there is little now that Japan can still learn cheaply, that is by absorbing foreign technology.

Foreign technology is absorbed in East Asia in two ways: through investment by foreign multinationals (MNCs), as in the 'gang of four', and without it, as in Japan. In the former case, foreign investors are courted for their technology and not for their capital. Notwithstanding its huge current account surplus, Taiwan still avidly encourages those foreign investments introducing new technology.

We now try to address three questions:

(a) Why is it that the 'gang of four' seem to benefit more from their dealings with the MNCs than do many other LDCs?

(b) Why is Japan more successful than others in acquiring foreign technology without foreign investment?

(c) Why is direct MNC investment needed for absorbing foreign technology for the 'gang of four', but not for Japan?

We shall first offer a tentative metaphorical theory of technology before turning to some facts of real life.

Technology is not science. As a complex of information, experience and insights in the possession of individuals (or teams) it pertains to the production processes at a particular location and time. Its value is measured by the ability of those possessing it to function effectively in their own environments. 'Production, American way' has to be adapted to become 'production, Korean way'. Formally, technology determines the set of production possibilities. The relationship that blue prints, operating manuals, experimental records (or other items specified in the agreements of technology transfers) bear to 'technology' is the same as that which pen, paper, ink, grammar and rhyming rules bear to poetry. The process of technology transfers is no different from the action of taking a college course, Poetry 201. One can pay a poet to teach poetry, one can send students to attend a class, but one cannot sue (successfully!) an instructor for malpractice if none of the students wins a laurel crown, or substitute class attendance for motivated hard work. Whether one really works hard defies monitoring and can only be inferred imperfectly from results. It helps if both parties, the teaching and the taught, have their hearts in the enterprise. It helps if the student already has some other form of writing skill. It helps even more if such skill was developed in some writing workshop, by some principle of 'learning to learn by learning'. There are many forms of writing skill. Blessed are those who have started with forms easier than poetry, perhaps when the former forms were more in vogue.

When Japan lost the first nuclear war in history, it had a tradition (and hence, self-confidence) of acquiring lethally effective technology from hostile aliens: the Tang

Chinese who sank the Japanese fleet, the Spaniards who seized the Philippines, the Dutch who colonised Java and Taiwan, and the Western powers who bombarded Shimonoseki. Further, Japan had already amassed enough technology by WWII to produce the largest warship (the Yamato) and an all-wood combat aircraft (the 'Zero' fighter). Compared to 'high tech' today, the technologies of the smokestack and engineering industries, then important, are perhaps easier to reverse-engineer for beginners. Then, under the pressure of the Korean War, America was ready to rely on Japan for offshore procurement, with certain technology transferred on easy terms. Furthermore, the entire Japanese society was convinced that Japan must import technology to survive and thrive by exporting. Thus, Japanese efforts and Japanese success are products of the right mixture of desperation and hope, both bestowed by Japanese history. Such has not been the pre-condition in Brazil, China, India, Russia or the 'gang of four'.

The 'gang of four' had to take a different road. 'Rich' in labour but poor in resources, their attraction is not their own markets but as export platforms for labour-intensive ware. MNCs come not as a cartel, but as competing capitalists. By mechanisms either Keynesian or neoclassic, the MNC investments create jobs, raise wages and reduce income inequality. They are rewarded by host governments: their highly profitable activities happen to make such regimes politically secure (and these economies, libertarian 'show cases').

However destitute they might be, local workers are never slaves. Thus, the MNCs cannot appropriate the 'capital gain' on this factor of production (labour), as promised by Stolper-Samuelson. Note that the reverse of all this holds true when MNCs invest in resource-rich economies.

By their very nature, transactions involving technology are between those who know (MNCs) and those who know not (LDCs). Yet under an outward-looking policy, profiteering MNCs must transfer and update such technology to make their products internationally competitive. This is not so under an import-substitution regime. For instance, the rapid rise of the Korean Hyundai Motors (backed by Mitsubishi, Japan) which are exported, poses a sharp contrast to the decade-long stagnation of the Taiwan Yueloong Automobiles (backed by Nissan, Japan) which caters to a protected home market. To take another example, the Brazilians pride themselves on cars indigenously designed for rugged roads. But such products for the 'have nots' are unfit for the world market of the 'haves', where volume ensures scale economy and competition spurs progress.

In the long run, what is important in an LDC is to transform its institutions as well as its habits, not the royalty paid, the profit remitted, and the unbundling of some specific, existing technology which will soon be obsolete. In hindsight, one may now suspect that, lofty intentions aside, the policies of many LDCs in dealing with MNCs have caused them to lag behind Hong Kong—an economy without a sovereign government of its own.

Incentive is crucial for the taught as it is for the teachers. Gaining a marketable skill in a market economy is what makes the indigenous personnel learn well. Competitive private firms pay employees bonuses when they are profitable. Thus their employees learn to be cost-effective. This is why state enterprises are usually not the best recipients of transferred technology, unless it is managed 'private style' (e.g., the Pohang Steel Works, Korea).

This is also why there seems to be much to be gained by keeping prices 'right' in economic development. The 'right' prices are what keep products in the world market: competition keeps the technological edge sharp. The 'right' prices need not be those under free trade. Among the East Asian Five, free trade is practiced in Hong Kong and

Singapore, and not in Japan, South Korea, and Taiwan. Since any performance differences among these five are not likely to be explicable by this factor alone, the case for static comparative advantage is at the best 'not proved'.

There seems to be conclusive evidence that the benefit of an 'outward-looking' strategy is dynamic. The initial measures for trade liberalisation and export promotion in Taiwan and South Korea were concentrated in a short few years. Yet the ensuing productivity gain was certainly not a one-off affair, nor does it appear to be a single effect arriving by distributed lags. The growth profile is neither a 'step function' nor a 'sealed exponential'. It resembles more the convex branch of a logistic curve. The likely explanation is induced international technological diffusion.

In the 'gang of four', one of the most potent means for technology diffusion is via labour mobility. Workers spread the technical information from firm to firm, and start new firms of their own, e.g., the eleven spawned by General Instruments, Taiwan alone. This threatens to 'hollow out' MNCs in the end.

Other mechanisms also exist. Serving as second-source subcontractors, firms in the 'gang of four' (e.g., shoemakers in Taiwan) simply cannot help but acquire some free technical information. Such opportunities are likely to be missed by firms under heavy bureaucratic regulation.

There is probably something more, because the East Asian Five are all resource-poor. They had to specialise in the labour intensive sectors of manufacturing at the outset. Now, skills acquired in manufacturing happen to be less sector-specific (e.g. between radio, television, television and computer monitor, etc.) than the extractive sectors of the resource-rich LDCs (e.g., between anchovy fishing, copper mining, and llama raising, etc.). Furthermore, trade ought make one vulnerable to external shocks. Yet, in recession and oil crises, the 'gang of four' fared relatively well.

The cases of the East Asian Five offer no panacea, but perhaps some food for thought. Not the least is the true benefit from trade: its invigorating effect, not its static trading gain. Thus, the key is not the trade volume per capita, but the openness to world competition. This benefit is open to all economies, small or large.

Deregulation in Reform: The Taking-Off of Korean Growth

Review of "Reform Unleashed Korean Growth"[*]

Foundation for sustained rapid growth This Article formalizes the view of Jones and Sakong (1980). With his foreign exchange reform, President Park refocused the Korean entrepreneurial effort to manage business well, rather than to seek rents from the unproductive activities of foreign exchange manipulations. This laid down the foundations for "the Korean Miracle".

History of Korean growth The Korean development was molded by eighteen years of micro-management under President Park, using directed credit and other means. It went through phases of globalization and then industry upgrading, away from the labor intensive exports. In this process, giant business groups amassed tremendous influence and dominated the economy ever since. The successful development of brand name products, like the cell phones from Samsung and the automobiles of Hyundai, comes at the cost of recalcitrant income polarization and repeated financial crises. See Hong (2002).

The micro-management of Park relied on mild inflation and, more importantly, directed credit. In this process, State banks offered short term loans at negative real interest rates to selected business groups. The latter made long term investment in heavy industry projects approved by Park. Thus, those fast growing business groups which dominated Korea with government favor would face certain ruin overnight, should the State banks call in their loans. Like the lantern genie in the Arabian Nights, the Korean business groups became powerful and obedient instruments of the ambition of Park for Korea. Eventually, Korea could match Japan in shipbuilding and displaces the latter as the world's chief supplier in computer memory chips.

Competing visions The heavy intervention and heavy industry bias of Korea under Park has been controversial, especially in the wake of the crisis of 1997–1998. Business groups became "too big to fail". Banks were overloaded with non-performing loans. Talented would-be entrepreneurs had little chance to

---

[*]This article is reprinted from the *German Economic Review*, Vol. 4, No. 1, pp. 19–34, 2003, published by Blackwell.

establish start-up firms, of the type in Silicon Valley in America, or Hsingchu in Taiwan. Some observers maintain that in terms of individual welfare, a policy more similar to what was in use in Taiwan can accomplish Korean goals at a lower cost. See discussion in Thorbecke and Wan (1999a and b), and Wan (2004). Regardless of the merit of this debate, for Korea, even a Taiwan-like policy would require a similar type of foreign exchange reform, which Taiwan also had a few years earlier than Korea.

Crisis and recovery in perspective Crisis 1997 marks the end of high growth for Korea. The debt crisis was sharp. The recovery was also quick. The restructuring of the economy was costly, but still carried out by and large (see however, McKinnon, 2004). Yet the uninterrupted high growth did not return. Banks tried to stimulate domestic demand by promoting credit cards. The inexperienced households accumulated unsupportable debts. The benefit was understandably short-lived.

Why should the high growth period come to an end for Korea at this time? Evidence suggests that by domestic demand alone, Korea cannot maintain a growth rate far above the advanced economies for long. Export expansion is limited by two constraints. First, past success appears to come from entering markets shared with Japan with a lower wage. This approach comes to an end when Japanese recession ended the rising Japanese production cost. Second, the loss of American markets to Chinese competition is not adequately compensated by expanding exports to China, in terms of generating the rate of growth. See Kim (2000). See also Article 12.

The lesson seems to be that globalization helps, and one cannot hope Korea to do much better. But this itself does not guarantee a specific rate of (high) growth.

German Economic Review 4(1): 19–34

Reform Unleashed Korean Growth

Henry Y. Wan, Jr.
Cornell University, New York

Abstract. *Before the reform in the 1960s, twin vicious circles perpetuated the shortages of foreign exchange and labor skill, and prevented the Korean economy from realizing its considerable growth potential. The breakthrough came when the Japanese labor shortage facilitated Korean exports, after economic normalization between the two countries. The reformed institutions reduced rent-seeking and refocused Korean managerial efforts to pioneering activities. The Korean takeoff scenario is a shared theme among all four Asian newly industrialized economies cited by Lucas (1988) as showcases.*

JEL classification: *D72, O12, O53, P11.*

Keywords: Rent-seeking; industrialization; Korea; regulatory reform.

1. INTRODUCTION

The cause of South Korea's rapid growth is still a subject of debate (Amsden, 1989; Rodrik, 1995; Bhagwati, 1999). Various factors have made contributions at various points in time. In addition, the country has always had much development potential.[1] This study focuses on a single issue: how was Korea's potential unleashed in the early 1960s? We maintain that while there is no single cause, there does exist a definite mechanism. Foreign exchange is crucial, and regulatory reform is indispensable. Lessons from Korea remain valuable to many developing economies today.

Our exposition relies heavily, though not exclusively, on Jones and Sakong (1980), both for their richly documented information and their highly convincing interpretation. Unless otherwise indicated, facts we cite will be cross-referenced to the page numbers in that volume. Based on the foundation of this relatively neglected work, we provide some simple analytic

---

1.   In 1961, among 74 developing countries, Korea ranked 14th in socioeconomic potential but 60th in per capita income (Adelman and Morris, 1967).

---

building blocks to streamline the argument. According to this view, it was specific institutional reform that refocused Korean managerial efforts to break into new export markets. The export of new goods never produced locally before is the mark of rapid growth in East Asia (Lucas, 1988).

We first identify the four interlocked hurdles impeding Korea's growth in the early 1960s and discuss how its components were overcome one by one. Nine stylized facts are then listed for context. Under the circumstances, there were two vicious circles perpetuating shortages of foreign exchange and labor skill. Following that, we introduce simple analytic building blocks to explain how the twin vicious circles formed and how they were broken by reform. In conclusion, we use the Korean takeoff to show how market forces contributed to East Asian growth, in spite of the differences among those rapid growing economies in government policy.

At President Rhee's fall in 1960, four interlocked hurdles plagued Korean growth:

(I)   A labor force did not have the training and experience versus countries like Japan.[2]
(II)   The strained economic tie with Japan deprived Korea the natural partner in trade.
(III) Businesses lacked the information, access and reputation to benefit from exports.
(IV)   The regulatory environment distracted entrepreneurs from managing well.[3]

Regarding hurdle I, improving labor efficiency takes time. It is best accomplished through learning by doing, in operations transcending the home market, which is limited in size and income. In this task Korea's natural partners at that time were Japanese traders. These traders were experienced in exports, but faced the rising Japanese wages. But because of hurdle II, co-operation was impossible until after Rhee.[4]

Yet working with the informed Japanese might make it more difficult for the uninformed Korean businesses to earn a reasonable share then and a better future later. They must give undivided attention to their business, to accumulate knowledge capital. In facing hurdle III, Korean businesses were not doing their best, until President Park arrived. The cause was hurdle IV. Before the reform, those in business were preoccupied with rent-seeking (and perhaps bribing) rather than managing well.

2.   Pages 25–26, Jones and Sakong (1980) for lacking experience in technical positions; p. 68, Amsden (ibid.) for lack of competitiveness vs. Japan.
3.   Page 96, Jones and Sakong (1980, pp. 276–278).
4.   Rhee was a lifelong exiled leader against the Japanese rule. But reconciliation always takes time. The normalization of economic relations with Japan took four more years even under the Japanese-educated Park.

Remarkably, in a few short years, the same business leaders, once denounced for amassing illicit wealth, emerged as visionary pioneers in industrialization.[5]

2. STYLIZED FACTS, VICIOUS CIRCLES AND THE BREAKTHROUGH

For context, we distill out of Korean history prior to 1960 nine *stylized facts*:

(A) *World market prices were not influenced by events in the Korean economy.* Thus, the 'small country' assumption in trade theory fits the Korean situation well.

(B) *Korean exports were highly price inelastic.* Early on, most of the Korean export was tungsten.[6] Such mineral exports could not be expanded much by cutting prices; thus, 'export pessimism' appeared to be realistic.

(C) *Imported inputs were indispensable for manufacture.* With no petroleum reserve and little iron, South Korea also had to import most machines.

(D) *The 'dollar shortage' was extremely acute.* A total of 82% of investment goods were financed by US Aid, which, according to President Park, '… was extremely tight fisted towards the productive facilities which we desired and generous with regard to consumer goods we did not require'.[7] Unlike the Marshall Plan for Western Europe, the US Aid for Korea was sometimes used as a tool for arm-twisting.

(E) *Under stringent exchange and import control, rent-seeking was widespread.* The distortion factor for the exchange rate was 272% in 1955 but 115% in 1965.[8]

(F) *Pioneering efforts in business have long-term benefits but take time to bear fruit.* Enos and Park (1988) have documented sector-by-sector how Korea introduced foreign technology. Stern *et al.* (1995) describe how Hyundai took a dozen years to realize its goal of entering the American market.

(G) *To seek rent on foreign exchange and to undertake pioneering manufacturing activities were mutually exclusive pursuits for top management.* This general situation is illustrated by the well-documented case of Mr Yi, the founder of the Samsung Group. Through importing, he made his fortune (including 17% of Korean commercial banks) under Rhee and pioneered various manufacturing industries under Park.[9]

---

5.   Pages 69–70, Jones and Sakong (1980, pp. 280–282).
6.   As mentioned in Park's State of Nation Message, 16 January 1965. In contrast, cotton textile was for import substitution and exports amounted only to 4.8% of total demand in 1963. Amsden (ibid.).
7.   Page 43, Jones and Sakong (1980). The share of capital goods in US Aid was 3.4% in 1953 and 11.7% in 1960 (p. 45; Amsden, ibid.).
8.   Page 88, Jones and Sakong (1980).
9.   Pages 349ff., Jones and Sakong (1980).

(H) *Interaction with Japan became mutually valuable, once the Japanese wage rose.* Kojima (1978) explains how labor shortages forced Japan firms to outsource their needs. Levy (1990) documents how Mitsubishi shifted its supply base from Kobe to Korea for rubber shoes exported to America. Kojima and Ozawa (1984) explain how Korea emerged as the most popular host for Japanese investment, after the normalization of economic relations in 1965.

(I) *Projects with scale economies became important in Korea's development only later.* Fact I implies that, for our present concern, President Park's 'heavy-chemical industry drive' (which promoted highly capital-intensive sectors from 1973 on) are not relevant.[10]

In the beginning, Korea faced *twin vicious circles*. First, facts A through D show that to earn foreign exchange, Korea needed manufacturing exports, but manufacturing industries needed inputs which Korea could neither supply at home nor afford by importing from abroad. In these circumstances, exchange control appeared to be a reasonable option. But this led to a vicious circle of a different kind. Second, facts E through G show that, to improve labor skill, the best way is through learning by doing and by exporting to the challenging world market. But the world market demands goods producible only with a skill that the country did not have and could not develop, with its entrepreneurs distracted by opportunities of quick profit through rent-seeking.

Before the first vicious circle could be broken with manufactured export, the multiple exchange rates under President Rhee were useful so that the government could extract rent out of the exports free from distortions, at least in principle.

Fact H shows that the turning point came when Japanese businesses ran out of low wage workers. Before that, the normalization of an economic relationship with Japan might be desirable in itself, but would have made little economic difference. Afterwards, both the economic estrangement from Japan and the exchange control system became binding constraints against growth.

With Japan experiencing a labor shortage, replacing Japan in its export market became far easier for Korea – especially with Japanese cooperation, at some middleman's fee. The terms with the Japanese would become gradually more favorable to Korea, if, by pioneering activities, Korean firms could demonstrate their ability in marketing, so they can go it alone without the middleman, if that becomes necessary. If pioneering efforts require the undivided attention of the top management, then their attention cannot be distracted to compete against each other in rent-seeking, which is what happened before the reform of the exchange rate system.

10. Stern *et al.* (1995).

When discretionary control operates in a state that lacks transparency, corruption usually takes place.[11] But under the above analysis, corruption is just a form of income transfer: it is relevant only in its moral aspect. Again it is often noted that corruption induces unproductive activity.[12] Here what is significant is that to wine and dine is costly not in material resources but rather in managerial distraction, especially in an economy in the throes of catching up.

We shall next use simple analytic building blocks to answer two questions:

- How did a vicious circle cause 'the export gap', and lead to the exchange control?
- How did the Japanese boom help Korean exports, with its benefit gradually realized after the institutional reform?

3. ANALYTICAL BUILDING BLOCKS

We focus on the single, eventful decade of 1955–65 in Korea, including the stagnation years of President Rhee up to 1960, the early growth under President Park since 1961, and the intermezzo under Chang Myon. In such a short-run framework, the effect of physical capital accumulation is omitted for simplicity.

We consider two sectors, namely, primary goods (agriculture and mining), and manufacturing. Each uses labor, L, and a sector-specific input, respectively, 'land', T, and imported industrial input, Z, measured in value terms. The primary sector produces Y_1. The manufacturing sector includes two separate industries, producing non-tradable, Y_2, and tradable manufacture, Y_5. Each unit of the latter combines m units of 'upstream' and one unit of 'downstream' components, Y_3 and Y_4. All in all, there are five outputs: the two components are intermediary inputs; the other three, Y_1, Y_2 and Y_5, are final goods.

The total supplies of labor and land are fixed. By selecting units, we set

$$L = 1 = T \tag{1}$$

The production process in the primary sector shows constant returns. Its output is:

$$
\begin{aligned}
Y_1 &= F_1(L_1, T) \\
&= L_1[1 - (L_1/2T)] \\
&= L_1 - L_1^2/2
\end{aligned}
\tag{2}
$$

11.   See, for example, Bardhan (1997).
12.   See Bhagwati et al. (1984).

where Y_1 and L_1 are, respectively, output and labor input of sector 1, and F_1 is the production function of that sector.

The production of non-tradable manufacture requires labor under a constant returns technology:

$$Y_2 = L_{2i}/a_2 \qquad (3')$$

The manufacturing process for good $i = 3$, 4 is of the fixed coefficient type,

$$\begin{aligned} Y_i &= F_i(L_i, Z_i) \\ &= b_i \min(L_i/a_i, Z_i) \quad \text{for } a_i, b_i > 0 \end{aligned} \qquad (3'')$$

where Y_i, L_i and Z_1 are, respectively, output, labor input and imported input of process i, and F_i is the production function of that process, with $i = 3$ and 4 standing respectively for the upstream and downstream components of the tradable manufacture, where a_i is the labor input for each unit value of imported input, and b_i is an output-augmenting efficiency indicator.

For simplicity, set

$$Y_5 = \min(Y_3, Y_4/m) \qquad (4)$$

where Y_5 stands for tradable manufacture and $m > 0$ is the constant for proportionality.[13]

The world market prices for primary goods and tradable manufacture are p_1 and p_5, respectively, and the price for imported input is 1.

The (private) utility function at home takes the form of

$$U(C_1, nC_2 + C_5) \quad \text{for } n > 0 \qquad (5)$$

which means non-tradable and tradable manufacture are perfect substitutes at home according to the $n : 1$ ratio.[14]

The welfare of the individual is assumed to be $U + W$ where W is an additive shift factor, showing how government uses funds, foreign aid, etc.

Define $X_i = Y_i - C_i$ as the net export of good i, $i = 1, \ldots, 5$.

We now assume that

$$X_i \leq R \qquad (6)$$

where $R > 0$ is the export bound of the country's export of primary goods before the reform. To recapitulate, we list the nature of all the goods mentioned above in Table 1.

13. We adopt the Leontief form of production function for simplicity. Like dealing with gold and the labor of a goldsmith in producing a gold ring, we find there is little point to state, 'the two components are substitutable, since more care by the goldsmith can save material, but their elasticity of substitution is assumed to be less than such and such a value, so that...'.

14. As a consequence of this perfect substitutability, although there are three final goods, the indifference curves are defined in the two-dimensional space.

Table 1   The nature of the goods $b_5 = 1/[(m/b_3)+(1/b_4)]$

	Productive input			Output			
					Manufactured		
						Tradable	
	Endowed		Foreign	Primary	Non-tradable	Component	Product
Good	T	L	Z	Y_1	Y_2	Y_3	Y_4	Y_5
Inputs				L, T	L	L, Z	L, Z	Y_3, Y_4
Export	n.a.	n.a.	n.a.	$\leq R$	No	?	?	Yes
Exchange a/c			-1	$+p_i$	n.a.	$-1/b_3$	$-1/b_4$	$p_5 - 1/b_5$

We next have the manpower balance:

$$L_1 + L_2 + L_3 + L_4 = L = 1 \tag{7}$$

also, at any equilibrium, there are the fixed coefficient relationships:

$$Y_4 = mY_3 = mY_5 \tag{8}$$

$$Y_i = Z_i = b_i L_1 / a_i \quad i = 3, 4 \tag{9}$$

as well as the accounting identities,

$$X_i = Y_i - C_i \quad i = 1, 3, 4 \tag{10}$$

and the balance of trade relationship:

$$p_i X_i + p_3 X_3 + p_4 X_4 = Z_3 + Z_4 \tag{11}$$

with the side condition,

$$mp_3 + p_4 = p_5 \tag{12}$$

If one is to close the system, one also needs the equilibrium relationship between the consumption of tradable manufacture and non-tradable (import-substituting) manufacture: since cost-conscious consumers would select between perfect substitutes. Thus, according to (5),

$$C_2 = 0 \quad \text{if } (a_2 + 1)/b_2 n > p_5$$

and

$$C_5 = 0 \quad \text{if } (a_2 + 1)/b_2 n < p_5 \tag{13}$$

To understand the grim realities of an economy facing an acute dollar shortage, one must consider the imported input requirements of exports for an economy having neither energy resources nor the capacity to supply sophisticated machinery.

4. THE STAGNATION EQUILIBRIUM

We now assume that, in the early days after the Korean War of 1951–54, the unit output value of the Korean manufacturing sector, p_5, could not cover the cost of its required imports:

$$p_5 \leq 1/b_5 \tag{14}$$

nor could that sector produce components to be separately exported. Therefore, there cannot be any positive net exports of components:

$$X_3 \leq 0 \quad X_4 \leq 0 \tag{15}$$

Thus,

$$X_5 = X_3 = X_4 = 0 = L_3 = L_4 = Z_3 = Z_4 \tag{16}$$

(there can be no manufactured export).

There are only two activities: primary good production and import substitution. The assumptions of the fixed coefficient production functions, and the perfect price inelasticity of the exports of agricultural and mineral primary products may have overstated somewhat the balance of payments difficulties, but not by very much. In fact, all import-substituting products need imported fuel. Without foreign aid, no import substitution is possible without export.

We can now show how the price inelasticity of exports allowed the government to extract rent through a multiple exchange rate system in Figure 1.

For simplicity, we assume that the utility function in (5) takes the quasi-linear form of:

$$U = V(C_1) + nC_2 + C_5 \tag{5'}$$

V being increasing and concave so that the shape of the indifference loci of the private sector would be independent of government rent extraction. We further choose units to make $n = 1$ in (5) in that, for domestic consumers, a unit of import substitute (good 2) is measured as the exact substitute for imported manufacture (good 5), one to one.

Equations (2), (3') and (7) yield a parabolic production frontier where the world prices p_1 and $p_5 = p_2$ of primary goods exported and (imported) tradable manufacture define the world market price line YC and select the production point Y. The price inelasticity of export gives rise to the export bound in (6), so that C is the highest attainable utility, at a marginal rate of substitution equal to the slope of the EC line, and different from the world market price

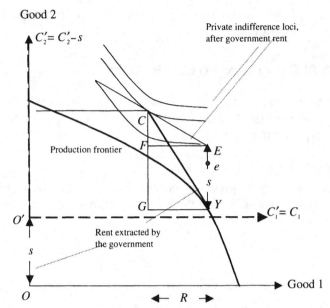

Figure 1   Export bound allows government rent extraction

ratio. This allows the government to impose a multiple exchange rate system and extract rent from the primary good export, ultimately at the expense of the owner of land *T*, who had no recourse.

To illustrate, we assume that state trading is imposed, so that the government takes over all export goods *GY*, sells on the world market at the world market terms of trade to acquire *CG* units of manufacture, then pays the exporters only *CF* units of that, which implies a domestic price ratio equal to the negative of the slope *CE*. The exporter will now sell the imported manufacture to others. The government retains a surplus *s*, equal to *FG = EY*, and the private consumption is measured with:

$$U(C_1', C_2') = U(C_1, C_2 - s)$$

with a shifting of the origin *O* to *O'*.

In reality, this is not what is literally done in the presence of a monetary economy. The government pays the exporters with the over-valued domestic currency to get all their foreign currency revenue, but the importers have to buy foreign currency from the government at a far different rate.

Since such imports may include heating oil and other essential goods, the government usually relents to take a share of rent less than the full amount *s* = the length of *EY*, but only the length of *eY* instead, by offering some importers a 'subsidized' exchange rate according to various exchange control or import control schemes. Case-by-case decisions are then imposed, according to the supposed merit of each case. That is when all types of rent-seeking behavior, lobbying (the least illegal type), outright bribing, smuggling and all forms of manipulation take place. In a prisoners' dilemma, each firm competes against rivals in such quasi-legal and illegal operations for sheer survival, and rivals try to denounce each other for engaging in inappropriate activities. The investigation and punitive procedures can be also corrupted in turn. After the fall of Rhee, major Korean businesses got their assets confiscated and leaders jailed, on account of amassing illicit wealth. In such an environment, the top management of business concerns understandably get distracted by such goings on.

5. REFORM AND BREAK-OUT FROM THE VICIOUS CIRCLES

The above model assumes the input and output coefficients are fixed in time. Actually, the labor usage coefficients (the a_i's) are functions of experience, especially when the activities (say, manufacturing goods of export quality) are new in the country. The output-augmenting coefficients (the b_i's) are functions of managerial activities, such as the exploration of new markets, the improving of production practices etc. These may take intensive effort of the top management, but sometimes faster than for the workers on the production line can accumulate experience.

There are two ways to conceptualize the *managerial activities*: either by assuming managers have different qualifications than workers on the shop floor, or by assuming that managers are part of a homogeneous labor force. They perform jobs different from shop floor operations. Although the truth lies somewhere in between, the second choice is far simpler analytically and adequate for the purpose at hand.

The key points are: the managers (a) form a very small portion of the labor force, so they can be overloaded, and (b) perform the distinct and critical chore that cannot be delegated entirely to others, namely, decision-making – such as determining whether to compete against rivals by (i) rent-seeking or (ii) managing the business better, by raising the productivity or the b_i's.[15]

Note that the effort level in *managerial activities* is subject to shirking. Thus, such jobs cannot be entrusted to anyone in the labor force. Nor is there much scope to design *legally* enforceable contracts for such jobs like accumulating *illicit* wealth. This is the chore of the top management, the membership of which is usually limited by kinship, during those days in Korea.[16] This

15. Strictly speaking, only 'direct labor' (in contrast to managerial labor) engages in fabrication. Before the reform, only the winner of the 'rent-seeking' games can secure the foreign exchange to buy the indispensable imported ingredients. After the reform, managerial efforts would increase production efficiency through irreversible improvement.

16. We assume the objective of the top management is 'lexicographical'. The first priority is the survival of the firm (capable to produce positive output). Then, for any surviving firm, its

limited membership gives rise to the prospect of possible overloading. A firm may manage well or 'bribe well', but not both.

To sharpen the argument, we can use the nested dominant player *game forms* in Tables 2 and 3, we identify the *outcome*, corresponding to each *profile of players' actions*. Over the discrete set of outcomes, the preference of the State or the Management over the set of outcomes is quite intuitive.[17] For example, the Chief of the State prefers the retention of power and avoids the chaos caused by a foreign exchange shortage for the government;[18] the Manager desires the retention of one's job, which would be lost if the firm cannot survive the competition against the rivals.

Overall, to analyze our problem with the most parsimonious model specification, we have adopted a nested decision process. Nature decides the State of the System (such as the international relative wage levels); Government Leaders, seeking political success, and taking note of the environment and their own personal background (such as Rhee's nationalistic constituency), select the policy regime; Managers, adapting to the policy regime of the successful leaders, choose business options to secure their own dominant position; Labor Force carries out operations under managers of the surviving firms. The decisions of government leaders allocate government resources that influence the well-being of all individuals in the State through an additively separable private utility function; the private choices are influenced only by the levels of private income. For government leaders and managers, leadership positions are desirable for their *libido dominani*, quite apart from any associated material rewards. Managers are the part of homogeneous labor who enjoy the trust to make critical decisions. For any productive activity, a small but constant portion of the labor force is deployed to carry out such managerial decisions.

Formally, one can set the managerial decision for rent-seeking as a dichotomous variable, $q = 1$ for rent-seeking and 0 for not doing so. Next one

management is assumed to maximize profit. Such an assumption is needed because under constant returns, the equilibrium profit is always zero for any firm, both the surviving and the failed!

17. Table 2 emphasizes the exogenous influence: the Japanese wage level determines the Korean export outlook. Alternatively, one might take a political economy view, identify the State with the chief executive. Their rise and fall are to be treated as historical events, not entirely decided by economic forces. Both Rhee and Park desired the continuation of their power. Rhee justified his autocracy by patriotism. Settling old scores against Japan and amassing foreign exchange to lessen Korea's dependence on American aid were popular with his core supporters. In contrast, Park had to find legitimacy in a Korea that had just rejected Rhee. In his own writings, Park (1970, pp. 39–40) identified the public will of people in Asia as pro-growth. Table 3 makes it clear that unless one can gain access to certain imported inputs, there might be no manufacturing process, well managed or otherwise.

18. This may be spent to enhance national defense as well as law and order.

Table 2 The State adjusts to the market prospect

		Nature	
Outcome		s_1: Export outlook pessimistic	s_2: Export outlook hopeful
The State	α_1: Exchange control	ω_1: The economy survives*	ω_3: Control is redundant
	α_2: De-control	ω_2: Insolvency and chaos	ω_4: Market force functions*

*Denotes the preferred outcome for the leader of the State, with ω_1 preferred to ω_2; ω_4 preferred to ω_3.

Table 3 The Management adjusts to the regulatory environment

		The State	
Outcome		α_1: Exchange control	α_2: De-control
The Management	$q = 1$: Seeking rents	Ω_1: Survives vs. rivals*	Ω_3: Losing opportunity
	$q = 0$: Managing firm well	Ω_2: Deprived of inputs	Ω_4: Survives vs. rivals*

*Denotes preferred outcome by the Management, with Ω_1 preferred to Ω_2; Ω_4 preferred to Ω_3.

can assume that:

$$(d/dt)b_i = (1-q)Y \quad i = 3, 4$$

Thus, rent-seeking ($q = 0$) means the derailment of learning.[19]

What caused the initial breakthrough was the Japanese boom driving up its wage and causing a labor shortage in labor-intensive industries. Korean export of manufacture became possible, and gradual economic cooperation with Japan made 'fragmented production' a reality.[20] Korean labor produced the product and Japanese intermediation opened the markets. In our formulation, if downstream means market service and upstream means fabrication, then once good 3 can be exported separately, it may earn on the world market a unit price: $p_3 > 1/b_3$.

By our convention, imported input has a unit price equal to unity, and goods using imported inputs are so measured to use one unit of imported input, if the firm level efficiency b_3 is unity. That means it will generate some foreign exchange to spare. Provided the wage is low enough, and a sequence of Korean devaluation made that possible, then the first vicious circle in

19. How Korean management has improved their capability is well documented by Enos and Park (1988).
20. About fragmentation, see Jones and Kierzkowski (1990).

© Verein für Socialpolitik and Blackwell Publishing Ltd 2003

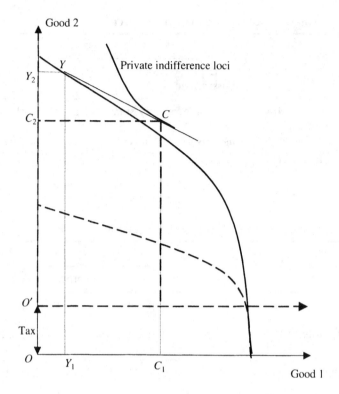

Figure 2   International division of labor permits reform

exchange shortage could be broken. With the reform, the distortion premium shrank, rent-seeking became unimportant, and efforts in management improved efficiency more and more. The second vicious circle was broken as well.

Figure 2 shows Korea becoming a net exporter of manufacture.[21] Government revenue was no longer dependent upon the surplus from the multiple exchange rate system. Soon it was on the way to becoming an economic miracle.

Korea's success in initial economic reform had some unusual referees. In those days, Koreans had relatively free and fair elections. As a coup leader, President Park did not enjoy broad support, but the growth of the economy earned him impressive approval in his re-election campaign. The reliability of the election results in those days is reflected by the fact that two elections later, due to financial crisis, he was almost defeated by Kim Dae Jung.

21.   As a percentage of total exports, the Korean manufactured export was 12.5% in 1960, and 60.8% in 1965 (Amsden, 1989).

6. CONCLUSION

The catching-up process includes two important components: the takeoff and the management of growth. Regarding the former, according to Kuznets (1982), development is not easy because to tap into the cumulated technology backlog of the developed world, one must remove various constraints. This involves 'substantial and time-consuming institutional changes' which have 'disruptive effects ... upsetting the relative standing of various groups in the society' and call for 'the increased international division of labor'. All the four Asian newly industrialized economies cited by Lucas (1988) have shared the same transformation. On the world market, Korea had to go beyond its status as a tungsten exporter, Taiwan had to transcend its status as a sugar and rice supplier, and Hong Kong as well as Singapore had to earn its living by shedding its exclusive role as an entrepôt. They all became highly competitive exporters of manufacture. These represent the shared theme that the current study focuses on.

Kuznets (1982) was written for Taiwan. The elements mentioned, such as institutional reform, international division of labor, tapping into existing foreign technology and upsetting the entrenched interest, fit just as well to assess the Korean development described above.

In contrast, managing the growth is a task that varies among Lucas's four examples from economy to economy. This reflects both the circumstance and the choice. For the Korean economy, strong government guidance, business groups and local entrepreneurship become the major characteristics, in contrast to the *laissez-faire* stance of Hong Kong, the small–medium enterprises of Taiwan, and the significant participation of multinational firms of Singapore.[22]

On managing the growth, there are important issues not yet settled. For example, is the role of the State so important for Korea? Lee (1996) offers some novel evidence. For context, one may refer to Thorbecke *et al.* (2002) about Taiwan and Hong Kong. Regarding how growth should be assessed, Prescott (1998) provides some insight. Concerning where the foundations of multi-sector growth needs further study, one might consult Jensen (this issue).

The main contributions of this study are the following. First, we highlight for any economy without energy reserves, how harsh the foreign exchange bottleneck can be, by formulating a model with crucial inputs which must be imported. Export is not an *important* requirement, it is the *indispensable* requirement, economically *and* physically. In Europe, this was the situation facing various countries at the time of the Marshall Plan. What confronted Japan and Korea at that time was no different.

Second, we identify the strategic role of managerial decisions in economic development. How else can one break through into new markets against the

22. See also Wan and Thorbecke (1999).

© Verein für Socialpolitik and Blackwell Publishing Ltd 2003 more entrenched rivals? Rent-seeking is harmful precisely because it distracts managers from their all-important task. For *developing economies*, no break-through means extinction for the hope of development.[23] On the other hand, a breakthrough in an export drive provides for a developing economy both the opportunity of learning-by-exporting and the discipline by the world market. The road of reform–exports–growth traveled by Korea is echoed by the experience of Taiwan, a few years earlier.

Korea's successful industrialization owes to both reform and the previous rise of Japanese wages, due to the mechanism of the product cycle. How such a mechanism operates in recent years is analyzed by Tung (this issue).

ACKNOWLEDGMENTS

The author has benefited from the comments by B. S. Jensen, S. Clemhout, and S. Ortigueira as well as discussions with R. Jones and E. C. Prescott when an earlier version was presented at the 2001 Dynamics, Economic Growth and International Trade Conference in Vienna. Two anonymous referees were also very helpful. Thanks are due to Andrea Williams-Wan for her professional editorial assistance. All remaining defects are the sole responsi-bility of the author.

Address for correspondence: e-mail: hyw1@Cornell.edu

REFERENCES

Adelman, I. and C. T. Morris (1967), *Society, Politics and Economic Development: A Quantitative Approach*, Johns Hopkins University Press, Baltimore, MD.

Amsden, A. H. (1989), *Asia's Next Giant, South Korea and Late Industrialization*, Oxford University Press, New York.

Bardhan, P. K. (1997), 'Corruption and Development', *Journal of Economic Literature* 35, 1320–1346.

Bhagwati, J. N. (1999), 'The "Miracle" that did Happen: Understanding East Asia in Comparative Perspective', in: E. Thorbecke and H. Y. Wan Jr. (eds.), *Taiwan's Development Experience: Lessons on Roles of Government and Market*, Kluwer, Boston, MA.

Bhagwati, J. N., R. A. Brecher and T. N. Srinivasan (1984), 'DUP Activities and Economic Theory', *European Economic Review* 24, 291–307.

Enos, J. L. and W. H. Park (1988), *The Adoption and Diffusion of Imported Technology: The Case of Korea*, Croom Helm, Beckenham.

Jensen, B. S. (2003), 'Walrasian General Equilibrium Allocations and Dynamics in Two-Sector Growth Models' (this issue).

23.   For the damage done by rent-seeking and corruption to an economy not necessarily at the threshold of development, compare Bhagwati *et al.* (1984) and Bardhan (1997).

Jones, L. P. and I. Sakong (1980), *Government, Business and Entrepreneurship in Economic Development: The Korean Case*, Harvard University Press, Cambridge, MA.

Jones, R. and H. Kierzkowski (1990), 'The Role of Services in Production and International Trade: A Theoretical Framework', in R. W. Jones and A. O. Krueger (eds.), *The Political Economy of International Trade: Essays in Honor of Robert E. Baldwin*, Blackwell, Oxford.

Kojima, K. (1978), *Direct Foreign Investment: A Japanese Model, Multinational Business Operations*, Croom Helm, Beckenham.

Kojima, K. and T. Ozawa (1984), *Japan's General Trading Companies: Merchants of Economic Development*, OECD Publications and Information Center, Washington, DC.

Kuznets, S. (1982), 'Modern Economic Growth and the Less Developed Countries (LDCs)', in: K. T. Li and T. S. Yu (eds.), *Experiences and Lessons of Economic Development in Taiwan*, Academia Sinica, Taipei.

Lee, J.-W. (1996), 'Government Interventions and Productivity Growth', *Journal of Economic Growth* 1(3), 391–414.

Levy, B. (1990), 'Transactions Costs, the Size of Firms and Industrial Policy: Lessons from a Comparative Case Study of the Footwear Industry in Korea and Taiwan', *Journal of Development Economics* 34(1–2), 151–178.

Lucas, R. E., Jr. (1988), 'On the Mechanics of Economic Development', *Journal of Monetary Economics* 22, 3–42.

Park, C. H. (1970), *Our Nation's Path*, Hollym Corporation, Seoul.

Prescott, E. C. (1998), 'Needed: A Theory of Total Productivity', *International Economic Review* 39, 525–551.

Rodrik, D. (1995), 'How South Korea and Taiwan Grew Rich', *Economic Policy*, April, 53–108.

Stern, J. J., J.-H. Kim, D. H. Perkins and J.-H. Yoo (1995), *Industrialization and the State: The Korean Heavy and Chemical Industry Drive*, Harvard University Press, Cambridge, MA.

Thorbecke, E., A.-C. Tung and H. Y. Wan (2002), 'Industrial Targeting: Lessons from Past Errors and Successes of Hong Kong and Taiwan', *World Development* 25(8), 1047–1061.

Tung, A.-C. (2003) 'Beyond Flying Geese: The Expansion of East Asia's Electronics Trade (this issue).

Wan, H. Y., Jr. and E. Thorbecke (1999), 'Some Further Thoughts on Taiwan's Development', in E. Thorbecke and H. Y. Wan, Jr. (eds.), *Taiwan's Development Experience: Lessons on Roles of Government and Market*, Kluwer, Boston, MA.

Moving Along the Upper Bound:
Singapore Reaching Out for its Potential

Review of "The Singapore Economy: Prospects for the 21st Century"[*]

Some perspective This Article states formally the obvious. In a world evolving by interdependent growth, what is the best expected performance for an economy like Singapore (or Luxembourg), namely, a small economy which is not the technological leader. First, in the long run, this economy cannot outperform the technological leader in growth rate. Second, conceivably this economy may enjoy a higher per capita real output than the leading economy. This possibility is based on the observation that in a large economy, per capita real output often differs from sector to sector and in an interdependent world, a small economy may contain more of the sectors with high real income. In the literature, the growth rate of an economy is often analyzed context-free. The case of Singapore examined in Article 6 may serve as a reality check for such a view.

The Singapore economy at work The above discussion focuses on what is the best achievable performance for some communities like Singapore, without addressing how such a potential may be realized. The history of Singapore offers much insight into this.

Conceptually, one can return to the teachings of Adam Smith (1776), a retired professor of moral philosophy: allowing the market force to play a proper role. Yet Smith was far from an *anarchist*. He maintained that the State has to do what the market cannot do well, taking care of what is called nowadays as coordination failures, to achieve what is good for the society. Given the problematic agency problem inside the government, with a shorter chain of command, in principle, the smaller societies can be governed better . The case of Singapore seems to corroborate this view. Specifically, this includes for example the following (see Lee, 2000).

---

[*]This article is reprinted from *The Singapore Economic Review*, Vol. 43, No. 2, pp. 1–11, 1998, published by the National University of Singapore, Department of Economics.

(a) The creation of advantages for the niche market:

1. The development of the Changi Airport for passengers from Australia and New Zealand visiting Britain, which in turn facilitates the establishment of the Singapore Airline, as well as a tourist industry;

2. The construction of modern port facilities at the Singapore Port to serve the traffic through the Malacca Strait, which in turn facilitates the creation of a petrochemical industry;

3. The setting up of a regional financial center at Singapore for the ASEAN region; and

4. The training of technicians with a curriculum jointly designed with foreign investors.

(b) The design of the Central Provident Fund provisions so that:

1. Household savings can be mobilized to finance infrastructure investment;

2. The labor cost can be insulated from short term macro-economic shocks; and

3. The ratio between the capital cost and labor cost can be manipulated to upgrade the industrial structure away from the labor intensive industries.

(c) The attraction of selected multinational enterprises to invest in Singapore, with:

1. Out-reach programs to provide information about Singapore;

2. Financial incentives like tax holidays;

3. Industrial estates (industrial parks) which reduce the cost of doing business;

4. Co-investment to share the risks of the new adventure; and

5. Labor institutions (such as the provisions for the compulsory arbitration of labor disputes) in order to ensure industrial peace.

The Singapore Economic Review Vol. 43 No. 2 **1-11**

THE SINGAPOREAN ECONOMY: PROSPECTS FOR THE 21ST CENTURY

Henry Wan, Jr.*

Cornell University and the National University of Singapore

Singapore has achieved sustained, rapid growth, at an unprecedented pace. Before the Crisis 1997, it surpassed both Japan and Hong Kong in per capita real income, and reached within 10% of the American level, which is the world's highest. The strategy initiated under Dr. Goh Keng Swee has succeeded beyond expectations. The prospect is to enjoy a per capita income path somewhat higher than America (by a "city effect"), at the American pace. There remain the challenges of decelerated growth, intensifying competition and sectoral adjustments like Finland had in the 1990s. One needs built-in resilience through human capital investment and entrepreneurship.

Anyone trying to describe the outlook for Singapore faces an immediate difficulty. And this is that the economy of Singapore is so unique...

Why Singapore Succeeds, Dr. Goh Keng Swee (1972)

1. INTRODUCTION

I appreciate this opportunity to offer this lecture honouring Dr. Goh Keng Swee.

When the 20th century comes to an end, posterity will look back at two major events. There is the successful effort along the Pacific Rim to catch up with the advanced economies; there is also the rise and fall of the economic experiment of central planning. As a professional economist and a scholar-statesman, Dr. Goh has contributed greatly to the catching up of Singapore by harnessing the market. It is proper in this context for us to focus on the prospects for this island republic.

Address for Correspondence: Henry Wan, Jr. Cornell University, Ithaca, NY 14853-7601, USA.
*This paper was given on March 24, 1999 as a public lecture at the National University of Singapore, when I served as the first Goh Keng Swee Professor of Economics. It conveys my personal opinion and represents the views of neither the Cornell University nor the National University of Singapore. I benefited from discussions with my colleagues and students at the National University of Singapore (in particular, Professor V V Bhanoji Rao) but I alone am responsible for all imperfections and limitations. Drs. Goh Ai Ting, Ho Kong Weng, and David Owyong as well as Mr. Kelvin Tan contributed to the logistic aspects of my presentation. I appreciated greatly the kind comments of Ms. Paula Parviainen on the recent recovery of the Finnish economy.

As our citation of Dr. Goh indicates, Singapore is challenging for researchers, because it appears to be *sui generis*. To an academic, the challenge is also the opportunity: the exception proves the rule. What is needed is the perspective and an applicable theory. This is true for Blust, combing the word lists of 200 Austronesian languages in search of the original home of all Malayo-Polynesian speakers,[1] or for Wolters, comparing Tamil, Chinese, European and Malay sources to determine the base of power of Srivijaya.[2] To study Singapore, we arm ourselves with the growth record of various developing and developed economies over the last four decades and invoke the recent research on the convergence hypothesis.

The standard practice today is to measure economic performance by two indices: (a) the per capita real income; and (b) its rate of growth.

Also often used is another derived measure, the *relative* per capita real income, calculated as the ratio of per capita real incomes between a particular economy and the one with the highest per capita real income among all economies. America has been holding that highest figure after World War II. At the end of the 1950s when Dr. Goh joined the government, Singapore was at about 15% of the American level. By 1996, the number stood beyond 96%, outpacing both Japan and Hong Kong (also Switzerland), in both the level and the rate of growth.

Table 1 provides another side of the story. Serving as a control group for the performance of Singapore in 1996 are the G7 countries (Canada, France, Germany, Italy, Japan, U. K. and U. S.), augmented by the four Scandinavians (Denmark, Finland, Norway and Sweden) as well as both Hong Kong and Switzerland. Their levels of per capita real income (by Heston-Summers) are paired with the average growth rates over 1990-1996.

By the above criteria, and given the initial conditions, the Singapore record merits the epithet, "a light unto the nations".

Various qualitative evidences corroborate the above assessment. First, Apple Computers maintained that its Singapore operation can move a product from the drawing board to production in half the time needed anywhere by all its other units. Such a record is surely not that of an imitator. Second, specialists claim that the American electronics industry can hold against Japanese competitors in the 1990s because of the efficacy of their associates in Singapore and other Asian lands.[3] Thus, apart from its size, Singapore has mattered on the global economic stage. Finally, by now the promise of local private firms has been proven by the respectable record of such firms as Creative Technologies.[4] The Singapore story is not merely the reflected glory of the expatriate multinationals.

---

[1] This is Taiwan, in his opinion. See, for example, Bellwood (1985)
[2] This is the special relationship with imperial China, in his view. See, for example, Andaya and Andaya (1982).
[3] See Borrus (1997).
[4] See Hobday (p. 146, 1995) for its role in establishing industrial standards.

Table 1. PER CAPITA REAL INCOME AND GROWTH — SELECTED ECONOMIES

	Per Capita Real Income, '96 (US $)	Average Growth, 1990-96 (%)
G7 Economies		
Canada	21,380	0.6
France	21,510	0.7
Germany	21,110	0.7
Italy	19,890	0.9
Japan	23,420	1.2
U. K.	19,960	1.5
U. S.	28,020	1.2
Scandinavian 4		
Denmark	22,120	2.1
Finland	18,260	-0.2
Norway	23,220	3.7
Sweden	18,770	-0.2
Switzerland	26,340	-1.0
Hong Kong	24,260	3.7
Singapore	**26,910**	**6.6**

Data Source: World Bank (1998)

2. THE FUTURE CHALLENGES — GENERAL FORCES

From current indicators, the Asian debt crisis of 1997 appears to be near its end, at least for both Korea and Thailand. Yet, for quite inherent reasons, the dawn of the new century will bring about new challenges not encountered before. So far as I can see, there are two types of challenges, those at the aggregate level and those that are sector-specific. We deal with the general type first. This relates to how the world economy operates around us.

For perspective, we refer to the data on pp. 333-4 of *The Textbook of Economic Growth* by Barro and Sala-i-Matin (1995). In four diagrams, each for four countries, the real per capita income over several decades is plotted against time:

1) for the four non-European countries of U.S. Canada, Japan and Australia;
2) for four large, non-Scandinavian European countries: U.K., France, Germany and Italy;
3) for four small, non-Scandinavian European countries: Austria, Belgium, the Netherlands and Switzerland; and
4) for four Scandinavian countries: Denmark, Finland, Norway and Sweden.

In each diagram, the four rising curves converge toward each other.

Next, we turn to the *relative* per capita real income of the five East Asian economies, Japan, Korea, Taiwan, Hong Kong and Singapore. Drawing upon the information of Figure 18.4 in Thorbecke and Wan (1999), we find that all these five economies are closing the gaps between themselves and America. Yet throughout all these decades, none of these economies has yet surpassed America in terms of real per capita income.

We summarise below the common pattern emerging from such information:

After World War II, the engine for growth was technological innovation. This spawned investment opportunities and therefore capital accumulation. Innovation caused investment, not vice versa. Four facts describe this world:

A. *(The leaders) Most major product innovations came from both North Atlantic shores, especially America: overall growth proceeded steadily but gradually.*
B. *(The followers) Compared against the advanced economies, a broad class of economies (covering much of Asia) had lower per capita real income, but higher growth rates. There was an early phase of trend acceleration, when the improved ability to acquire information caused the growth rate to increase with income. But as the catching up process progressed, the exhaustion of learning opportunities caused the eventual slackening of the growth rate. This is the "β-convergence" of Barro and Sala-i-Matin.*
C. *(The late-comers) For all economies catching up with the advanced countries their growth followed the path described above. The ratio of per capita real income, between a follower and a late-comer will also evolve toward unity. This implies the "σ-convergence" of Barro and Sala-i-Matin.*
D. *(The city effect) The presence of a low-income rural sector tended to reduce the average per capita income. Thus, a follower-economy without a rural sector may overtake the leader-economy with a rural sector. In the semi-log graph, the follower-cum-city state had its time path converging to an adjusted asymptotic path which lies above the regular asymptotic path by a fixed constant.*

At the risk of oversimplification, we can graphically summarise the essence of the above points in panels a through d of Figure 1.

Some elaboration is in order.

(1) For the last half a century, almost all major new products for the world market — from micro-processors, to the internet, to various advanced material — appeared in America first. America has the initial advantage, the massive R & D spending, the ability to attract the best foreign researchers and the wherewithal to tap foreign discoveries by cross-licensing or other means. The fact that America leads in per capita real income is no surprise. In per capita real income, Japan rose toward America from below, even though in growth rate Japan slowed down toward America from above. The best one could do is like Switzerland, approaching America extremely slowly.

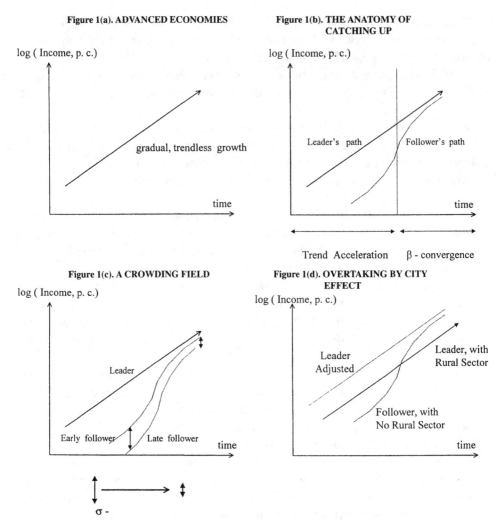

Figure 1(a). ADVANCED ECONOMIES

log (Income, p. c.)

gradual, trendless growth

time

Figure 1(b). THE ANATOMY OF
CATCHING UP

log (Income, p. c.)

Leader's path   Follower's path

time

Trend Acceleration   β - convergence

Figure 1(c). A CROWDING FIELD

log (Income, p. c.)

Leader

Early follower   Late follower

time

Figure 1(d). OVERTAKING BY CITY
EFFECT

log (Income, p. c.)

Leader
Adjusted

Leader, with
Rural Sector

Follower, with
No Rural Sector

time

σ -

(2) Japan surpassed American per capita income in nominal but not in real terms. This is because foreign goods, be they American, German or Korean, find it hard to penetrate Japanese administrative protection, making the Japanese cost of living inflated, as a consequence.

(3) Among non-oil producers, if any country is going to surpass America in per capita real income, Singapore is likely to be the first, for the following reason. In all countries, urban income leads rural income. America and Japan have a rural sector, but a city state like Singapore has none. Plotting growth rate against in-

come level, the Singapore curve lies above that of Japan (or America) by some constant. Figure 1, panel d shows such a "city effect": Singapore surpasses Japan in growth rate, when both have the same per capita real income.[5]

Some tentative conclusions can now be drawn for Singapore. Because of the "city effect", Singapore has some breathing space left, to plan for adaptation and adjustment. After that, what is attainable — *if all goes well* — seems to be a soft-landing toward "an American rate of growth", coupled with a "higher-than-American per capita real income". In short, what seems achievable is the overtaking of America, by the *level effect*, but not by the *growth effect*. Our reasoning is as follows.

(a) The production technology presently used by workers in Singapore has been mostly introduced from outside, with minor modifications. By and large, such technology cannot be said to be more productive than that used by American workers.

(b) Capital flow is essentially free between Singapore and America.

(c) The Singapore economy is largely dominated by multinational firms, so that the "quality of decision making" is comparable to what goes on in America as well.

(d) Although Singapore has yet to catch up with America in terms of technology, as reflected by the comparison in per capita real income, Singapore can outperform America in terms of growth rate: as a leader, American growth only comes from R and D; Singapore can make further gains from technology transfers from outside.

(e) Once Singapore has caught up with the *properly adjusted* path of America (taking into account the negative "rural drag" America sustains), there is nothing left for Singapore to outgrow America with. This can happen sooner than expected.

To some extent, the above analysis may reach conclusions which resemble those of Tan and Lee (1999) on sustainable growth, via "growth accounting". But a careful reader will notice the differences in both the premises and implications.

The main task for Singapore is to see that *all goes well*. Even then, two types of general challenges remain:

(1) By β-convergence, growth deceleration is inevitable, for ALL countries along the catch-up path. The deceleration happening to Japan now will happen to Singapore, sooner or later.

(2) By σ-convergence, ALL countries which have managed to catch up will see their competitive edge eroded relative to their close followers. The market pressure faced by Japan from Korea will be faced by Singapore from some of its present competitors.

---

[5] In 1996, the real per capita income of Luxembourg was 34,480, higher than that of the U.S.

The reduced rate of growth is not a problem in general, unless government or business plans are based upon unrealised growth expectations. For Singapore, the situation is not clear: in the past, growth was the source to finance defence.[6]

3. THE FUTURE CHALLENGES — SECTORAL ADJUSTMENTS

All the effects analysed above are in aggregate terms, treating all outputs and jobs as homogeneous and perfectly substitutable. Such a view is inadequate, when we consider the other major event in our century, leading to the ultimate failure of the Soviet system, in East Germany as well as Russia. With their forced saving approach, Soviet accumulation always outpaced the West, at least in the beginning. Assuming "a car is a car is a car", the CIA estimates on the East German economy were never really wrong, except for that all-important assumption. In output expansion, the East German Trabant was *never outdone* by the West German Volkswagon. But once it had to fight the Volkswagon for the surviving niche of the consumer's garage, the Trabant was instantly *done in*, en masse. By the owner's estimate, a Trabant was no more valuable, then, than a full tank of gasoline.[7] In the market place, nothing is more awesome than *creative destruction*.

Technological (and market) risk is present, even for the advanced industrial economies. Risk is heightened when all eggs are in one basket. Not all risks must be always avoided; that is not possible. But the moral remains: reduce risk if you can.

The case of Finland, 1970-90, is instructive.[8] Although a late-comer among the Scandinavian countries in industrialisation, Finland grew at an average rate of 5 per cent over 1970-94, which outpaced the average OECD economies, thus making the country comparable to Austria, Belgium and Norway in per capita GNP. The forestry industry (including paper) accounted for 56 per cent of the 1971 exports. Over the next 20 years, the forestry industry was caught in a price-wage squeeze. Under a low real interest, firms borrowed heavily to invest in very large plants and seek scale economy. Debt crisis and bankruptcy eventually came, raising the unemployment rate from 3 per cent in 1990, to 20 per cent in four years. Although the ultra-generous unemployment benefits may offer part of the explanation, the high concentration of resources in a single sector seems to be the major cause of the vulnerability.[9] With the telecommunication boom, the unemployment rate finally fell to the European Union average of 11-12 per cent.[10]

The moral is: the vicissitudes which visited a creative and energetic people like Finland can equally cause havoc to any other high-income, small economy. As it

---

[6] See citation in Chin (p. 298, 1999).

[7] The joke at the German unification was: Q. How do you double the value of a Trabant? A. Fill it up.

[8] Our main source is Honko (1994).

[9] A competing explanation of the Finnish recession is the implosion of the Soviet Union, which took 1/4 of Finnish export in the late 1980s when Finnish exports amounted to 16% of the GNP.

[10] Data supplied by Ms. Parviainen.

stands, Singapore faces three types of potential specific challenges, each related to the specific features of the economy.

(a) To attain a high income, small countries must deploy resources in selective concentrations. Singapore has been no exception. In some recent years, 39 per cent of the manufacturing value-added came from electronics, with 10 per cent from hard disk-drives alone (see Martin *et al.* (1997)). For perspective, today, 20 per cent of Finnish exports can be accounted for by the firm Nokia alone.[11]

(b) Much emphasis has been placed on Singapore's role as a regional headquarters city.

(c) Entrepot trade continues to be important for Singapore.

There is no question that such features bring much current economic reward. Yet, in the long run, each feature carries some risk of technological obsolescence. First, all manufacturing industries are vulnerable to technological obsolescence. The issue is more acute for economies dependent on foreign firms. Once their investment in the host country loses viability, the managers of such firms are obligated to their owners to withdraw. In relating the closing down of such factories, Dr. Goh Keng Swee clearly recognised years ago how things would stand.[12]

Second, with the arrival of video-telephones and tele-conferences, the corporate need for regional headquarters may well decline in the future.

Finally, many locations in and around the Atlantic were once important as sites of "coal stations" or sources for "naval stores". The passing of coal-fired steamers and sail ships have left such countries "high and dry". Both the future of container shipping and the possible construction of the Kra Canal are events which can potentially affect the importance of Singapore in transportation.

4. SOME RECOMMENDATIONS

The answer to these challenges is not to abstain from all that is presently profitable, but to build into the economy flexibility and resilience. Our discussion can be grouped under two headings — entrepreneurial environment and specific topics.

4.1   Entrepreneurial Environment

One desirable development is to nurture more locally-based high-tech enterprises. It is in the headquarters of such firms that one would find the skilled personnel for strategic planning and product development. These are the talents who can build in resilience for an economy.

---

[11] Correspondence from Ms. Parviainen.
[12] For his views, see Goh (1972, 1977, 1995).

Ever forthright and clear-sighted, Dr. Goh recognised in his writings years ago, that, on these scores, Taiwan is more advantageously positioned than Singapore. There is much more "industrial entrepreneurship", and also more "reverse brain drain", in terms of repatriate scientists and engineers who bring home years' worth of field experiences and personal connections.

More specifically, take the electronics industry for example. This is an industry with great importance to both Singapore and Taiwan. This is also an industry notable for its many spin-off firms, like those which have populated Silicon Valley. In the business literature, the term "hollowing out" was born in Taiwan, when former staff at General Instruments in Taiwan left that firm and started eleven spin-off firms. The natural question is whether there has been some similar development in Singapore. The answer seems to be a heavily qualified "yes", judging from the information in Lee and Low (1990).[13] How to provide a policy environment no less effective than the *benign neglect* of Hong Kong and Taiwan seems to be the main puzzle.

Only carefully-designed field studies on issues like comparative regulatory routines can unravel such riddles.

4.2   Specific Topics

There is much scope for Singapore to enhance its prospects for growth and stability. The opportunities come under two categories:

(A) Short-term opportunities
My general impression about Singapore is one of optimism. The economy is already doing well. Yet, there is still much scope for improving the marketing prowess of Singaporean businesses, for designing more attractive products and for providing more competitive services.

In modern business, marketing involves much more than supplying reliable quality at reasonable prices. International commerce today has become more and more customer-centred and system-oriented. The ability to anticipate the clients' needs often becomes a major advantage. Efforts in this direction do not have to involve high technology, even though modern technology can usually help. Two examples should suffice to make the point.

1. A Swiss supplier of bakery equipment keeps all its clients on file, together with their location and the fastest air-route to reach them. Service staff of this firm are ever-ready with their supply of parts and toolkits for service calls around the world. Buyers of their products can rest assured that any equipment breakdown will not cause them to lose much business.

---

[13] The first three cases in their chapter 2 concern industrial entrepreneurs. Chapter 4 contains some penetrating analysis.

2. For its product design, Shimano, the Japanese producer of derailleurs for bicycles collects gravel samples from European and American roads. This safeguards riders of bicycles (with the Shimano product installed) from losing control while shifting gears.

In Singapore today, progress in a similar direction is not easy because of the following vicious cycle.

a. (The product) To enhance the resilience of the economy, it is desirable to develop top-of-the-line consumption goods (as in most small, high-income European countries), which enjoy "brand loyalty" from their clients, through thick and thin.
b. (The entrepreneur) To develop products for the up-market sector, local firms must be more forward looking in planning such ventures.
c. (The technology) To succeed in producing such goods in a high-wage, no- natural-resource location like Singapore, one must have the know-how to supply better-designed, better-packaged, and better-marketed goods than is currently being done.
d. (The market) To strike out on such unfamiliar paths in selling consumption goods on the basis of taste and image rather than demonstrable cost advantages, one needs a larger clientele than what is locally available.

Rather than waiting for the gradual improvement of the situation, one can break out of the cycle by judicious policy-making. Measures may include:

1) Popularising user-friendly designs through the media.
2) Emphasising business communication skills in business education.
3) Providing consultancy services to help small and medium enterprises.
4) Promoting good design and creative customer services by giving awards.
5) Purchasing of key technology with public funds before licensing to private firms.

In economic theory, certain technologies such as some canning operations in food preparation have the nature of a "non-rival" good: its utilisation by one firm does not preclude its use by others. It is quite proper for the state to acquire it and then transfer it to private individuals. In fact, Taiwan has adopted such policies regarding the production of semiconductors.

(B) Long-term opportunities
In Europe, states like Belgium, Luxemburg and Switzerland have all benefited from hosting various supra-national organisations and institutions related to the European Community or CERN. Within the French-speaking sphere in Europe, Brussels often plays the role as a second venue to Paris for writers and artists. When intra-Asian intellectual and cultural interactions intensify in the coming decades between South Asia, Southeast Asia and East Asia, Singapore will have its pan-Asian role to

play. However Utopian that prospect may sound today, any preparatory step Singapore takes for that day will have its immediate benefits in inspiring synergetic activities for a multi-ethnic society.

Much progress can still be made on the eve of a new millennium.

REFERENCES

Andaya, B. W. and L. Y. Andaya (1982) *A History of Malaysia*, London: MacMillan.

Barro, R. and X. Sala-i-Matin (1995) *Economic Growth,* New York: McGrawHill.

Bellwood, P. S. (1985) *Prehistory of the Indo-Malaysian Archipelago*, Sydney: Academic Press.

Borrus, M. (1997) Left for Dead: Asian Production Networks and the Revival of the U. S. Electronics. In B. Naughton (ed.), *The China Circle, Economics and Electronics in the PRC, Taiwan and Hong Kong*, Washington: Brookings Institution Press, pp. 139-163.

Chin K. W. (1999) Singapore: Towards Developed Country Status — The Security Dimension. In L. Low,   (ed.), *Singapore, Toward a Developed Status*, Singapore: Oxford, pp. 290-311.

Goh Keng Swee (1972) *The Economics of Modernisation and Other Essays*, Singapore: Federal Publications.

——————— (1977) *The Practice of Economic Growth,* Singapore: Federal Publications.

——————— (1995) *Wealth of East Asian Nations*, Singapore: Federal Publications.

Hobday, M. (1995) *Innovation in East Asia: The Challenge to Japan*, Aldershot, UK: Edward Elgar.

Honko, J. (1994) *Competitive Strategy of Small Industrialised Countries*, Berlin: Rainer Bohn Verlag.

Lee, T. Y. and L. Low (1990) *Local Entrepreneurship in Singapore, Private and State*, Singapore: Times Academic Press.

Martin, P. *et al.* (1997) *Singapore: A Developmental City State*, Chichester: Wiley.

Tan, K. G. and W. K. Lee (1999) Beyond Regionalisation, Basis for Sustainable Growth and Potential Source of Expansion. In L. Low, (ed.), *Singapore, Toward a Developed Status*, Singapore: Oxford, pp. 87-121.

Thorbecke E. and H. Wan, Jr. eds. (1999) *Government and Market: Evidences from Taiwan*, Amsterdam: Kluwer.

World Bank (1998) *World Bank Atlas, 1998*, Washington: World Bank.

To Have and Have Not an Industrial Policy:
The Hong Kong-Taiwan Comparison

Review of "Industrial Targeting: Lessons from Past Errors and Successes of Hong Kong and Taiwan", jointly with Erik Thorbecke and An-Chi Tung[*]

Industrial policy case histories In this Article, the record of Hong Kong and Taiwan shows that industrial targeting is neither an panacea, nor a mere placebo. Relative to the hands-off policy of colonial Hong Kong under its British financial secretaries, the effectiveness of Taiwan's industrial policy varies over time. In earlier days, it was often ill-conceived and ill-designed, sometimes less than *laissez faire*. But at other times, those effective measures in the 1970s and 1980s, taken to promote high tech and nurture heavy industry, had laid down a fine foundation for the local industry. These are superior to policies practiced in Hong Kong, for their residents. The latter had left that economy open to eventual de-industrialization and income polarization, after the British were gone.

Industrial policy misconceptions Industrial policy concerns the transformation of the industrial structure to advance national interest. It is a subject often misunderstood. It is often believed to be a Japanese invention under the Ministry of International Trade and Industry (MITI), with dubious effectiveness. Its supposed reliance on trade restriction, with a beggar-thy-neighbor orientation has past its days, against the World Trade Organization (WTO) rules, especially in today's globalized world when the *laissez faire* precepts of Adam Smith (1776) is promoted in the American Century.

All these are false. When the MITI practiced administrative guidance most actively in the 1950s, the term "industrial policy" did not appear. In contrast, the substance of what is known as industrial policy was cogently formulated in the Report of Manufacture by Alexander Hamilton in 1791, as commissioned by the American Congress two years earlier. The promotion of infant industry was then advocated by Frederick List, the inspiration for the successful Zollverein, a customs union of the German states, even before their political union under Bismarck at Paris. Industrial policy resembles medicine, with effects potentially

---

[*]This article is reprinted from *The World Economy*, Vol. 25, No. 8, pp. 1047–1061, 2002, published by Blackwell.

both bad and good, but certainly not always ineffective. It has been implemented effectively in countries like Singapore, where its Lilliputian domestic market rules out restrictive trade policy. So not all industrial policy can be intrinsically against the rules of WTO.

Industrial policy in nature *Public enterprises* by the government as in the post-World War II France, are not always called for under the industrial policy. The failure of the centrally planned economies in the 1980s clearly proves there is no reason that public employees always outperform their counterparts in private industry. What government officers do best is to offer their good office as umpires, to internalize externalities against coordination failures. An example comes from Cheng (2001), when small Taiwanese footwear firms asked the government to use public authority and enforce the quality standards for export, agreed upon in a social compact among themselves. Viewed this way, the industrial policy deals with externalities, which is conceptually equivalent to public goods, the provision of which justifies the existence of the government, according to Adam Smith. It is not by nature to *beggar-thy-neighbor*. Yet as all actions affect the entire world, an industrial policy may benefit some neighbors, at the expense of others.

Industrial policy in practice Industrial policy has been characterized as case by case innovation, rather than systematic design (Kuo, 1999). Similar description was made by both Korean and Japanese economists about the actual implementation of such programs in their countries. Thus, Wan (2004) offers the novel interpretation that by nature, industrial policy is a *contingent plan*, formulated in response to both the *past history* and *current events*, to carry out some consistent *policy goal*. Hence in negotiations, no government can be expected to hold on to preconceived courses of action, at any cost.

Industrial Targeting: Lessons from Past Errors and Successes of Hong Kong and Taiwan

Erik Thorbecke, An-Chi Tung and Henry Wan, Jr.

1. INTRODUCTION

W E review here the roles of the government and the market[1] in Taiwan and Hong Kong over the period, 1950–1990. This exercise has two purposes. First, since all Chinese economies now operate under World Trade Organisation (WTO) rules, these episodes show that some (but not all) of Taiwan's industry targeting is not only effective but compatible with both WTO rules and free trade, quite contrary to popular belief. Second, a comparison between Hong Kong and Taiwan over these 40 years provides fresh insight: industrial policy appears to be unnecessary in early industrialisation, but essential later.

Such a discussion is relevant to the proposed re-industrialisation of Hong Kong today. We believe re-industrialisation is both feasible and desirable. It also has some historical precedents. The Dutch economy had once shifted focus from industry to high-valued agriculture in the early nineteenth century, only to be re-industrialised again toward the end of that century.[2] Living standards rose in each stage. We regard the feasibility as quite certain with government leadership. Some practices effective in Taiwan appear to be compatible with WTO rules. We define desirability here as a win-win game, beneficial to both Hong Kong and the Chinese Mainland.

In the next section, we explore the compatibility between free trade and industrial policy. The following two sections compare the records of Hong Kong and Taiwan over two periods, (a) in the 1950s, and (b) for the period of 1960–1990. After that, we comment about what we view as the long-term interests of

ERIK THORBECKE is from Cornell University. AN-CHI TUNG is from Academia Sinica. HENRY WAN, JR. is from Cornell University. While the authors are responsible for all the residual imperfections, the professional editorial assistance of Andrea Wan-Williams is deeply appreciated.

[1] More specifically, the industrial policy or its absence.
[2] See Mokyr (1976).

the Mainland Chinese economy. The concluding section addresses the general context of industrial policy.

2. FREE TRADE AND INDUSTRIAL POLICY

The essence of free trade is that in a trading world, all agents act as price takers. No economy should 'beggar-thy-neighbour', to benefit domestic agents by imposing tariffs, quotas, subsidies and so forth. This should not prevent agents from seeking self-improvement, for example raising their own productivity through formation of capital, in physical or human form.

WTO rules respect free trade and are not opposed to investment, be it as a result of individual decision, or collective (or public) action. Such action includes the upholding of intellectual property rights with effective patent and copyright laws, in order to remedy market failure. This would encourage citizens to be more creative, and hence more competitive against all comers. Such action may take other forms, like the supply of 'public goods', that is, goods of a 'non-rival nature'. Such goods may take physical form, such as roads and bridges, or non-physical form, such as information acquired through publicly funded projects. The point is, information valuable to many individuals – be they consumers or producers – might not be forthcoming in adequate amounts, without some action by public choice.

This valuable information may come from a feasibility study, a laboratory experiment, or a pilot project. This pilot project may take the form of a firm launched with public funding since it is both too risky for any private party alone and too valuable for its demonstration effect to be scrapped.[3] It may well be that under public, rather than private ownership, the expected loss of this experimental enterprise will be somewhat higher, due to lower efficiency. That detail ought not to affect the conclusion that the project should go ahead at public expense but to the benefit of privately owned firms. So long as the increased private profit is adequate to cover the loss of the public owned pilot firm through taxation, the national interest is served.[4]

Industrial policy is any public policy that improves the industrial structure of an economy. The launching of an information-gathering but loss-making project is such a policy. Well informed, and hence efficient, firms make a prosperous country like a form of well endowed natural resource. A public policy of developing such information is no different from the development of natural resources by laying pipelines from a natural gas field. Now, firms gain competitive advantage in the export market because their production costs are

---

[3] This is the Kemp Criterion of Itoh et al. (1991, p. 45).
[4] This is the Bastable Criterion of Itoh et al. (ibid., p. 43).

lowered by the availability of better information. In this case, their foreign rivals should have nothing to complain about. Yet, some rivals may claim that, in this case, a government has used public funds to give an (undue) advantage to a private firm to increase its market share, just like giving a cash subsidy, or subsidising research. Some people may draw the line at the pre-commercial stage.

We argue the merit of such public supported firms, but note that, in such matters, the issues are resolved judicially case by case and there are no comprehensive codes.[5]

Now suppose (a) an economy has an export industry that sells outputs and buys inputs, at home as well as abroad, all at world market prices, (b) the economy is too small to affect input prices and (c) the public policy is used only to improve the efficiency of the domestic suppliers of such inputs. Thus, the ultimate result enriches industries that deal with exporters, but does not enrich exporters themselves. Then such an industrial policy should be even more immune to challenges by any foreign firm, in particular, foreign suppliers of those inputs. After all, in this case, the inputs always change hands at the same world market price.

Such domestic input suppliers are linked to the world market, one step removed. Market competition makes sure that they sell at the given input price on the world market. As their costs get lower, they become richer and so does the country. Typically, in the worldwide production of that input, this economy gains a larger share than before. Even in the special case, where the input market share remains the enrichment results hold. Notice that according to (b), the world input price remains the same. So, for any specific foreign competitive supplier who takes exactly the same world input price as given, it can produce the same output and earn the same profit as before. Such a foreign firm has no ground to claim that it is a victim.

This lengthy discussion is historically relevant because, as a concrete example, Taiwan has developed very efficient upstream industries in both the synthetic fibre and the semiconductor industries by using such a novel type of industrial policy. Firms wholly or partially financed with public funds were used to spearhead the development of these industries.

3. THE HONG KONG–TAIWAN COMPARISON: THE 1950s

Over the period from 1950 to 1990, the British government in Hong Kong practised *laissez faire*. In contrast, Taiwan adopted industry targeting, even though the policy package changed greatly over time. This section focuses on the 1950s, before the reforms late in that decade gradually made Taiwan an outward-oriented economy.

---

[5] On this point, we thank Professor Robert Baldwin for his discussion, in private communication.

Through the 1950s, exchange control and import licensing, as well as control over the establishment of plants and land use were all resorted to in Taiwan. The powerful influence of American advisors who held the indispensable purse of US Aid directed industrialisation efforts to the private sector rather than the public firms favoured by the ruling Chinese Nationalists on Mainland China.[6] Target industries were set up by selected entrepreneurs such as Y. C. Wang, under the forceful and strong-willed K. Y. Yin, as well as technocrats like K. T. Li with which he surrounded himself.[7]

Over the decade of the 1950s, Taiwan's heavily assisted recovery from the nadir about 1950 has often been interpreted as credible growth. Extrapolating from this record, prior to the exhaustion of import substitution, some economists seem to doubt the causal role of the outward-oriented reform that started in 1958.[8] Moreover, other economists believe that import substitution policy in this period was necessary for the subsequent export expansion. Since economics is a non-experimental, empirical discipline and since history only happens once, what would have prevailed in Taiwan without import substitution seems to be a topic fit only for idle speculation.

However, in this case, economists are lucky. For all the four Asian NIEs, the textile industry played a leading role in early development. In both Hong Kong and Taiwan, the textile industry started with immigrant industrialists from the *same* Shanghai area, at about the *same* time. Comparison between these *Siamese twins* provides us much information.[9]

From five different angles, we shall consider the performance of the textile industry, before assessing the industrial environment in general.

a. Five Aspects About the Textile Industry

First, in terms of export volume, the *unprotected* industry in Hong Kong out-performed the *protected* industry in Taiwan, not only inside the British Common-wealth where Hong Kong might enjoy certain preference, but also in the American market.[10] In per cent share of US imports in 1962: Hong Kong dominated Taiwan 27.1 to 3.7 in textiles and 11.5 to .9 in clothing. One might argue that these lopsided figures reflected quota allocations under the Multifibre Agreement

---

[6] See Gold (1986), especially chapter 5.

[7] For the founding of the Formosa Plastics, one may refer to Wade (1990, p. 90).

[8] See for example, Rodrik (1995).

[9] On the textile industry in Taiwan, see Wade (ibid., pp. 79–80). On the textile industry in Hong Kong see Wong (1988). Though unsuccessful, the Rong family which is prominent in Hong Kong also tried to invest in Taiwan. The same Far Eastern Group has been active in both economies.

[10] The American market is important. England (1971, pp. 225–6) regarded that along with capital and technology, 'American market outlets' is an important asset, brought by the migrant capitalists from Shanghai to Hong Kong.

(MFA). However, today's large quotas are based on yesterday's large exports. So such reasoning only confirms Hong Kong's advantage at an earlier date.

Second, in terms of loom activities, according to Owen (1971, p. 148), even as late as 1966, the percentage of automated looms in factories was 100 per cent for Hong Kong but only 63 per cent for Taiwan. Moreover, the hours worked per loom in a year were 8,160 in Hong Kong to 4,864 for Taiwan. The *fuller* use of *better* facilities is surely a mark of efficiency.

Third, in terms of informed opinion, according to Wong, ibid., Shanghai merchants in Hong Kong were frustrated by Taiwan.[11] According to Wang (1974), Y. C. Shu, an authority in textile management,[12] had reported after his visit to Hong Kong, that institutions had prevented Taiwan from performing as well as Hong Kong (such as marketing shirts in America). What is noteworthy is that from both Hong Kong and Taiwan, contemporary sources gave similar views about Taiwan's industrial environment.

Fourth, in terms of the quality of policy makers, Taiwan tried hard to promote the cultivation of cotton, a crop clearly unsuitable to Taiwan.[13] In this case, policy makers seemed to be either wilful, or ignorant, or both.

Finally, in terms of policy support, according to Liang and Liang (1980), serious excess capacity developed in the textile industry near the end of the import substitution system, making it unsupportable.

It is true that according to Wong, more of the Shanghai textile capitalists went to Hong Kong than to Taiwan, and they had a longer connection with the former than the latter. Yet they could invest in both places and some did. Ironically, though they were the favourites of Taiwan's industrial policy,[14] they found the policy environment there less favourable than Hong Kong where they were not specially favoured.

b. General Environment for Industries

More generally, the main problem of import substitution is that it imposes a plethora of restrictive laws and regulations on the economy, administered by policy makers who either have inaccurate perceptions about the economy or are plainly ignorant about the laws of economics. Apart from this, regulations provide some administrators the chance to abuse their power. The following information provides an impression of Taiwan's general industrial environment in the 1950s.

---

[11] Rong's project in 1948 ended because Taiwan did not supply the needed electricity. The government limited output expansion throughout the 1950s, to prevent market saturation. In contrast, the British in Hong Kong were flexible and responsive, though not farsighted (ibid., pp. 22–25).

[12] Shu came to Taiwan from Shanghai.

[13] See Wan and Thorbecke (1999, p. 422).

[14] The main beneficiaries of the industrial policy were textile firms from Shanghai and Shangtung. See Tung (2001c, p. 34).

First, regarding inappropriate laws and regulation, according to K. T. Li (1998), in 1960 there were eight clauses of tax code and four articles of land use regulations that were unfavourable to attracting foreign direct investment.

Second, regarding the perceptions of policy makers at that time, it is now known that they (a) subscribed to 'export pessimism',[15] (b) underestimated the entrepreneurship of Taiwan's small and medium enterprises[16] and (c) maintained that each export commodity deserves a suitable exchange rate of its own.[17] Subsequent history showed that under a *unified* exchange rate that cleared the market,[18] *vibrant* SMEs helped Taiwan's exports to achieve *record growth*.

Finally, regarding the abuse of power by the administrators of the over-regulated system, we can also cite the following:

(a) According to Chang (1999, p. 45), around the middle 1950s, his shipping line had to deal with ten regulatory agencies. Officials therein abused their positions to secure jobs for their kin, who often quickly became loafers. 'It was a case of emotional blackmail at its worst'.
(b) According to Wade (ibid., pp. 286–9) outright corruption in Taiwan was never too damaging (in his words, *garden variety* and not *gangrene*). But it declined further only after the importance of growth and export to the economy became recognised in the society around the 1960s.[19]

To sum up, if the purpose of import substitution is to promote learning by doing in the targeted industries, then when the technology of an economy is still relatively simple, firms can often afford the cost for learning without protective measures.[20] Thus, on the one hand, industry targeting yields little benefit. Yet, on the other hand, to administer industry targeting requires bureaucracy, and hence imposes transaction costs on all traders. There is no net advantage when the remedy for *minor* market failure induces *major* government failure.

4. THE HONG KONG–TAIWAN COMPARISON: THE 1960s–1990s

Even twenty-six years before Hong Kong's actual Handover, Hopkins (1971) wrote on the first page of the preface of his well cited volume on Hong Kong: 'In

---

[15] See Tsiang (1984, p. 306). In resource allocation, this is like asking the gardener to preserve *all* weeds and flowers with impartiality.
[16] See Yin (1954).
[17] See Chen and Mo (1992, p. 85).
[18] Reached after a trial and error process.
[19] Customs officers would spare exporters and importers of electronic parts but extort importers of foods.
[20] One of the authors was informed that, in the 1970s, for a worker attending spindles in a textile factory, the upper bound for learning is reached after three to four months. Users of new textile machines would not need to call machine suppliers for trouble-shooting after half a year.

1997, the greater part ... is due to be handed back. ... It is highly unlikely that the remainder will be ... viable as a separate unit.' The recognition of this *finite horizon effect* made the British unwilling to plan ahead for Hong Kong. Industry upgrading is left for the working of 'trading up', that is, output shifts into greater value-added grades under a volume quota. This perhaps describes the reason behind the 'Positive Non-interventionism' of Cowperthwaite, Haddon-Cave and their successors as the financial secretary of the colony. Even before the Handover, de-industrialisation proceeded apace after the Chinese reform of 1978.[21]

In contrast, under the name of 'second stage import substitution', Taiwan has been working hard to upgrade its industrial structure by going upstream, throughout the three decades, 1960–1990. According to Chen and Ku (1999), the targeted industries produce capital goods or intermediate goods and enjoy economy of scale. For a relatively small economy like Taiwan, such industries can develop only when the downstream industries have reached sufficient volume. The founding of such industries goes hand in hand with the maintenance of the downstream industry. Such a setting turns out to be quite advantageous for two reasons:[22] (a) Since the downstream firms must meet international competition, the public-owned firms upstream can never charge prices for their outputs above the world market; (b) under such market discipline, losses of the public-owned firms can never be hidden. Thus, such firms never become bottomless pits for public funds. The transaction between the upstream and downstream firms is completely domestic. Therefore it is the least vulnerable to challenges by anyone from outside, under WTO rules.

The effect of such policy measures is that during the last decade, Taiwan has become the third largest exporter of information technology (IT) products (only after America and Japan) and the largest supplier of polyester, even though with the minuscule size of Taiwan's economy in the world, these rankings are not expected to last very long.

To illustrate the conditions under which such an industry may be established, we provide the example below and a formal model is contained in the Appendix.

Example. The economy currently exports 120 units of a downstream product y. Each unit of y uses one unit of importable good x, with a world price of $1. Good x may be partly supplied at home. To do this, one needs:

(a) To launch the industry, which incurs a once-for-all cost of $25,

and also

(b) To start a firm.

---

[21] See Sung (1997).
[22] See Chen and Ku (2001).

For each period, a firm can supply only 100 units of x after a fixed cost of $10. The marginal cost is 80¢ under public management, but 70¢ under private management.

Each period, there can be a single new firm entering the industry.

The interest rate is 10 per cent per period.

An old firm must list the unit price one period before the sale.

Analysis

- No private firm would volunteer to be the pioneering firm.

To be a pioneer, any private firm in the first period can list the unit price as $1, and earn $100¢ - 70¢ = 30¢$ per unit for the first 100 units and pay the current fixed cost of $10. That means a first period profit is $20.

During the second period, its list price must not be higher than 80 cents, since this is the stay-out price. Otherwise, a new firm can break even by selling at 80 cents per unit for the first 100 units, while paying a fixed cost of 10 dollars and a marginal cost of 70 cents per unit. But charging a list price of 80 cents means this private firm cannot make any profit either.

But then the $20 of first period profit will not be enough to cover the industry-launching cost of $25.

- A public firm would never break even. This is because the public firm has an even higher marginal cost than the private firm.
- A public firm serving as a pioneer will lose $25 - $10 = $15, since it can only earn profit in the first period, and, being a public firm,[23] the profit is $10 only. But then with a pioneering public firm in place, listing $1 from the second period on (the public firm would not be able to sell and break even in any case), a private firm will enter in the second period, earning a profit stream of $20 per period. This yields a present value of $200 = $20/.1. Out of this one can assess some tax to cover the $15 loss of the public pioneering firm.

The continuing posting of the $1 list price by the *non-operating* public firm from period 2 on can save any private firm from posting a list price of 80¢.[24] If the public firm ceases operations altogether, then, after entry, any private firm will list a price of 80¢. Less profit now goes to upstream firms, but more profit goes to any downstream firm that can get the domestically supplied good.

- Alternatively, the pioneering public firm can be privatised, and cover the loss from the first period (when it was public).

---

[23] With a higher marginal cost than the private firm, by assumption.

[24] One may more realistically assume that the public firm still has to pay the fixed cost. Little is changed.

In Taiwan, firms partially or fully owned by the public have been used as pioneers. These are either marginalised through competition by private firms as in the synthetic fibre sector,[25] or privatised through public stock offering as in the semiconductor sector. The need of public funds to spearhead new ventures is well documented in the latter case. Both UMC and TSMC could be founded only through the partial support of public funds, yet their successes soon attracted private firms to enter the field. For a detailed discussion of both the initial policy options and their eventual successes, see Tung (2001a and 2001b).

The lesson here is that, after the initial industrialisation, industry targeting can be used for industry upgrading by using the public firms as the pioneer for new industries. For an analytic treatment of the topic, one may consult Itoh et al. (1991).

5. THE COMMON INTEREST OF THE THREE CHINESE ECONOMIES

Section 2 has explained how industry targeting remains feasible for WTO members. Sections 3 and 4 have demonstrated through the Hong Kong–Taiwan comparison that industry targeting is unnecessary in the initial phase of industrialisation but is quite justified at later stages.

By now, after the entry of WTO, the economic interactions among the Chinese Mainland, Hong Kong and Taiwan are likely to increase further, by merely following the market force. Two issues stand out: first, whether this is the best for the three Chinese economies and second, if there is some other course that is superior to the evolutionary path in some win-win sense, what enabling policy instruments remain admissible under the WTO rules. Against some policy measures, there can be legal challenges by other WTO members. In the latter context, the record of industrial targeting in Taiwan over the period from 1950 to 1990 may serve as useful reference.

We note that the use of industry targeting in the last section is beneficial to an economy itself, with no harm done to any others. That is to say, it is a Pareto improvement.

A word should be said now about the economy of Mainland China and its interaction with Hong Kong and Taiwan. The unprecedented growth of the Chinese economy in the last two decades is certainly notable by any standards. Nonetheless, in the catching up process, the same progress also reflects how far that economy has to go and should go.

Using World Bank data, we have the information presented in Table 1. In words, a dollar's worth of China's product is accepted by the world market at 28¢. In contrast, one dollar's product by Japan and Hong Kong are accepted at the

---

[25] See Chen and Ku, ibid.

TABLE 1

Per Capita GNP 1997	Nominal	PPP	Nominal/PPP
Chinese Mainland	860	3,070	28%
Hong Kong	25,200	24,350	103%
Japan	38,160	24,400	156%
USA	29,080	29,080	1%

world market as $1.56 and $1.03 respectively. For a considerable time, Mainland Chinese have been able to produce goods with highly challenging technical requirements, for example, in the aerospace industry. The principal difficulty for China is to produce export goods to the required specifications, at a stable quality, and by cost-effective methods that allow punctual delivery. Remarkable progress has been made in recent times. Yet, 20 years after China's reform in the late 1970s, there is still continued dependence on the service of middlemen for external trade, as documented in Sung (2001). Causal empiricism suggests that, after Taiwan's own outward-oriented reform in the late 1950s, somehow, Taiwan seems to have graduated much faster from its 'middleman dependence'.

In recent decades, both Hong Kong and Taiwan have served as bridges for the Mainland economy to acquire production technology and to market products to the outside world. Such a function will be better served if Hong Kong and Taiwan stay industrialised, at least until the Mainland economy has gained enough capability to interact with the world market. It would not be to the interest of the Mainland economy for Hong Kong to completely de-industrialise and specialise in such service industries as hotels, restaurants and tourism. To invest in such service sectors in the rest of China may provide Hong Kong capitalists much profit, but this way the Mainland economy would be left with an eroded bridge to the outside world. By this token, the re-industrialisation of Hong Kong is desirable for the Mainland economy, as well as for Hong Kong.

From the pure economic angle, the adoption of industry targeting by Taiwan to slow its de-industrialisation should also be beneficial to the Mainland Chinese economy. A metamorphosis of Taiwan into a second Hainan Province is not in the economic interest of the Mainland Chinese.

6. CONCLUDING REMARKS

In a broader context, industrial policy is usually associated with the policies of Japan in the 1950s and 1960s and of Korea in the 1960s and 1970s, before trade liberalisation has placed constraints on what governments can do for domestic firms.

In addition, as Kikkawa and Hikino (1999) wrote:

The Japanese economy stumbled and American economy soared, and the interest in industrial policy evaporated in the 1990s.

Likewise, the Korean crisis in 1997 also has dampened the enthusiasm of development economists in industrial policy.

This study places matters in a different light. Industrial policy has been practised effectively in places other than Japan and Korea. It can take forms both different from the Japanese and Korean varieties and compatible with liberalised trade policies. The facts we cite are from Taiwan, and the intended application concerns Hong Kong. The major relevant policies of Taiwan relate to two areas, the launching of new industries that we discussed before, and the contribution to R & D efforts we should mention now.

According to Ng and Tuan (1995), the difference in policy stance between Hong Kong and Taiwan has had a pronounced impact on the development of the consumer electronics industry in these two economies: Taiwan showing a trend of upgrading but Hong Kong staying at the low-tech level.

We would further argue that, in the case of Taiwan, the government contribution to R & D is not only consistent with the spirit of trade liberalisation, but can even help to ameliorate the over-concentration of market power in the world market. In the case of derailleurs for the bicycles, the top four suppliers in the world are Shimano and SunTour of Japan, Machs of Germany and Champaignole of Italy. Together they control 800 patents which deters the entry of small emerging firms like those in Taiwan. The Industrial and Technology Research Institute (ITRI), a government-sponsored outfit in Taiwan, has responded to the request of local small and medium firms in the Taiwanese bicycle industry to develop independent designs of derailleurs and transfer it to these small local firms.[26]

Certainly, the theory and practice of industrial policy deserves much further attention from researchers.

APPENDIX

Incentive for the Pioneer: A Diagrammatic Treatment

For a domestic plant producing y, an input for exported good, let:

$m > 0$ be the marginal cost which is finite up to Q, but infinite above Q,
$F = E + F_0$ be the fixed cost,
E be the pioneering cost, that takes the value,
$\quad E_0 > 0$ if no firm has produced y in the economy before and
$\quad E_0 = 0$ otherwise,

---

[26] The source of information is from ITRI.

$F_0 > 0$,

r be the rate of interest,

p be the c.i.f. unit price of an imported unit of y.

Adopt now the assumptions:

(1) $m + (E_0 + F_0)/Q > p$,

and

(2) $p > m + (rE_0 + F_0)/Q$.

We have some obvious facts in:

Lemma 1

(3) $m + (rE_0 + F_0)/Q > m + F_0/Q$.

We can construct Figure 1 with the total cost curves over $0 < q < Q$:

(4) $C_1(q) = (E_0 + F_0) + mq$,

for the pioneer firm that must absorb all pioneering cost in 1 period,

FIGURE 1
The Anatomy of Market Failure

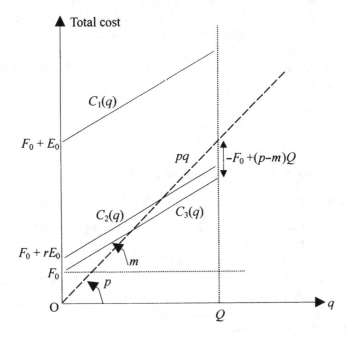

(5) $C_2(q) = (rE_0 + F_0) + mq$,

for the pioneer firm that can spread the pioneering cost over all periods,

(6) $C_3(q) = F_0 + mq$,

for the late-coming firm that is allowed to free-ride, and

(7) pq,

for the cost of importing the input.

We have actually established:

Proposition 1

Under the adopted assumptions:

    A. It is socially desirable to have a pioneer firm in view of (2),
    B. No pioneer firm can break even if all pioneering cost must be absorbed in one period in view of (1), and,
    C. No firm would choose to be a pioneer if late-coming firms can free-ride on its effort, in view of Lemma 1.

    Alternatively, the maximum operating profit in any period is:

(8) $P = -F_0 + (p - m)Q$,

From this, one can deduce:

Corollary 1

A firm may be induced to serve as a pioneer if it is granted the power of monopoly over the domestic market for at least N periods, where:

(9) $P[1 - (1 + r)^{-N}]/r > E_0$.

For example, in promoting its artificial fibre industry, the Japanese government induced Toray to serve as the pioneer firm by restricting market entry of all other firms. See Suzuki (1999). The minimum period of monopoly may be written as:

(10) $N^* = G(rp, m, F_0, E_0, Q_0)$,

where Q_0 is limited to plant capacity Q or market size M, whichever is lower. In fact, one can expect that:

Corollary 2

(11) $\partial G / \partial M \geq 0$,

For Taiwan, given the limited size of the home market and the uncertainties about the world market conditions, entry restriction may not be a credible inducement to potential pioneers. This may explain the practice in Taiwan of using public financed firms to serve as pioneers.

REFERENCES

Chang, Y.-F. (1999), *Tides and Fortune* (Singapore: Times Books International).

Chen, T.-J. and Y.-H. Ku (1999), 'Second-stage Import Substitution: The Taiwan Experience', in G. Ranis, S. Hu and Y.-P. Chu (eds.), *The Political Economy of Taiwan into the 21st Century* (Cheltenham, UK: Edward Elgar).

Chen, T.-Y. and C.-P. Mo (1992), *The Reminiscences of Dr. S. C. Tsiang* (Taipei: Institute of Modern History, Academia Sinica), Chinese.

England, J. (1971), 'Industrial Relations in Hong Kong', in K. Hopkins (ed.), *Hong Kong: The Industrial Colony* (Hong Kong: Oxford University Press).

Gold, T.B. (1986), *State and Society in the Taiwan Miracle* (Armonk, NY: M. E. Sharpe).

Hopkins, K. (1971), Preface in K. Hopkins (ed.), *Hong Kong: The Industrial Colony* (Hong Kong: Oxford University Press).

Itoh, M., K. Kiyono, M. Okuno-Fujiwara and K. Suzumura (1991), *Economic Analysis of Industrial Policy* (San Diego: Academic Press).

Kikkawa, T. and T. Hikino (1999), 'Industrial Policy and Japan's International Competitiveness: Historical Overview and Assessment', in H. Miyajima, T. Kikkawa and T. Hikino (eds.), *Policies for Competitiveness* (Oxford: Oxford University Press).

Ng, L. and C. Tuan (1995), 'Evolution of Hong Kong's Electronics Industry under a Passive Industrial Policy', *Managerial and Decision Economics*, **16**, 5, 509–23.

Li, K. (1998), 'Preface', in I. Yang, *Fabulous Strategies of Morris Chang* (Taipei: CommonWealth Magazine), Chinese.

Liang, K.S. and C.H. Liang (1980), *Trade Policy and the Exchange Rate of Taiwan* (Taipei: National Taiwan University Press).

Mokyr, J. (1976), *Industrialization in the Low Countries, 1795–1850* (New Haven, CN: Yale University Press).

Owen, N. (1971), 'Economic Policy', in K. Hopkins (ed.), *Hong Kong: The Industrial Colony* (Hong Kong: Oxford University Press).

Rodrik, D. (1995), 'Getting Interventions Right: How South Korea and Taiwan Grew Rich', *Economic Policy*, **20**.

Sung, Y. (1997), 'Hong Kong and the Economic Integration of the China Circle', in B. Naughton (ed.), *China Circle: Economics and Technology in the PRC, Taiwan, and Hong Kong* (Washington, DC: Brookings).

Sung, Y. (2001), 'Export-oriented Foreign Directed Investment in the People's Republic of China: Division of Value Added between Source and Host Economies', in L.K. Cheng and H. Kierzkowski (eds.), *Global Production and Trade in East Asia* (Boston: Kluwer Academic Press).

Suzuki, T. (1999), 'Industrial Policy and the Development of the Synthetic Fibre Industry: Industrial Policy as a Means for Promoting Economic Growth', in H. Miyajima, T. Kikkawa and T. Hikino (eds.), *Policies for Competitiveness* (Oxford: Oxford University Press).

Tsiang, S.C. (1984), 'Taiwan's Economic Miracle: Lessons in Economic Development', in A. Harberger (ed.), *World Economic Growth* (San Francisco, CA: ICSP).

Tung, A. (2001a), 'Taiwan's Semiconductor Industry: What the State Did and Did Not', *Review of Development Economics*, **5**, 2.

Tung, A. (2001b), 'Taiwan's Integrated Circuit Industry', in L.K. Cheng and H. Kierzkowski (eds.), *Global Production and Trade in East Asia* (Boston: Kluwer Academic Press).

Tung, A. (2001c), *Economic Design and Economic Miracle: A Study of Taiwan's Economic Planning* (Taipei: Institution of Economics Academia Sinica), Chinese.

Wade, R. (1990), *Governing the Market, Economic Theory and the Role of Government in East Asian Industrialization* (Princeton: Princeton University Press).

Wan, H. and E. Thorbecke (1999), 'Some Further Thoughts on Taiwan's Development Prior to the Asian Financial Crisis and Concluding Remarks', in E. Thorbecke and H. Wan (eds.), *Taiwan's Development Experience: Lessons on Roles of Government and Market* (Boston: Kluwer Academic Press).

Wang, C.-I. (ed.) (1974), *Annals for Mr. Yun-Chang Shu* (Taipei: Institute of Modern History, Academia Sinica).

Wong, S. (1988), *Emigrant Entrepreneurs, Shanghai Industrialists in Hong Kong* (New York: Oxford University Press).

Yin, K.Y. (1954), 'Adverse Trends in Taiwan's Industrial Development', *Industry of Free China* **2**, 2, Chinese.

The Win-Win Game of Intermediation: The Hong Kong PRC Connection

Review of "Hong Kong: The Fragile Economy of Middlemen", jointly with Jason Weisman[*]

The middleman's role Mainland China re-entered the world market, after its 1978 reform. This launched Hong Kong onto the new career (its third) as a middleman, shedding the earlier roles of an entrepôt, and then an exporter of manufacture. With a model of general equilibrium under information asymmetry, this Article studies how the Hong Kong-China nexus enables China to produce goods of better quality — thus earning a higher level of value-added — and reward Hong Kong for its service. It further speculates whether and how any wide-spread rent-seeking after Hong Kong's handover to China in 1997 will influence the operation of the middleman. As it turned out, such concerns were overblown. For a while, the economic re-integration of Hong Kong with Mainland China seems to be a win-win game. But that is also an over-simplification.

De-industrialization for Hong Kong History shows that the real challenge for Hong Kong is the exodus of its factories and income polarization. On the one hand, 11 million Chinese workers in the Pearl River Delta now work in factories under Hong Kong management; on the other hand, the manufacturing jobs in Hong Kong went from 905,000 to 226,200 between 1984 and 2000. Simultaneously, the ratio of income going to the richest 10% to the income going to the poorest 10% went from 17.7 to 38.0 between 1976 and 1996. So the capitalists gain and the workers lose. Domestic demand has sagged and real estate price has slumped, even though the overall growth rate stays positive.

Then, Crisis 1997 led to the raid of the Hong Kong dollar, the raise of interest rate as its successful defense, but this caused the recession as well. The subsequent lean years were only ameliorated somewhat when tourists from a booming China provided some badly needed business. Nevertheless, re-industrialization remains a much discussed and unattainable goal.

---

[*]This article is reprinted from the *Review of International Economics*, Vol. 7, No. 3, pp. 410–430, 1999, published by Blackwell.

It is also one of the inherent facts of life that, over time, the two parties the middleman intermediates for become well acquainted with each other so much so that there is scarcely any more need for a middleman.

The Hong Kong connection on Chinese development For China, the interaction with Hong Kong is an unmixed blessing. Consider the example of Shenzhen for instance. In 1979, Shenzhen was established as China's first Special Economic Zone, administered separately on the border of Hong Kong. By now it has grown into a metropolis in its own right, with four million residents. Like a magnet, it attracts investment from abroad and labor force all over China into its industries. Like a radiator, it generates backward and forward economic linkages with its neighboring districts in China. For China, it has served both as a window and a laboratory for introducing the market force. The only justification for Shenzhen's existence is its proximity to Hong Kong.

While the success of China's reform is a showcase of gradualism, the catalyst for such gradualist reform is the economy of Hong Kong. Even today, Beijing makes it clear that the movement of people and goods between Hong Kong and the rest of China remains highly regulated. Whatever was the motive behind this gradualism, such a program has worked far better than the "shock therapy" practiced in Russia, or during the German Reunification. This Chinese experience fits well the proposal "to globalize at optimal speed" of Bhagwati (2004). It is a topic deserving further research.

Review of International Economics, 7(3), 410–430, 1999

Hong Kong: The Fragile Economy of Middlemen

Henry Y. Wan, Jr and Jason Weisman*

Abstract

The paper shows that standard trade models can be adapted to address crucial policy issues in our dynamic, imperfect-information world. It also shows that intermediated trade is essential to the modernization of the 1.2 billion-person Chinese economy; yet, notwithstanding sincere intentions in Beijing and Hong Kong, subtle changes may deny Hong Kong its irreplaceable catalyst role, leaving China ultimately to technical stagnation.

1. Introduction

With the approach of *la fin de siècle*, it is tempting to speculate about what will be counted as the most important legacies of the latter part of this century. Three candidates seem to be obvious: (1) the microelectronics revolution, (2) the entry of East Asia into the trading world, and (3) the rise and fall of centrally planned economies. The first development spawned the globalized economy and quickened the product cycle. The second led to the rise of Japan and the Asian NIEs as major players in the world economic system. The third allowed China to open up and re-enter the world society after a 30-year hiatus.

Without 1.2 billion-person China, East Asia's impact on the world economy would be only modest in scale. Without modernization, even an "open" China would have only a marginal impact on the rest of the world. Without Hong Kong's involvement, China would face a much more difficult, if not impossible, task of successfully growing and modernizing its economy. Therefore, given the importance of Hong Kong in China's recent success and the ramifications of this relationship for the entire global economy, a deeper understanding of the role played by Hong Kong in mainland China's development is much needed.

Sung (1991) pointed to several important functions of Hong Kong in this relation ship: (1) provider of a variety of trade and transport services, (2) source of capital and foreign exchange, (3) market for Chinese primary goods and light manufactures, (4) channel of information between China and foreign businesses, and (5) middleman between China and other countries. The first three factors are associated with tastes, technology, and factor endowments, the importance of which is easily grasped by most policymakers. With the development of Shanghai and many other regional ports along the eastern coast of the mainland, over time these traditional economic contributions are likely to decline in their importance. The last two functions (i.e., conveyor of information and middleman in trade) are more basic and crucial to Hong Kong's role in bringing about long-term sustained development.[1] At the same time these factors are the least understood by both laymen and academics. It will be argued, however, that it is in large part because of Hong Kong's success in these roles that Chinese manu-

---
* Wan: Cornell University, Ithaca, NY 14853, USA. Tel: (607) 255-6211; Fax: (607) 255-2818; E-mail: hyw1@cornell.edu. Weisman: GE Capital Structured Finance Group, International Country Risk, 180 Glenbrook Rd, Stamford, CT 06902, USA. Tel: (203) 359-9479; E-mail: jlw12@cornell.edu. The second author wishes to state that this work was done privately, and the views expressed do not purport directly or indirectly to represent the official or unofficial views of GE Capital, any unit or officers thereof.

facturing exports have scored unprecedented growth in the past two decades, in quality as well as in value.

With Hong Kong's participation as an intermediary/catalyst, trade in "challenging" goods provides China the incentive to gain information and technology required to successfully participate in the dynamic global economy. This is the same self-sustaining mechanism which benefited Japan and all the NIEs. On the other hand, the absence of strong ties with the more advanced economies made development of Brazil, India, and the former Soviet Union extremely difficult. In this century of fast-moving technological frontiers those who fail to keep up with the latest developments quickly suffer technical obsolescence. In fact, no economy has ever managed to catch up with the industrially advanced world without a close linkage to it.

We believe that the quick modernization of China has and will continue to depend critically on Hong Kong facilitating connections between Chinese enterprises and the more technologically developed world. For historical and cultural reasons Hong Kong is uniquely suited to provide this linkage, and in fact, China needs this linkage more than any other developing economy. This seems to be broadly recognized in Beijing as well as Hong Kong. However, the degree of understanding may not yet be sufficient to preserve the fragile mechanism which maintains this relationship. It is illustrated below that owing to the nature of the "middleman economy" there is a clear risk that Hong Kong's current role may well dissipate unless it is assiduously safeguarded. So, now that the handover is over, a proper study of Hong Kong's important middleman role in mainland China's economic maturation may be essential to all concerned.

This paper examines from the perspective of economic theory the role of middlemen in bringing about economic efficiency. Understanding the middleman's role is also important in other cases, so the Hong Kong–China relationship is far from unique. Currently, Singapore serves a similar role for other ASEAN economies, and in other parts of the developing world new middlemen may conceivably emerge.

Section 2 introduces several stylized assumptions about the important features of an economic system in which middleman trade is carried out within a rapidly evolving world economy. These assumptions are justified by examples from recent experiences of East Asian development. Section 3 is the core of the paper, laying out an explicit model for the middleman economy. In that section it is shown that, owing to an asymmetry in information available to buyers and middlemen, there may be benefits for all involved from the middlemen's participation, bringing about the possibility of moving the economy from stagnation to dynamic growth. On the other hand, using that same model it is shown that the equilibrium with middleman participation may be quite fragile, possibly disintegrating if corruption is allowed to creep into the system. Section 4 discusses the relevance of this model and its results for China and Hong Kong in the wake of reunification. Section 5 concludes.

2. Some Preliminaries

A Stylized World

For simplicity, a stylized world with rapidly changing technology is considered. We focus on manufactured goods, Y, which differ in quality, $q \in \mathcal{R}$, with goods ranked along some quality ladder (Grossman and Helpman, 1991). A good of quality q is denoted by $y(q)$, with the minimum quality which poses challenge denoted as Q. A cardinal fact of life is:

STYLIZED FACT 1. *A developing economy can keep up (let alone catch up) with the current technological advances only through the learning effect of manufactured goods production.*

To capture the principle of "bounded learning" (Young, 1993) it is taken that:

STYLIZED FACT 2. *What is relevant for catching up is to produce manufactured goods of such quality which pose challenge, specifically $q \geq Q(I, t)$. Here the "challenge threshold," $Q(I, t)$, is specific to the country (I) and variable over time (t). What is usefully challenging for Korea at time t may not be so for Japan at the same instant, nor for Korea later, by the mechanism of the product cycle.*

Still another fact one must contend with is:

STYLIZED FACT 3. *Only by exporting can developing economies afford to produce manufactured goods posing challenge. In symbols, if $q \geq Q(I, t)$ then $y(q)$ is not affordable to consumers in developing country I at time t.*[2]

Our three stylized facts are neither deduced from more general assumptions nor expected to hold exactly in all possible worlds. By nature, the validity of these is tested empirically. The central role of manufacturing exports in the catching-up process has been observed in the ongoing econometric inquiry by Hong et al. (1998). Independently, Chapter 2 of *Emerging Asia* (Asian Development Bank, 1997) and Coe et al. (1997) provide descriptive corroborative evidence of this phenomenon.

Some discussion of the plausibility of these stylized facts is now in order. To be sure, the learning effect is also present in many primary industries. Yet, in comparison, manufacturing activities are much less dependent on sector-specific natural endowments. Furthermore, unlike activities such as prospecting minerals, tending tropical plants or harvesting marine products, skill and information in manufacturing is much less industry-specific in nature. Hence, in the context of catching up with the developed world, the learning effect arising from manufacturing activities is most conducive to rapid and sustained growth. This characteristic is important, and perhaps increasingly so in our time, when new technologies and products have caused the rapid and widespread obsolescence of older ones. Few people today care much about the elaborate, time-honored art of the *mahout*; i.e., taming the elephant.

In general, there is also less point today in pursuing specialized expertise for extended periods. Indeed, not everything can be learned overnight. Yet in a fast-moving world with intense cross-product competition "the best may well be the enemy of good." This underlies the principle of bounded learning. One does not have to go so far as Nathan and Ross (1997) to derogate the newly developed Chinese fighter planes as "the most perfected obsolete planes in the world." The difficulty of going it alone in technology is well understood to all, the Chinese leadership included.

Most modern technology calls for costly, specialized equipment. For example, clean rooms for fabricating memory chips come at a cost of one billion US dollars each. Facing such a fixed cost, a developing economy—even one as large as India or China—has few domestic consumers who can afford such products with sufficiently challenging qualities to bring about learning. Hence, for producers of such goods, to export is to survive. Conversely, for developing economies, to de-link is to resign from the game.

Moreover, in East Asia, export activities are often collaborative ventures between the developing South and the more developed North. In the intense North–North competition, reliable outsourcing to the low-cost South, when done before one's rivals, offers Northern firms a clear edge. The same holds for the Northern suppliers of key parts to Southern assemblers/exporters. It therefore pays for individual Northern firms to selectively tutor their Southern partners.[3]

Furthermore, to be complete, one may add that Northern firms can hardly use the potential benefit of such tutoring as a bargaining chip to entice Southern firms. Managerial decisions in the South are not generally swayed by the potential efficiency gains of their footloose Southern workers. Poorly developed Southern capital markets would never support Southern workers to work for even lower wages just for the sake of learning. In such deals, therefore, weakness is strength.

Korean Lessons

We now demonstrate the essential validity of the above discussion using an example from economic history: evidence from South Korea over the last four decades. On the whole, postwar Korea stagnated before the early 1960s under President Rhee and Premier Chang, but took off after the export drive of President Park.

First, it can be seen that exporting is important, yet not all exports are equally important. Following up the Filipino-Korean comparison of Lucas (1993), it is noted that the early export of wigs from Korea eventually led to textiles, which after time led to supertankers and computer chips.[4] However, sugar exports from the Philippines now cannot even hold their own against Thai competition in that market. Skills Koreans learned in exporting wigs—quality control and punctual delivery—have allowed them to move on to pursuits with ever-increasing challenge.

Second, industry upgrading is important. The Korean aspiration to catch up could hardly have had much future if they continued to specialize in wigs after 30 years.

Third, for industries with learning potential such as automaking, the home market of a developing economy hardly supplies the clientele necessary to stimulate dynamic learning. This is partly a matter of numbers, partly a matter of income, but also partly a matter of "cosmopolitan" tastes. For example, to earn US dollars in the 1950s automakers had to produce stylish high tailfins. Close attention to Northern consumer tastes help to explain why in world markets Korean cars have far outsold their Brazilian, Russian and Indian rivals, all of which were designed with domestic consumers in mind. The parallel experience of Japan served as a blueprint for the Koreans, which further laid the foundation for the Malaysian movement, "Look East."

The Sino-Hong Kong Context

We have introduced a few symbols to sharpen our discourse, but have made no attempt to fully analyze this problem as a dynamic general equilibrium system. The formulation in Wan (1993) supplies a basis for doing just that, assuming Stylized Facts 1 and 2.[5] For our purpose now, however, such a complex exercise would serve only to distract readers from the main focus. In fact a convenient shortcut is readily available in this analysis. That is, although the crux of our study may be dynamic, *to continue the catching-up process*, one may well focus upon its static dual; i.e., *to escape from the steady state of stagnation*.

To sum up, we take as given that for China to modernize, it must produce goods of ever-more challenging quality, and with export appeal. This is consistent with the observation of Lucas (1988) that for economies with sustained rapid growth (the NIEs) goods produced primarily for export were not produced domestically in the past. Lucas's focus is that these goods are not new globally, only locally; our focus is on the fact that *what is new is exported—to the North*.[6] In our model the main benefit of trade comes from the dynamic effect of learning, not merely from increased employment, higher wages or larger reserves of foreign exchange, as discussed in the Ricardian tradition of static gains.

Furthermore, we note that that even today Russia remains far more technically advanced than China. Yet, in the former Soviet era that nation's economy stagnated owing to isolation. Still today, in areas in which it is isolated, the Chinese economy apparently faces similar difficulties. We believe the mechanism of learning-by-exporting will remain essential to the Chinese effort to modernize for many years to come.

Under "reform and opening" policies of the last twenty years China has supplied labor-intensive goods of foreign design, produced with foreign technology, to foreign markets. Thus, conveniently, the small country assumption in trade theory applies well even for the most populous nation in the world. This is because waiting in the wings are economies like Vietnam, Myanmar, and several African countries, ready to enter these same markets with wages even lower than China's. Thus, we have formally:

STYLIZED FACT 4. *The prices (and designs) of exports from rapidly growing developing countries are set by world markets.*

A stunning implication of our argument is that, notwithstanding its recent raging growth, Chinese development can still be stunted (like the former Soviet Union's) unless its exports are continuously upgraded with an appeal to Northern tastes. In the past such upgrading depended on the intermediation of Hong Kong, a process which as is shown below to be quite fragile. To assess the future of Hong Kong, one must have a firm grasp of (a) *what* function intermediation served in the past, and (b) *whether* the environment will be conducive to such intermediation in the future. A critical question is: precisely which features of the former environment, if any, may defy emulation? The answer to this turns on both the aspects of information and incentives existing in the intermediation process. These issues are examined more closely in the following sections.

3. The Economics of the Middleman

The role of middlemen is critically related to an asymmetry in information available to these market intermediaries and to consumers. Employing a simple bargaining model with search costs, Rubinstein and Wolinsky (1987) were the first to present an explicit model showing how middlemen serve to create more efficient markets by facilitating contacts. Contributions by Yavas (1994, 1996) generalized the basic framework by endogenizing various aspects of the trading process, providing conditions under which the existence of middlemen results in positive welfare effects. Biglaiser (1993) developed a bargaining model to show that middlemen who have large present and future stakes in a market can resolve inefficiencies when adverse selection exists. Biglaiser and Friedman (1994) discussed how the existence of intermediaries can improve quality of products by acting as quality inspectors. They observe that the existence of intermediaries can have several types of effects on markets; including reducing search costs, reducing selling costs, reducing the price premium needed to induce firms to produce better quality goods, and resolving the adverse selection problem. For our part, the model introduced below is most closely linked to this last issue.

Although the works cited above on middlemen have motivated our analysis, in order to more efficiently study the interactions among various economies, we have instead fashioned a much more tractable model out of four building blocks, familiar to researchers in trade and growth.

First, for the international division of labor, we follow the production specification of Dornbusch–Fischer–Samuelson (1977). A representative good can be produced in a continuum of quality grades, $q \in \mathcal{R}$, using Ricardian technology. This model has been extended by Collins (1985) to apply to a three-region trading world, including the North, the South and the newly industrialized economies (NIEs). In contrast, our focus is on the vertical division of labor between a developing economy (China) and a NIE (Hong Kong), which coordinate to export goods to the North. To focus on the price-taking behavior of exporting firms we take as given that all equilibrium prices of goods are determined in the world market.

Second, on the issue of dynamic evolution, we adopt the well-known "principle of bounded learning" of Young (1993); i.e., learning is possible only when producers venture beyond the current-day "mature technology." Thus, we can concentrate on the question of "escaping from stagnation" rather than its less tractable dual of "achieving sustained growth." In doing this we actually demonstrate the versatility of Young's principle in a model where conclusions are in direct variance with Young's.[7]

Third, in dealing with trade under imperfect information, we build upon the models of Chiang and Masson (1988) and Pomery (1984), which show that when consumers cannot easily differentiate products of individual firms, adverse selection (the "lemons" problem analyzed by Akerlof (1970)) may ensue. Consequently, a firm which undertakes the expense of improving the quality of its products will not receive the full benefit. At the same time, those firms which do not attempt to produce better goods gain by free-riding. In this situation a suboptimal equilibrium may result wherein no firms in the economy are willing to undertake costly improvements in the qualities of their products. Chiang and Masson suggest various methods to internalize this negative information externality, including industrial consolidation, limiting export licenses and industrial export quality standards. Our departure from them is to study the effect of a neutral middleman in resolving this adverse selection problem.

Lastly, in discussing the effect of increased corruption, the model developed here treats the gathering of quality information as costly in terms of labor and importable inputs, under a standard production function. Hence, we can measure the effect of corruption on the system, including determining the particular critical point where intermediation becomes economically nonviable.

Formally, we introduce and characterize three different types of equilibria: (1) the perfect-information equilibrium, (2) the (unintermediated) imperfect-information equilibrium, and (3) the intermediated equilibrium. Like Chiang and Masson, we show that quality of exported goods is lower in an unintermediated imperfect-information equilibrium situation than it is when buyers have perfect information about the products they purchase. We also illustrate that, under suitable conditions, the intermediated equilibrium implies the same equilibrium product quality as under perfect information. We then show that if corruption erodes the effectiveness of intermediation, beyond a threshold level of corruption, intermediation stops and equilibrium product quality and net social welfare decline. Under the condition that equilibrium product quality levels under imperfect information correspond to mature technology only, the learning process may then come to an end and the economy cease to grow.

Practically speaking, the information asymmetry we consider is clearly evident in China owing to the character of its social and economic systems. As observed in *Emerging Asia*, the most dynamic and export-oriented components of China's economy today are the rural cooperatives and foreign-related joint venture enterprises. These institutional arrangements vary widely from case to case. However, high transaction costs and low transparency in laws and regulations remain the rule, not the exception. To get the best deal, foreigners need the Hong Kong-based Chinese, who are well-informed about China but not located on the mainland. Their effectiveness in this endeavor rests not only upon their understanding of China, but also on their independence, and here there may be some problem.

To be more precise, in the context of the middleman's role, the perception of independence (in this case by Westerners) is more important in driving this system than the reality. So whether or not Hong Kong continues to have "a high level of autonomy" after the return of sovereignty is less important than whether this perception is maintained, particularly in the minds of Westerners. That is why the role of the popular press is so crucial in this case. As a typical example of popular impressions, seven months before the return of sovereignty of Hong Kong, Gargan (1996) reported in *The New York Times* that "in many respects China—its businesses, its way of operating, its politics—have so permeated this territory that little is left to be done but to lower the Union Jack." Given his description in the same article of key "mainland business practices—bribery, padded commissions, reliance on political contacts to cut deals," it is not surprising that there is some concern in the minds of potential business partners about the stability and independence of Hong Kong's middlemen.

In that same article Gargan described an unusual defense used by the lawyer for the chairman of a Hong Kong company who was accused of dumping his company's shares. The lawyer argued for a light sentence for his client on account that he was "an honorary citizen of China," and because it was necessary for him to have contact with officials in the future. Now, whether or not that defense was successful in winning a more lenient punishment in that particular case is somewhat besides the point.[8] What is quite telling is that, at least as perceived by the lawyer, that line of argument had some chance of being considered positively by a supposedly impartial justice system. Widely held perceptions today about the utility of special connections, if pervasive throughout many levels of the society, may turn out to become self-fulfilling prophecies.

The Model

We adopt the following seven assumptions and definition.

ASSUMPTION 1. *There are three economies in the world, including:* A, *the Advanced economy,*[9] B, *the Backward economy, and* C, *the Catalyst economy.*

ASSUMPTION 2. *In each period, all output prices* p_t *are determined by* A, *with agents in* B *and* C *acting as price-takers in the market for their exported goods.*

ASSUMPTION 3. *Labor is the only primary input, supplied to each economy* I *in fixed quantity,* L_I.

ASSUMPTION 4. *There are* N *firms in* B, *with identical, constant returns to scale, Ricardian technologies. The unit labor requirement for output of a representative good of quality* q *at time* t *is* $a_t(q)$, *which is increasing in* q *since more labor is needed to produce higher quality goods.*

ASSUMPTION 5. *Individuals in* A *are risk-neutral with respect to quality, the precise meaning of which will be clarified below.*

ASSUMPTION 6. *The wage rate in B, w_B, is determined by market forces acting to clear the labor market*

$$L_B = \sum_i li, \tag{1}$$

where l_i is the labor employed by firm i.

ASSUMPTION 7. *In B, given wage w_B, each firm i chooses an ordered pair of labor force employed, l_i, and product quality, q_i, in order to maximize current profit*

$$\pi_i = \rho_i(q_i, .)y_i - w_B l_i = l_i \left\{ \frac{\rho_i(q_i, .)}{a(q_i)} - w_B \right\}. \tag{2}$$

The (net) unit price received by the firm is $\rho_i(q_i, .)$, which is increasing in q_i but defined differently under different concepts of equilibrium, discussed in more detail below.

(1) Under the *perfect information equilibrium*:

$$\rho_i = p(\mu_i), \text{ and } \mu_i = q_i, \tag{3}$$

where $p(\mu_i)$ is a continuous, increasing function describing the price buyers in A are willing to pay for goods produced by a firm i which are perceived to have quality μ_i, and with perception in this case mirroring reality.

(2) Under the *imperfect information equilibrium*:

$$\rho_i = p(\mu_i), \text{ and } \mu_i = \frac{q_i \hat{y}_i + \sum_{j \neq i} q_j \hat{y}_j}{\sum_j \hat{y}_j}, \tag{4}$$

where μ_i is the perceived quality of goods produced by firm i, and $\hat{y}_j$ is the expected output of firm j, using information from previous experience. Since buyers cannot identify products of individual firms, they form perceptions on the basis of a weighted average of all firms' production levels.

(3) Under the *intermediated equilibrium*:

$$\rho_i = (1 - f)p(\mu_i), \text{ and } \mu_i = q_i, \tag{5}$$

where the quality perception (of the buyers in A) mirrors reality and sellers in B pay a fee for the services of middlemen in C, who provide information about the quality of goods of specific exporting firms. The fee structure is such that a fixed fraction f of the sales price is paid for this information, with f dependent on conditions in C, as further explained below.

DEFINITION. *Each equilibrium concept encompasses an ordered triplet:*

$$\left(w_B^*, (l_i^*, q_i^*)_{i=1, 2 \ldots, N} \right) \tag{6}$$

which satisfies the twin conditions pertaining to perfect competition:

$$0 = \max_{q, l_i} l_i \left\{ \frac{\rho_i(q_i, .)}{a(q_i)} - w_B \right\} \quad \text{(competitive profit condition),} \tag{7}$$

$$0 = L_B - \sum_{i=1}^{N} l_i \quad \text{(full employment condition)}. \tag{8}$$

Remark 1. Having assumed that all firms share identical technology and market access, it is reasonable to focus attention on symmetric equilibria, where

$$l_i^* = L_B/N \text{ and } q_i^* = q_1^* \ \forall \ i = 1, 2 \dots, N. \tag{9}$$

Remark 2. Any monotonic transformation of the value of quality leaves all quantities produced and purchased unchanged, hence, without loss of generality units of quality may be redefined such that

$$q = p(q), \tag{10}$$

which reflects the marginal consumer preference in A for a known quality of good.[10] The weighted average of "quality" reflects the weighted average of the marginal utility to consume goods. Under risk neutrality this justifies equation (4).[11] It is now clear that equations (7) and (8) define a Cournot–Nash equilibrium. Players' qualities affect each other through what buyers perceive about a "Made in China" label.

Remark 3. Figure 1 illustrates the implication of equation (7). By definition, from any equilibrium, however reached, a firm can never make more profit by changing its quality decision, given the value of l_i. Nor can one make more profit by changing l_i. Under constant returns, profit must be zero anywhere on the horizontal line illustrated, which maximizes the revenue per worker, given the wage rate and other firms' production decisions. Therefore no individual firm will gain by deviating from the symmetric equilibrium shown in the figure.

Results

From the above analysis we can deduce the following proposition.

PROPOSITION 1. *Under a perfect information equilibrium:*[12]

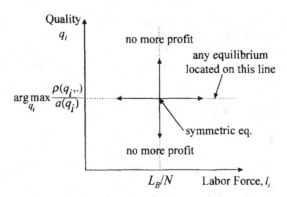

Figure 1. Illustration of a Firm's Optimization Decision

$$q^* = q_i^* = arg\ max_q[p(q)/\,a(q)] = arg\ max_q[q/a(q)]\ \forall\ i = 1, 2, ..., N. \qquad (11)$$

PROOF. If the claim is false, there exists some q_0 such that

$$[q_0/a(q_0)] > [q^*/a(q^*)]. \qquad (12)$$

Since firm i is free to choose independently its product quality and labor force, it can hire the same labor force but produce q_0 instead of q^* and increase its profit by an amount $\{[q_0/a(q_0)] - [q^*/a(q^*)]\}l_i$, contary to equations (3) and (7).   □

COROLLARY 1. *Under a perfect information equilibrium:*

$$w^* = max_q[q/\,a(q)]. \qquad (13)$$

PROOF. This follows directly from equations (6) and (7).[13]   □

Remark 4. In a perfect information equilibrium, l_i is indeterminate. If symmetry is assumed, however, $l_i = L_B/N$.

Remark 5. The above findings hold even if arg $max_q\ [p(q)/a(q)]$ is a set with more than one element, in which case there are multiple potential equilibria.

To sharpen the analysis, the quality elasticity of per unit labor input, $\varepsilon(q)$, is defined as

$$\varepsilon(q) \equiv \frac{da(q)/a(q)}{dq/q} = \frac{qa'(q)}{a(q)}, \qquad (14)$$

with assumptions[14] that:

ASSUMPTION 8. $\varepsilon(q)$ *exists and is a continuous, strictly increasing function of output quality.*[15]

ASSUMPTION 9. *There exist some* q *and* $\bar{q}$ *such that:*

$$\varepsilon(q) < 1/N\ \forall\ q < q,$$

$$\varepsilon(q) > 1\ \forall\ q < \bar{q}.$$

COROLLARY 2. *For the perfect information case, a necessary and sufficient condition for equilibrium is*

$$\varepsilon(q^*) = 1. \qquad (15)$$

PROOF. Note that profit is

$$\pi_i = l_i \left\{ \frac{p_i(q_i, \cdot)}{a(q_i)} - w^* \right\} = l_i \left\{ \frac{q_i}{a(q_i)} - w^* \right\}, \qquad (16)$$

using equation (3). The first-order condition for profit maximization, choosing quality level results in equation (15) as a necessary condition for profit maximization for each firm. Assumption 9 along with continuity guarantees the existence of some equilibrium quality. Uniqueness is assured since elasticity increases with increasing quality level.   □

COROLLARY 3. *For the symmetric, imperfect information case a necessary and sufficient condition for equilibrium is*

$$\varepsilon(q^0) = 1/N. \tag{17}$$

PROOF. Profit is

$$\pi_i = l_i \left\{ \frac{\rho_i(q_i, .)}{a(q_i)} - w^0 \right\} = l_i \left\{ \frac{q_i + \sum_{j \neq i} q_j}{Na(q_i)} - w^0 \right\}. \tag{18}$$

The above expression is obtained using equation (4) along with the assumption that firms are perceived by buyers in A to be equal in size; i.e., $\hat{y}_j$ are identical for all j. The first-order condition, maximizing profit with respect to quality choice for firm i, gives the desired necessary condition. Existence and uniqueness follow as above for the perfect-information case.   □

Hence, the quality/cost tradeoff is affected by the spillover effect of a shared image: a firm receives just $1/N$ of the fruits of its effort to improve the collective image of the quality of goods, but bears the full share of costs. Figure 2 illustrates and provides some intuition about the effect of imperfect information on the quality level of firms' products.

We can now surmise the consequences of imperfect information.

PROPOSITION 2. *Under an unintermediated, imperfect-information equilibrium, both the equilibrium product quality and market-clearing wage rate are lower than in a perfect-information equilibrium.*

PROOF. That the equilibrium quality level is higher under perfect information is obvious from Assumption 8 given the results from equations (15) and (17), since there

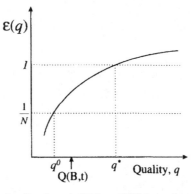

Figure 2. Equilibrium Quality Levels With and Without Intermediation

are assumed to be many producing firms in B $(N > 1)$. Next, to show that the wage rate under perfect information is higher than it would be under imperfect information, note that w^* has been found to be the unique solution to the unconstrained maximization of $q/a(q)$. In a symmetric, imperfect-information equilibrium the zero-profit condition using equation (16) gives

$$w^0 = q^0/a(q^0),$$

(19)

which since $q^0 \neq q^*$ implies $w^* > w^0$.

Now we consider the intermediated equilibrium, in which a large number of perfectly competitive firms in economy C charge a proportional fee, f^* per unit of goods, to provide buyers in A perfect information about the quality of products.

Remark 6. Economies B and C are small and therefore have no effect on world prices. The incidence of the middleman's fee must fall on individuals in B.

Remark 7. With intermediation, economy B can export under conditions of perfect information, guaranteeing that the quality level of products would be the same as q^*, above. The wage rate under perfect competition in B is

$$w_B^{**}(1 - f^*) q^*/a(q^*).$$

(20)

Alternatively, under imperfect-information equilibrium, the wage rate would be

$$w_B^0 = q^0/a(q^0).$$

(21)

A symmetric, intermediated equilibrium exists only if no firm would find it profitable to sell low-quality goods in order to avoid the middleman's fee. The equilibrium exists, therefore, as long as

$$(1 - f^*)q^*/a(q^*) \geq q^0/a(q^0).$$

(22)

Remark 8. Information gathering is costly. The magnitude of f^* depends on the efficiency of economy C in that activity, and that effectiveness may erode because of corruption, which enters as a parameter to the production function for information gathering.

We illustrate this situation with a simple example based upon some special assumptions. To determine the quality of goods produced by each unit of labor in economy B, the required resources for this activity are described by a linear homogeneous production function of the form:

$$F(a_M, a_C; \theta) = 1.$$

(23)

Here a_M and a_C are the unit requirements of imported capital and local labor, respectively. θ is an institutional parameter describing the efficiency of the intermediation activity, equivalent to the degree of corruption in C, with $\theta = 1$ denoting "normal" (or "uncorrupted") institutions and $\theta = 0$ the maximum level of corruption in the society. For concreteness a Cobb–Douglas technology for intermediation is assumed, with capital and labor used as inputs. This production function is represented by

© Blackwell Publishers Ltd 1999

$$F(a_M, a_C; \theta) = \theta a_M^{1-\gamma} a_C^\gamma \tag{24}$$

With all of C's labor force employed in intermediation activities, in equilibrium

$$a_C^* = L_C/Y, \tag{25}$$

where L_C is the size of the labor force and Y the total quantity of exports from country B. Using the above production function for intermediation, this implies a corresponding value of a_M^*. Given the world market price for imported inputs, m, and the implied marginal rate of factor substitution from the production function for intermediation, the market-clearing wage for country C, w_C^*, can be obtained. Finally, using the fact that the market for intermediation is perfectly competitive, the unit cost (price) of the value of intermediation services (k) is derived:

$$k(w_C, m; \theta) = a_C(\theta)w_C(\theta) + a_M(\theta)m. \tag{26}$$

With the cost of intermediation set as a fixed fraction of the price of exported goods, independent of quality level, this condition determines the fee schedule:

$$f^* = k(w_C^*, m; \theta)/p(q^*). \tag{27}$$

Note that since the intermediation process is quality-neutral, a proportional fee schedule will not affect the choice of product quality by firms in B[16] provided that

$$p(q^*) - p(q^0) \geq k(w_C^*, m; \theta). \tag{28}$$

If this condition is not met then firms in country B would opt to sell their products directly to world markets, forgoing intermediation.

Using the above Cobb–Douglas form to describe the intermediation activities, the quantity of capital imported to C is

$$M^* = \left(Y/L_C^{1-\gamma}\right)^{1/\gamma} \theta^{-1/\gamma}. \tag{29}$$

The wage rate for labor in C is

$$w_C^* = \frac{(1-\gamma)mM^*}{\gamma L_C}, \tag{30}$$

with the imputed value of intermediation services therefore

$$kY = \frac{mM^*}{\gamma}. \tag{31}$$

In fact, the intermediation process described above is no different from any production process in C which incurs some real "cost of doing business" in order to transform a "quality lottery" into its sure-quality component. Analytically, to receive the higher value for quality-certified products, agents in B treat the for-fee service from C just like a transport cost under the "iceberg" hypothesis in the trade literature.

PROPOSITION 3. *With Cobb-Douglas technology for intermediation, a small incremental decrease in efficiency (increase in corruption), $d\theta$, will result in: (1) an increase in the level of imported capital by $[M^*/(\gamma\theta)]\, d\theta$, (2) an increase in wage rate of country C by* *(wᶜ*/(γθ)dθ, and (3) a decrease in income of country B by (m/γ²) (Y/L<ᶜ¹⁻ᵞ)¹ᐟᵞ θ⁻⁽¹⁺ᵞ⁾ᐟᵞ dθ.*

PROOF. The first result above can be obtained by taking the natural logarithm of equation (29), differentiating with respect to θ and rearranging the result. The second expression follows similarly after substituting (29) into (30). The third relation results from the fact that country B's income equals $[1 - f^*(\theta)]q^*Y$, with $f^*(\theta) = (mM^*)/(\gamma q^*Y)$ from equation (27) and $p(q^*) = q^*$. Substituting for M^*, differentiating with respect to θ and rearranging gives the desired expression.   □

Ironically, as efficiency declines in C owing to increased corruption, incomes decline in country B but not C. The quality choice for exports by B is unaffected. If corruption proceeds to the point where

$$q^* - q^0 < k(w_C^*, m; \theta),\qquad(32)$$

country B will revert to the unintermediated equilibrium, with product quality declining to q^0 from q^*. This is equivalent to the condition that $\theta < \hat{\theta}$ in Figure 3. Once the intermediary role is lost, individuals in country C would be exactly like those in B, a situation residents of Hong Kong faced under Japanese rule during the Second World War.

This bleak scenario is a cautionary tale, certainly not inevitable. Over time, B may have no need for intermediation. Corruption in C may not go unchecked, or C may find other export of its own, beside serving as a middleman. On the other hand it is a logically consistent scenario, not to be dismissed out of hand. A rather gloomy passage in Lucas (1993) seems to corroborate our view.[17]

We now come to the heart of our inquiry, namely, export is essential to the Chinese ambition to modernize. As we move from a static to a dynamic analysis, quantities are now labeled with time indices. For this analysis we adopt Young's Principle of Bounded Learning and assume that with experience producing "challenging goods" labor productivity increases and costs of production decline.

PROPOSITION 4. *For some "challenge threshold" level,* $Q(B, t)$, *in country B*

$$a_{t+1}(q_i) < a_t(q_i),\ for\ all\ q_i \geq Q(B, t),$$

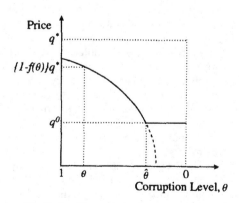

Figure 3. Price Received by B for Exports vs. Corruption Level, θ

$$a_{t+1}(q_i) = a_t(q_i), \text{ for all } q_i < Q(B, t).$$

Some observations are in order. First, it has been assumed that labor turnover in B is so high that firms would not sacrifice current profits just to make their labor force more experienced. Next, under autarky economy B would produce only for domestic demand and output may be positive only for goods with quality lower than some level, $q'(B, t)$, since in general less-developed countries have little demand for goods near the frontiers of current technology.

LEMMA. *If* $q'(B, t) < Q(B, t)$ *learning is impossible without trade and an import substitution policy would be futile.*

This brings up the rather disturbing possibility that an import substitution policy provides some initial benefit, but proves to be ultimately futile after much of the labor force is trapped in "uneconomic" production activities. This situation may describe what happened to many Eastern European nations after the Second World War. For those countries inward-looking policies sustained some degree of technological progress for a time, but eventually led to stagnation.

PROPOSITION 5. *Intermediation may improve product quality, thus presenting the possibility of firms in B securing dynamic learning.*

As illustrated in Figure 2, if at some point in time the challenge threshold $Q(B, t)$ for country B is in the range between q_i^0 and q_i^*, then the availability of intermediation by C would spell the difference between perpetual stagnation and sustained growth.

4. Discussion

What Hong Kong Provided

At this point, some institutional discussion is in order. We take for granted that the quality decision is made by management but the benefit of learning accrues to workers. The possibility of labor turnover will consequently make learning into an externality from the perspective of individual firms.

In contrast to the buyer, the advantage enjoyed by the middleman is partly cultural but also partly a matter of scale. Individual importers in country A need not purchase repeatedly. They are in no position to keep tabs on individual suppliers in country B and pose the threat of the "grim trigger" strategy; i.e., no future business if the quality standard is not met. On the other hand, the middleman, whether as an independent professional or in the employment of a multinational firm, is distinguished by both capability and intention. Such an actor plays for the long haul, and has his own reputation to care for. As a group, free entry into the ranks of middlemen serves to keep incumbents honest under competitive pressure. In short, the middlemen intermediate best when rent-seeking is conspicuous by its absence.

It is significant that professional middlemen thrive in an environment with an independent judiciary, laws against restrictive business practices, as well as an administration tempered internally by checks and balances and externally by public hearings and an uninhibited press. Formally speaking, the mechanics of governance does not have to be multiparty parliamentary democracy. Certainly, during the former period of the British Crown Colony, residents of Hong Kong had little political role to play compared with citizens of most participatory democracies. Yet, there has been the rule of law, not the rule of men, especially since 1974 with the establishment of the Hong Kong Independent Commission Against Corruption.

What China Needs

The People's Republic of China arose out of a baptism of revolutionary fire. In the first three decades after its founding the PRC confronted both superpowers with arms and fought border wars with India and Vietnam. An argument might be made that in times like those judiciary independence and so forth cannot rank high in the list of public priorities. Understandably, when the survival of the Great Cause is not yet assured, the separation of powers means a divided command, which can only cause mischief and grief. At any rate, the Constitution of the People's Republic of China states that the nation's economic system is based on "socialist public ownership of the means of production, namely, ownership by the whole people." How effectively middlemen can intermediate in this environment seems to be rather a non-sequitur. It is no coincidence then that after 1978, when the "Four Modernizations" became the Chinese national policy and economic growth was promoted to a top priority, the Chinese economy has been intermediated by Hong Kong, and not Shanghai—a metropolis with twice the population and a much larger and centrally placed hinterland. Institutionally, Hong Kong was uniquely qualified to be China's middleman.

The Intermediated Equilibrium with Corruption

In analyzing the future of Hong Kong we are least impressed by some Western media perceptions that Hong Kong capitalist captains are threatened by Beijing ideologues. Even in China, political leaders are trying hard to convince the people that their rule is good for China as a state and for the population in bringing people greater economic benefits. Ideological purity is far from the top item in the current government's agenda. More likely, any threat to the system after the handover will come from Hong Kong rent-seekers perverting a status quo which has been crucial to the long-run benefit of the Chinese economy.

A foretaste of this occurred in 1994 when, two years after it opened its largest restaurant in the world in downtown Beijing, McDonald's was evicted from the site by the Beijing Municipal Government in order to make room for another project. Apparently McDonald's 20-year lease was no match for the behind-the-scenes influence of a consortium controlled by one of Hong Kong's richest men, property developer Li Ka-shing (Roberts, 1997). Whatever the merit of this particular case, Mr Li has apparently gained and Chinese credibility lost in Western eyes. *Ipso facto*, the vigor of Hong Kong capitalism can be easily lost by leaving matters to the most successful Hong Kong capitalists.

To begin with, judging from how much the People's Republic has tried to develop the Shenzhen Special Economic Zone in Hong Kong's image, it should be apparent that the Chinese leadership recognizes: (1) it is to the interest of the mainland for Hong Kong to survive and thrive, (2) Chinese economic institutions are not to be transplanted to Hong Kong, and (3) the administration and economic policy of Hong Kong can be best handled locally. However, we shall argue below that this recognition need not be sufficient at all to preserve the middleman role of Hong Kong.

Certainly, our analysis of these issues in this essay does not imply we are pessimistic about the future of the Hong Kong–China relationship. From an academic perspective these issues should be discussed and possible economic pitfalls addressed. Certainly, nothing is inevitable. Even if Hong Kong can no longer serve as middleman, for some time to come at least, Hong Kong businessmen can still contribute their current skill and information to Chinese development, and receive economic benefit in the bargain. It is a matter of Chinese prestige that Hong Kong should prosper. At the worst, Hong Kong can serve as a second Beidaihe—the Chinese answer to the Soviet government resort towns of Yalta and Sochi. Yet, in the large scheme of things, without Hong Kong as intermediary, the continued upgrading of Chinese manufacturing exports would prove difficult—to the detriment of Chinese development.

Rather than burdening our discussion with analytic formalism, we shall try to make our point with a few purely hypothetical scenarios below. The degrading of Hong Kong's ability as a middleman must take one of two forms: (1) an erosion of efficiency of intermediation, or (2) the development of distortions. It is neither hoped nor predicted that either of these will occur, yet each of these possibilities must be examined dispassionately. The point of departure is to see how the end of the colonial period may trigger such happenings.

Erosion of Efficiency

Hong Kong became effective thanks to the Darwinian process of market competition. First, however imperfect, judiciary independence, a rule of law and certain traditions against conflicts of interest as well as restrictive business practices came with the British system. Second, the top of the colonial administration had insufficient local contact to develop suffocating corruption. Certainly, it is not true that the playing field was ever really level or that British merchants never profited from their privileged positions. Far from it. But the point is that there was still breathing room left for emerging entrepreneurs (mostly, but not all, Chinese) to survive and thrive. From the ranks of the obscure, those both capable and lucky could still emerge (Chau, 1993). Finally, historically opportunities to succeed in Hong Kong were in enterprises related to foreign commerce.

After the return of sovereignty all these things are changed, and not clearly in ways favorable to the trade of middlemen. It is possible that now the cost of doing business may rise so much for intermediaries that Chinese exporters can no longer benefit from Hong Kong middlemen. In this event Hong Kong would be functionally no different from Shanghai—in the period before Chinese reforms.

Development of Distortions

Specific bias may arise to directly compromise the intermediation function. For example, suppose it is well understood by all that a would-be Hong Kong investor in China is personally very close to a high official in Hong Kong. Seeking advantage for her own investment interest, this would-be investor recommends to a Hong Kong middleman a very well-connected (but quite inexperienced) Chinese supplier who "just might prove to be useful" for some ongoing deal. Although it is not the usual practice to select an inexperienced supplier, this middleman has a critical petition (say, the confirmation of the temporary operation license) coming soon under a discretionary government review. A quick cost–benefit calculation causes this Hong Kong-based middleman to feel obliged to select the recommended Chinese supplier for the foreign client.

Now, the intermediated deal eventually goes wrong. Under normal circumstances any deal has some possibility of failing, but given the conditions described here, more deals will go wrong than previously expected. Sooner or later foreign firms would begin to feel less confident about Hong Kong middlemen as well as the Chinese suppliers of goods. This change in attitudes towards the region may result in foreign firms shifting their choice of suppliers from China toward competitors from other countries, to Southeast Asia or elsewhere. By that time the damage would be already done to Chinese national interest. The ultimate effect of this process would be to shift the equilibrium quality in Figure 2 back toward q^0.

Such a development may have happened even if Hong Kong had remained under the Union Jack. Yet, no matter whether the British are or are not more corrupt than the Chinese, for reasons of "cultural distance" the transaction costs of lobbying are certainly much lower now than before. When nonprofessional considerations enter into professional decisions, unjustified risks will be taken more often, and things begin to go sour. In the political economy literature this is the well-known principle of "logrolling" among lobbying parliamentarians. Such practice is present in London and New Delhi, and it is not realistic for anyone to seriously guarantee its absence in Hanoi or Beijing.

Worthwhile to notice is that the change (for the worse) in our hypothetical scenario happens without a single move (good or bad) made by any Mainland Chinese. And yet the perception about the Chinese system as compared with the departed British system has played a role somewhere. Chinese "connections" are believed to be more essential. It does not really matter what is the truth and what is the perception, or where indeed may be some "source most foul" promoting such perception. The critical question is how to head off this type of mischievous development in advance. As has been shown here, it is in the economical interest of both the Chinese mainland and Hong Kong to take preventive countermeasures, soon.

5. Conclusion

It is clear, especially now that Hong Kong is formally a part of the People's Republic of China, that the destinies of these two regions are fundamentally linked. Although Hong Kong has been designated as a Special Administrative Region with a "large degree of autonomy," still the Basic Law of Hong Kong is subordinate to the Constitution of China. Without a doubt the economic future of Hong Kong hinges on the success of Chinese development and the benevolence of the mainland leaders. So, today and in the future what is good for the Chinese mainland will also prove to be good for Hong Kong.

Part of the measures necessary to avoid decay of this mutually beneficial middleman system may rest on what may be called "openness." During the British period, the press was fully free and economic scandals involving Colonial officials presumably could be laid bare by the press. Parliamentary questions could also be raised in London if there were serious economic scandals. Although local residents of Hong Kong never had any formal means to vote out any particular Royal Governor (let alone to affect how Royal Governors were appointed), at least the perception was that officials under suspicion would be readily investigated and probably removed. It is presumably achievable for Beijing to demonstrate the presence of some similar mechanism with respect to Hong Kong corruption now that the territory is under the sovereignty of China.

Part of such measures concern how to deal with potential conflicts of interest between local businesses and the local administration. Again, this presumably can have no ramifications one way or another on the internal security or stability of China. Yet, it should be understood in Beijing that in economically thriving Western societies monopolies and cartels are treated as public enemies. Restrictive business practices are and have been guarded against in Britain under both Labor and the Tories. The anti-trust provisions in America are not just propaganda nor a means to bamboozle the proletariat. These policies serve to preserve free entry against currently entrenched firms, so that the economy can have sustained vitality. Just a few years back Intel and Microsoft were fledgling firms challenging the incumbents.

Capitalism withers if capitalists are not under leash. If Hong Kong is to enjoy fifty years of thriving economic conditions, the current capitalists must be under proper legal constraint, as is standard under capitalism anywhere else. With capitalism everywhere else surviving as before, a prematurely withered capitalist Hong Kong will be to neither the credit nor the interest of Chinese socialism.

References

Akerlof, George A., "The Market for 'Lemons': Quality Uncertainty and the Market Mechanism," *Quarterly Journal of Economics* 84 (1970):488–500.

Asian Development Bank, *Emerging Asia, Changes and Challenges*, Manila: Asian Development Bank (1997).

Biglaiser, Gary, "Middlemen as Experts," *RAND Journal of Economics* 24 (1993):212–23.

Biglaiser, Gary and James W. Friedman, "Middlemen as Guarantors of Quality," *Journal of Industrial Organization* 12 (1994):509–31.

Chau, Leung Chuen, *Hong Kong: A Unique Case of Development*, Washington, DC: World Bank (1993).

Chiang, Shih-Chen and Robert T. Masson, "Domestic Industrial Structure and Export Quality," *International Economic Review* 29 (1988):261–70.

Coe, David T., Elhanan Helpman, and Alexander W. Hoffmaister, "North–South R&D spillovers," *Economic Journal* 107 (1997):134–49.

Collins, Susan M., "Technical Progress in a Three-Country Ricardian Model with a Continuum of Goods," *Journal of International Economics* 19 (1985):171–9.

Dornbusch, Rudiger, Stanley Fischer, and Paul A. Samuelson, "Comparative Advantage, Trade and Payments in a Ricardian Model with a Continuum of Goods," *American Economic Review* 67 (1977):823–39.

Gargan, Edward A., "China Already Entrenched as a Hong Kong Capitalist," *New York Times*, 5 December, 1996.

Grossman, Gene M. and Elhanan Helpman, "Quality Ladders in the Theory of Growth," *Review of Economic Studies* 58 (1991):43–61.

Hong, Yongmiao, Man-Lui Lau, and Henry Y. Wan, Jr, "A Non-parametric, Panel Study of Convergence, and the Trade-Development Nexus," unpublished manuscript, Cornell University, 1998.

Kim, Kihwan and Danny M. Leipziger, *Korea: A Case of Government-Led Development*, Washington, DC: World Bank (1993).

Lau, Man-Lui and Henry Y. Wan, Jr, "The Hong Kong–Guangdong Nexus," in *Proceedings of the International Conference, Financing Development in Guangdong*, Hong Kong: City Polytechnic University of Hong Kong (1994).

Lucas, Robert E., Jr, "On the Mechanics of Economic Development," *Journal of Monetary Economics* 22 (1988):3–42.

———, "Making a Miracle," *Econometrica* 61 (1993):251–72.

Nathan, Andrew J. and Robert S. Ross, *Great Wall and Empty Fortress: China's Search for Security*, New York: Norton (1997).

Pomery, John, "Uncertainty in Trade Models," in Ronald W. Jones and Peter B. Kenen (eds.), *Handbook of International Economics*, Vol. I, New York: North-Holland (1984):419–65.

Roberts, Dexter, "Maybe Guanxi Isn't Everything After All," *Business Week* (International Edition), 24 February, 1997.

Rubinstein, Ariel and Asher Wolinsky, "Middlemen," *Quarterly Journal of Economics* 102 (1987):581–93.

Sung, Yun Wing, *The China–Hong Kong Connection: The Key to China's Open–Door Policy*, Hong Kong: Cambridge University Press (1991).

Van, Pham H. and Henry Y. Wan, Jr, "Emulative Development Through Trade Expansions: East Asian Evidence," in John Pigott and Alan D. Woodland (eds.), *International Trade and the Pacific Rim*, London: Macmillan (1998).

Wan, Henry Y., Jr., "Trade, development and inventions," in Horst Herberg and Ngo Van Long (eds.), *Trade, Welfare and Economic Policies: Essays in Honor of Murray C. Kemp*, Ann Arbor: University of Michigan Press (1993).

Yavas, Abdullah, "Middlemen in Bilateral Search Markets," *Journal of Labor Economics* 12 (1994):406–29.

———, "Search and trading in intermediated markets," *Journal of Economics and Management Strategy* 5 (1996):195–216.

Young, Alwyn, "Learning by Doing and the Dynamic Effects of International Trade," *Quarterly Journal of Economics* 106 (1991):369–405.

———, "Invention and Bounded Learning-by-Doing," *Journal of Political Economy* 101 (1993):443–72.

———, "Lessons from the East Asian NICs: A Contrarian View," *European Economic Review* 38 (1994):964–73.

Notes

1. In Lau and Wan (1994), the emphasis was placed on information. What will be argued here is that the best means of acquiring information is through intermediated export trade. The two views are thus intertwined.

2. The special cases cited by Van and Wan (1998) suggest that only by satisfying the quality requirement for developed countries can producers in developing countries learn to improve their technology.

3. For a collection of case histories, see Van and Wan (1998).

4. Kim and Leipziger (1993) documented this type of transformation of the Handok Company over the fifteen years between 1971 and 1985.

5. Stylized Fact 3 may take more doing since it is complicated by heterogeneous preferences.

6. See Young (1993) for an example of a model in which production of challenging goods provides a means of learning-by-doing and brings about the possibility of escape from technical stagnation. In contrast to Coe et al. (1997) which focuses on trade in general, this specification emphasizes export as the trigger for learning.

7. Young (1991) shows theoretically that autarky promotes growth for less-developed regions, while Young (1994) gives empirical evidence that trade is irrelevant for dynamic gain.

8. The insider-trading tribunal fined the businessman one-third the maximum allowable penalty, and banned him from his company for one year, deferring the ban for 12 months.

9. Alternatively, A may be the "rest of the world" relative to B and C, which includes some advanced economies.

10. Quality is an ordinal variable, so any monotonic transformation can be adopted.

11. That is why, should the market care only about the average quality, purchasing a good under information imperfection is equivalent to a quality lottery.

12. This implies that for a given cost of production the producer has achieved the maximum value of output.

13. This means equilibrium profit must be zero under constant returns and free entry; wage is equal to the average product of labor when labor is the only input of production.

14. It is possible to use weaker assumptions to derive the results below. For simplicity and to avoid distracting the reader from the main focus here, these more straightforward and intuitive conditions are utilized.

15. If ε is increasing but not strictly increasing, then there may be alternative equilibrium product mixes of output, some of which imply stagnation and others allow for continued progress. We appreciate the comments of an anonymous referee which alerted us to this possibility.

16. This is because including a multiplicative constant (independent of quality level) in the firm revenue relation will still result in the same quality choice; i.e., $q_i^* = \arg \max[p(q_i)/a(q_i)]$.

17. Lucas (1993) acknowledged the success of the Asian NIEs while expressing his pessimism about the situation after the handover by noting, "never before have the lives of so many people undergone so rapid an improvement over so long a period, nor (with the exception of Hong Kong) is there any sign that this progress is near its end."

© Blackwell Publishers Ltd 1999

Challenges for a Billion-People Economy:
A Prognosis for the Development of the PRC

Review of "How Size Matters to Future Chinese Growth: Some Trade Theoretic Considerations"[*]

Implications of Size Size and the Chinese economy seems to be inseparable concepts in the discussions of trade issues today. To clarify matters, this Article takes an abstract approach, without delving into any historical institutional factors which shaped the Chinese development.

All in all, there are three aspects to consider: (a) the static issue of providing jobs; (b) the dynamic issue of achieving development; and (c) the ultimate issue of stabilizing the world economy. This Article focuses on the first.

On jobs For a billion-resident economy, the employment problem can be fully solved only through domestic demand. The Chinese population is large both in the absolute sense, but also relative to its resource base — with 21% of the world's population, living on 10% of the tillable earth, and its per capita available water only a quarter of the world average. Trading seems the natural solution. A comparison with India in the last paragraph shows how at the present, China has benefited from trade. But excessive trade expansion may cause trade friction because of the exports sold, the strategic imports demanded (oil, iron ore, etc.) and the pressure generated on environment, etc. To serve as the world's largest shipbuilder may be a feasible way to help Korea solve its employment problem. But with a population 27 times the Korean size, China can never satisfy its need to create jobs in the same manner. These are issues relevant to China for sure, but also soon to India, and Russia, Brazil and Indonesia in due course. China may be important, but what can be learned is also relevant under broader contexts.

On global impact The shortest path to catching-up lies in trade, spearheaded by the export of labor intensive products, if the record of the last 60 years carries any weight. It has been so for Japan then, for the four NIEs, and now for China. Through trade, there comes technology, and hence the opportunity for investment

---

[*]The article first appeared in *Critical Issues in China's Growth and Development*, Yun K. Kwan and Eden S. Yu (eds.), pp. 41–65, 2004, published by Ashgate. The author is grateful to Prof Kwan and Prof Yu who own the rights to the article for granting the permit to reprint in this volume.

and the scope for growth. The road for development opened for the NIEs when the Japanese wage rose; the chance for export brightens for China when labor shortage pervades throughout the NIEs. With the size of the Chinese labor supply, rising Chinese wage is not to be expected any time soon. For China, foreign investment brings capital, technology, and hence gain in productivity. Due to the tardy wage advance, this means gain in profit, and still more foreign investment and more growth, though it also means more income inequality. But for the rest of the developing economies, what hope can they entertain? This sensitive issue must be solved with mutual understanding and goodwill.

On growth There may exist subtle effects on the world economy with the successful, rapid growth of large, developing economies. As it stands, the world's terms of trade are decided mainly by the developed economies because of their domination in total income. That obviously may change with the rapid growth of economies with more than a billion residents. But the implication goes much beyond that. The household budgets of most individuals in every society are mostly spent on non-traded goods. Unlike houses, many of these may be tradable but the prices are not right to export, given the transportation cost. This is precisely "the Keynes case" in the classical transfer problem of trade theory. The mechanism goes as follows. If the whisky-producing British and the beer-producing Germans consume both types of drinks, each buying proportionally more of what each produces, then a rising of the whisky price relative to the beer price would enrich the whisky producer at the expense of the beer producer, and their respective tastes will drive the price ratio further, favoring whisky. What is involved is that at the equilibrium in question, the income effect dominates the substitution effect, so that any price shift away from that equilibrium would lead to larger price deviation. So there must be more than one other equilibrium terms of trade bracketing this particular price pattern. There is no reason why one equilibrium price pattern will appear rather than the others, when external shocks arrive. Hence this can cause instability.

A comparison with India for context In Sachs and Warner (1995), a rich natural resource endowment is a curse. The theoretical reason is not always convincing. In most recent WTO figures, with populations of 1.08 and 1.30 billions, both India and China are the most populous countries with little natural resources: manufacture accounts for 74.5% and 91.4% in commodity exports.

However, India is "less open" than China to the world market. The trade to GDP ratios differ considerably: 28.7% for India to 58.9% for China. In the world's exports, shares of India are 0.83% in goods and 1.86% in services, while shares of China are 6.48% in goods and 2.92% in services. In the entire world's exports, goods to services stand at a 4 to 1 in ratio.

In goods, India ranks as the 30th and 23rd largest among exporters and importers respectively; China ranks as the 3rd largest in both. In services, India ranks as 16th and 15th, to the Chinese's 9th and 8th.

The per capita incomes in nominal and PPP terms are respectively $641 and $3,114 for India, to 1,271 and $5,493 for China.

The destinations for export also differ. For India, EU outranks US and Japan; for China, US outranks EU and Japan.

Although in software, an item with high value-added and produced by skilled labor, India exports more than China. In total trading gain, undoubtedly China has earned much more than India. China serves as the workshop of the world, even though this is with paper-thin value added. Much of this development is due to the migration of textile and information technology industries from other East Asian economies to Mainland China. The large inflow of foreign investment into China is the other side of the coin of such industry migration.

It may well be that the bureaucratic paractice of Indian commodity trade has both its impact on the relatively modest Indian export of goods relative to China, also the steering of Indian high skilled labor toward software development. At the same time, the rapid accumulation of the foreign exhange reserves in China may suggest that the RMB is still under-valued.

A Note on Chinese Industrial Policy In recent decades, the Chinese industrial policy can be described as Comparative-Advantage Following (CAF) strategy advocated by Lin (2005), moderated by the needs of job creation, including infrastructure projects in rural sectors. It is decidedly different from what Japan and Korea focus on — a surfeit of heavy industry, but little foreign investment.

How Size Matters to Future Chinese Growth: Some Trade–Theoretic Considerations

Henry Wan Jr.[1]

Introduction

It is both a distinction and a challenge to contribute a chapter honoring Professor Gregory Chow, especially in this conference devoted to the Mainland Chinese economy. As a leading econometrician and a researcher with deep insight, Professor Chow himself has contributed greatly to this subject. In addition, there already exists a voluminous literature on the institutions and economic performance of China. As a novice to this area, I shall focus on some aspects that are closely related to my background and less studied by others.

Since the 1978 reform, the Chinese development has depended heavily on its 'openness' to the external markets. Such interactions with the trading world follow certain regularities. These are evident from the development experience of other economies which are in some fashion, similar to China. It is useful to question whether and how does China's size influence the interactions between China and the rest of the world.

Whenever the Chinese economy is being discussed, what first comes to one's mind is often its 'size' in area, population, or total output value. In research, we have to decide *what* exactly 'size' means, *how* that matters in analytic terms, and *whether* size poses special opportunities or challenges to China. These issues are important to policy making, like a navigation chart is to a pilot. Most such issues concern the relative strength of a country in international transactions. They may thus be studied from the trade–theoretic angle. A systematic survey of all these aspects should be useful for policy analysis.

We approach the matter from a variety of viewpoints: (a) the population size, and related to it, the aspect of factor proportions; (b) the issue of reciprocal demand, between a country and the rest of the world, and hence the terms of trade; (c) the economies of scale; (d) the strategic trade aspect, namely market power; and finally, (e) the co–ordination aspect, when in real life, decentralized decisions are made in 'incomplete markets'. We relate such discussions to the performance of the Chinese economy in its recent past as well as the economic prospects for its future.

Size and factor proportions

Today, China is the most highly populated nation. Its population of 1.24 billion in 1998 is almost five times as numerous as the American population of 275 million. Located largely in the temperate zone, these two countries are broadly comparable in territorial size. Yet within its territory, China is often less well endowed than America in its total amount of many kinds of natural resources. The following comparison in Table 3.1 is far from exhaustive. It serves only for illustration.

Comparison may also be made in terms of the endowments in standing timber, fresh water, iron ore, etc. Not only in per capita endowment of natural resources, but also in both physical and human capital, however measured, China is much less well endowed per capita than America today. In the history of trade theory, what qualifies as America's abundant factor of production has become the subject of the Leontief Paradox. However, in its trade with America, or most of the other countries, Chinese export is definitely labor intensive.

In principle, large economies need to trade less than small economies. Their endowments tend to be more balanced. Different regions may complement each other. But compared to other East Asian economies like Japan and Korea, the Mainland Chinese economy is no more self–sufficient in natural resources, in spite of its size in area. In many ways, the supposedly large size of China actually means abundant labor, coupled with the relative scarcity in various other resources, skilled manpower included.

For such a crowded country, the slowing down of its population growth rate is a desirable achievement. Soon, China would not be the most populous country. But it benefits the world as a whole more on environmental grounds, than it benefits China in terms of trade. Facing the same trading world, the terms of trade of every labor–abundant country must deteriorate in response to the unchecked population growth, whether in China or anywhere else. In trade theory, this is the lesson of the 'integrated equilibrium' for the trading world. In other labor–abundant countries, population growth has remained unchecked. Thus, fierce Chinese population control may delay global warming for the world, but will not save China from the worsening terms of trade against labor intensive products.

Soon the aging Chinese population, with its rising dependency ratio, will be at a competitive disadvantage relative to a labor–abundant country whose birth rate starts to drop later: its share of working age in the population will be larger than the Chinese. This will be even more true, if the child labor laws remain unenforced. As a remedy, China has to accumulate physical and human capital to change its comparative advantage, in a timely fashion, like Japan had been successfully doing.

Even in physical capital formation, one needs some perspective. For example, beyond some point, Chinese infrastructure construction must take account of some global limit for growth. A thought experiment should bring us some realism. Today, many industries have easily migrated across the Taiwan Strait. Any difference in production technology among the Chinese on both shores is marginal and temporary. Thus in the foreseeable future, the per capital output value in

Table 3.1   Comparative endowments: China and USA

	China	USA
Crude petroleum (million bbls.)	24,000	22,317
Coal reserve (million tons)	114,500	240,518
Farm land (thousand hectares)	166,902	393,471

Mainland China should reach Taiwan's level today and the consumption patterns may converge in short course. Today's person–to–motor vehicle ratio stands at 4.3 in Taiwan to 128 in the rest of China. By then, the expected motor vehicle ownership in China could be 288 million, which is more than 80% of the total American automobile ownership today (the vehicle/person ratio for the 275 million Americans being 1.3). Given the highly inelastic world supply and demand of petroleum,[2] such a prospect should be approached with some forethought.

Vehicles do not travel in a vacuum. Tomorrow's transportation is likely to be carried on roads built today. Americans presently travel on the highway system laid down in the Eisenhower years. Thus, when infrastructure is constructed in China nowadays, it is time to give thoughts to how the economy might look in 50 years. Hopefully such a vision is not based upon the hypothesis that a growing Chinese economy has no appreciable effect on Chinese import prices. (That is, the *small* country assumption in the trade theory literature). It is the unthinking urban sprawl that makes the energy demand difficult to control for the richer societies today.

It is worthwhile to note that the average income is much higher in Hong Kong than in Taiwan, but the person/vehicle ratio is only 13.1. This comparison shows that the energy demand of high income societies is far from inflexible. Thoughtful urban design today can make a great deal of difference tomorrow.

The question of reciprocal demand

What we have just discussed concerns factor proportions, on the supply side. Now we turn to the demand side. From the viewpoint of resources per capita, China today may not be that different from South Korea, in the early 1960s. Being populous is a relevant fact to China. Size is clearly a constraint here, not a strength. Now in the N–goods general equilibrium setting, modeling the demand of the (heterogeneous) 'rest of the world' analytically is not a simple task.[2] But even a less formal approach can be quite convincing.

Let us say, at time t, Korea has exported M units of some particular output. This means with a population of 46 million in 1998, on a per capita basis, Koreans have exported M/46,000,000 units of that good in question, and gained certain benefit from that transaction. This product may be textile, steel, automobile,

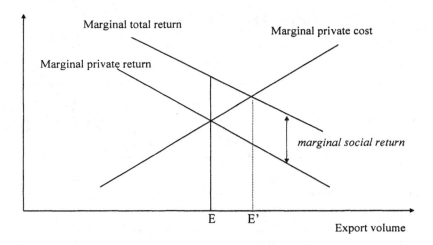

Figure 3.1   Export externalities

dynamic random memory chips (DRAMs), whatever. Now if China is to achieve the same effect by exporting M/46,000,000 units per person, the world market must absorb nearly 30M units, since the Chinese population is almost 27 times that of the Korean. Common sense predicts that this export goal is hard to meet, even if China can produce goods of the same quality but charges a much lower unit price. For example, if Korea has exported microwave ovens, but where can China get 27 times more new foreign customers? In the trade literature, this mental experiment may appear unfamiliar. But logically, this is just an extension of the theory of *immiserized growth*.

But the implication does not stop here. Exporting brings many benefits besides the static gains from trade, conventionally measured. It offers the opportunity for a developing economy to acquire technology (through customers' feedbacks) and experience unavailable at home.[4] It brings forth contact and reputation. It imposes discipline on inefficient domestic enterprises, demanding labor unions and sometimes corrupt government administrators, once it is recognized by the general public that export performance is in the national interest, not to be jeopardized for private gain. It motivates the society to accumulate the specific human capital for foreign trade. All these benefit the economy as a whole, rather than any particular trader or producer in the export business. For convenience, they shall be called collectively, 'trade externalities'. These are public goods with a non–rival nature, relevant to a country with any size. For example, labor mobility across firms facilitates the diffusion of best practices inside national borders. In conventional welfare analysis, the situation is shown in Figure 3.1. Thus, there is a cause for any State devoted to economic development to promote export activities, moving the equilibrium in Figure 3.1 from E to E'.

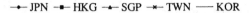

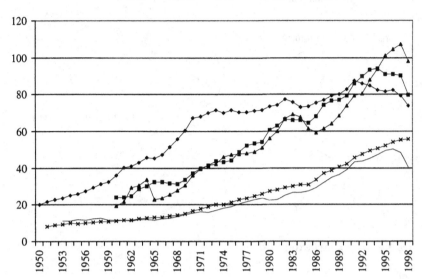

Figure 3.2   The East Asians catching up with the US

It is reasonable to believe that such external benefits from trade are particularly important for developing economies where current practices need improvement. This is also empirically verifiable. In the second half of the century, cross–Pacific trade blossomed between Japan and the four Newly Industrialized Economies (Korea, Taiwan, Hong Kong and Singapore) on one side and America on the other. There is no intrinsic reason that the static trading gain would benefit America less than America's trade partners. In contrast, the less developed East Asia has much more to gain from trade externalities than the developed America. Thus, the testable implication of trade externalities is that with expanded trade, East Asia would begin to catch up with America in this last half century, narrowing the differences in per capita real GDP.

We use data from the Penn World Table version 6.0 to plot the results in Figure 3.2, where each series of the Asian per capita real GDP is shown as a percent of the US data. The hypothesis of trade externality is not falsified by evidence.

One may question whether trade expansion is the key cause for catching up. We gain more insight from Figure 3.3, in which the series for Argentina is added. Clearly, Argentina was ahead of all the East Asia Five in the early 1950s but eventually fell behind all these five.

In fact, Argentina is not all that atypical among the developing economies. The real question is whether and by how much the catching up performance can be attributed to the openness of an economy. For verification, we use the series of the

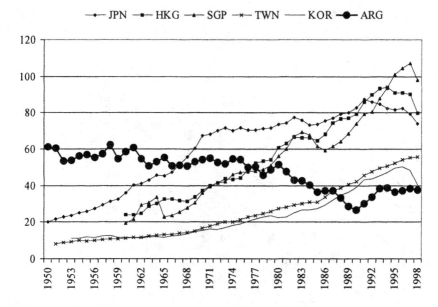

Figure 3.3   **Argentina falls behind**

'openness index' = (Export + Import)/GDP, available from the Penn World Table 6.0. The 'openness' for these six economies is depicted in Figure 3.4 for the years 1956, 1966, 1976, 1986 and 1996. Thus the hypothesis that openness facilitates catching up cannot be rejected. Argentina is the least open among the six, for all the five selected years, with the possible exception of 1996, where the Japanese economy is slightly less open. But by then Japan is an advanced industrialized economy, openness does not provide the trade externalities urgently in need.

From the viewpoint of the Mainland Chinese economy, what Figure 3.1 and Figures 3.2–3.4 convey is that openness benefits the catching up process. Since on the per capita basis, the conventional gains from export—a private returns—are likely to be small for China relative to say, Korea, it appears that the Chinese State should make effort to magnify the effect of the private returns for acquiring external benefits. This seems to be a *prima facie* call for export promotion.

On the other hand, our previous analysis of reciprocal demand indicates that the size factor works against the degree of Chinese openness. On a per capita basis, one cannot hope for Chinese exports to match what the other East Asian economies achieved earlier, unit for unit. Even though a straightforward approach to trade promotion cannot work very well, the State should amplify the private returns from trade for the sake of trade externalities.

Can such a policy work? History suggests yes, and Japan is a clear example. Facing severe dollar shortages in the 1950s, the entire Japanese society identified export as a top priority, under the slogan, 'export or starve'. Since then, to

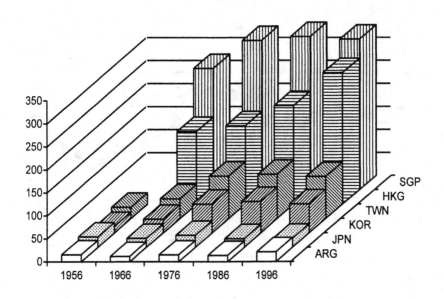

Figure 3.4   Openness index

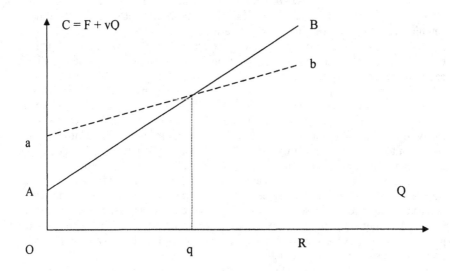

Figure 3.5   Economy of scale

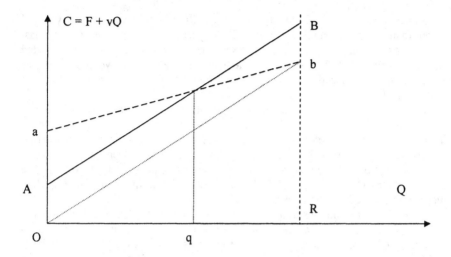

Figure 3.6   Sunk cost does not matter to the entrenched firm

ameliorate international trade friction, Japan has repeatedly accepted 'voluntary export restrictions'. Therefore, Japan has benefited from 'trade externalities' even though in terms of the openness index, Japan is far less open than Korea and Taiwan.

The point of avoiding trade friction is also relevant to China. Already China's Asian neighbors, Singapore included, are concerned that Chinese trade expansion would displace Southeast Asia economies in the export market and as a destination of direct foreign investment.[5] When necessary, the pursuit of both export promotion and voluntary export restraint by Japan seems to form a viable precedence.

Western historians often puzzle over the fact that just before Prince Henry of Portugal promoted the national capacity for navigation, in the hope of profiting from the China trade, Ming China had stopped the Chinese naval excursions into the South Seas. The above discussion should go far to solve that 'mystery'. For the Chinese, the asymmetry in size between China and its trading partners had diluted the static trading gain, and hence government interest.

Of course, by hindsight, the development of ocean shipping has contributed to the subsequent rise of the West, and trade externalities were overlooked by China in the Ming dynasty.

The supply side once more—increasing returns

Leaving population size aside, we now consider 'size' in total gross national product (GDP). In terms of purchasing power parity, China ranks second in the world, between America and Japan. In nominal GDP, the Chinese economy is still larger than every developing country (having surpassed Brazil during the last decade), and is only smaller than America, Japan, Germany, France, the United Kingdom and Italy.[6] The sizeable difference between these two measures has grown in the last decade, and is relatively unusual in the world. This is to be addressed later.

We are now considering the issue of absolute size in productive operations rather than the size relative to other countries. Since industrialization is such an important aspect in development, and industrial production often exhibits internal or external scale economies, 'big push' has been a favorite concept in the literature of growth and development. Can China get much advantage from this angle? The answer seems to be yes, in principle, but not necessarily all that much. A simplified diagram in Figure 3.5 illustrates the point.

Figure 3.5 is the simplest model where up to some level, R, the total production cost of a certain product can be divided into two components: one proportional to the units produced, the other a constant. Two types of technology are depicted: the solid line is less costly up to the break even point q; the dotted line represents an alternative process that is more efficient above the critical point q.

Now for a country engaging in trade, what matters most is maximizing the per capita value–added, whatever the product mix. There are four reasons why the presence of economies of scale does not imply that country size confers national economic advantage. First of all, an economy can produce high–value niche products, with a worldwide demand below the point q in Figure 3.5. The advantage of mass production associated with the cost curve ab is simply out of place. Second, even small economies can enjoy major world market shares of goods they export. For example, Singapore can satisfy a significant portion of the world demand for computer hard drives. Large country size is not needed. Third, the efficiency of increasing returns may benefit all consumers of such a product with no special advantage for the country producing it.[7]

Finally, Figure 3.6 illustrates an example where the market demand is at a particular volume R, with the price equal to the average cost of the entrant firm (with a higher fixed cost but a lower variable cost), as well as the variable cost of the entrenched firm.

$$[v + F/R]_{entrant} = p = [v]_{entrenched}$$

Under the reasonable assumption that all fixed cost is sunk cost, the entrenched firm has nothing more to lose at this equilibrium, and the entrant firm can never make any positive profit. This seems to describe well the situation facing such industries like shipbuilding, automobile, and steel making, etc. In the world market, all these industries have developed excess capacities. Those producers with large market share may reap zero or negative economic benefit: the non–positive profit margin is precisely what serves as the barrier to entry.

Such a scenario prevails in a world experiencing rapid technological change. Economic obsolescence is a constant threat to industries with large fixed equipment, that is, the industries with significant internal increasing returns. Of

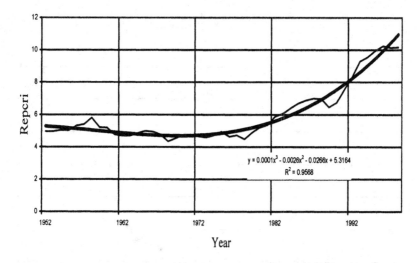

Figure 3.7   The relative per capita real income (REPCRI) of China

course, external increasing returns to scale are also very important. But, with the rise of global supply chains, such externalities become cross–national in nature. Thus, country size loses much of its importance. In fact, Ernst (2001) questions the South Korean strategy to specialize in DRAMs with massive capital spending, without mastering first the high–end technology.

The perspective of 'strategic trade theory'

In trade negotiations more than in other aspects, size may provide China the clear advantage of wielding significant bargaining power,[8] because of what the Chinese market already is, also because of what it can easily become. The critical questions are what is the nature of such power, and how should it be deployed.

Market power comes from what a country can promise to buy, or offer to sell. What China exports today is based upon a large pool of hardy, intelligent labor, ready and eager to learn. In comparison with what is available in Korea and Japan, their formal training and industrial skill can improve, and also need improvement. Unlike Mideast oil producers, China has nothing irreplaceable to withhold from the world market. In the final analysis, it is the size of China's domestic market that is particularly appealing. To any trade partners of modest size, to capture a sizeable share of this large potential market is advantageous. This is because there are economies of scale in marketing just as in production. The crucial question for China is what to bargain for from these relatively smaller partners? More succinctly, where does China's long term national economic interest lie? Knowing

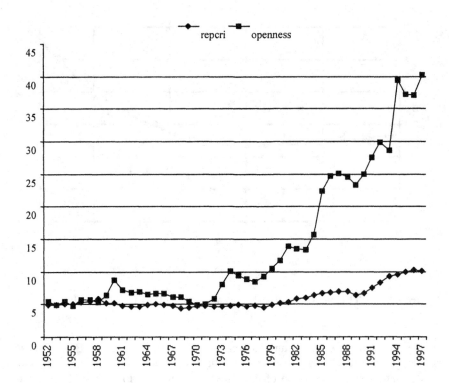

Figure 3.8   The relative per capita real income (REPCRI) and openness index of China

well which way the economy can grow is the prerequisite of getting there. Our previous analysis suggests that China should not bargain with these small trading partners for market access, just to acquire static trading gain. On per capita basis, the benefit cannot be very significant, in any case. It is far more important to bargain for market openings which facilitate skill accumulation. That will allow Chinese to receive more reward for what they already produce, from the world market. More will be said on this important but complex topic.

Size, marketization and future growth

The economy of China forms a class by itself. Prior to 1978, it was a command economy with relatively sluggish growth, leaving intact the income gap between itself and the advanced economies. Among all Communist economies, China is one of the first to embark on market reform. Decentralization improved the system performance. Its cautious opening to the world market has introduced more advanced technology from abroad. This has allowed productivity to rise with only

Table 3.2   Catching–up Regression, China, 1952–98

Dependent variable: Growth rate of REPCRI

	Coefficient	t–value	
Intercept	0.106	1.86	–
REPCRI	–0.027	–1.90	–
Openness	0.005	2.33	–
Adj. R Square	–	–	0.093
Observations	–	–	46

Note: REPCRI = relative per capita real income

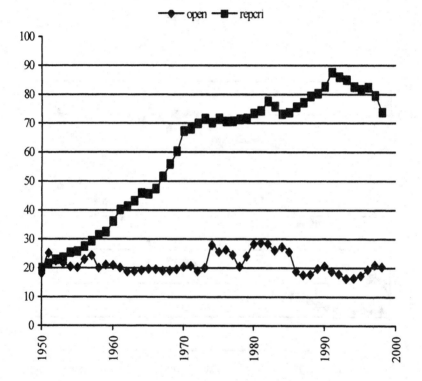

Figure 3.9   The relative per capita real income (REPCRI) and openness index of Japan

modest indigenous R & D Under the reformed system, the process of catching up resembles the workings of a private ownership economies. Emulation is a contact game. Contact depends upon trade and foreign investment. The catching up process slows down as the remaining technology gap begins to close.

As a transition economy, this gradualist approach has allowed China to score considerable growth but avoid gross instability, with its political system preserved

Table 3.3   Catching–up regression, Japan, 1950–98

Dependent variable: Growth rate of REPCRI

	Coefficient	t–value	
Intercept	0.155	4.004	–
REPCRI	−0.002	−4.663	–
Openness	−0.001	−0.513	–
Adj. R Square	–	–	0.358
Observations	–	–	38

Note: REPCRI = relative per capita real income

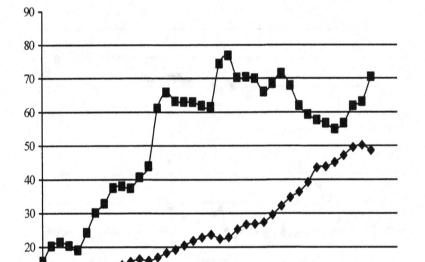

Figure 3.10   The relative per capita real income (REPCRI) and openness index of Korea

up to this day. The institutional transformation entails a sequence of devolution of decision power. When each round of deregulation begins, local decision makers in government units and the state owned enterprises seize newly gained power for rapid expansion. In a world of incomplete markets, such exuberance intensifies coordination failure, and causes the economy to overheat.   The inexperienced decision makers and inadequate laws and regulations soon open the doors to additional inefficiency, corruption and instability. With rising prices and material shortage threatening social stability, the central authority then tightens the rein, through credit squeeze or administrative measures. Stabilization then ushers in slower growth, until the government has regained the confidence to decentralize the system further.   Such recurrent boom–bust cycles of reform often mask the process of the catching up process.

In this process of reform, the size of the country complicates the oversight task of the government.

In a nutshell, so far, the interplay of four elements has shaped Chinese growth:

(1) As a developing economy—provided certain conditions are met—the catching up process operates under appropriate conditions to narrow down the income gap from the advanced economies.

(2) Some levels of trade and foreign investment are essential to help technology acquisition from abroad and allow the catching up process to function.

(3) Because China was once a centrally planned economy, the Chinese reform has taken the form of a sequence of structural transformations through deregulation, and repeated boom–bust cycles.

(4) The size of the country makes it especially challenging to ameliorate those boom–bust cycles.

The performance of the economy in the recent past

Using the Penn World Table version 6.0, we plot the relative per capita real income (REPCRI) series for China over the period 1952–1998 in Figure 3.7. As we recall, this series is the ratio of per capita real GDP (measured on the basis of purchasing power parity by the Heston–Summers method) between a particular country and the USA. The convex parabolic trend might appear to fit the data well. But for reasons explained in the last section, such temporal interpolation is misleading, since it does not reflect the working of the four factors (1)–(4) discussed above.

Next, we plot REPCRI and the openness index of China against time, in Figure 3.8. Note that the openness index exceeded 10% only once in the 27 years before 1978, but in every one of those 19 years after 1979. It has reached 40% in 1997. Likewise, the relative per capita real income of the China has hovered around 5% of the American level, showing no trend in the first period, but risen more or less steadily to 10% by 1997. This reduces the income gap from America.

We run a regression of the catching up rate (the growth rate of REPCRI) against both the level of REPCRI and the openness index. The result is shown in Table 3.2.   The rate of catching up depends positively upon the openness index (significant at the 2.5% level) and negatively upon the level of relative per capita real income.

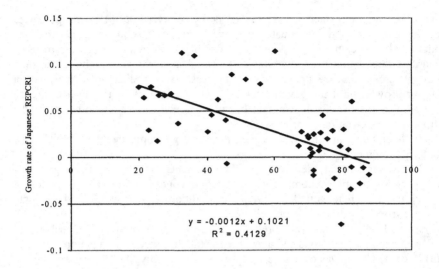

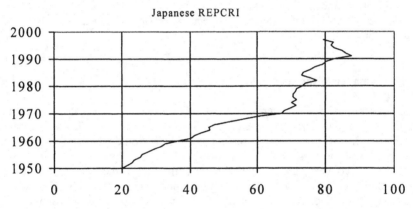

Figure 3.11   The Japanese economy settles at a 'limit gap'

For comparison, we plot the corresponding Japanese and Korean data in Figure 3.9 and Figure 3.10. Tables 3.3 and 3.4 display the regression results for those two countries.

Within these samples of observations, the openness index changes little for Japan throughout the entire period and fluctuates at a rather high level for Korea over much of the latter part of the observed period.   Understandably, it is insignificant in explaining the Japanese catching up process and of marginal significance (at about 10%) for the Korean catching up.

The Japanese regression is highly significant both for the positive intercept and the negative REPCRI coefficient. For the Korean regression, the negative REPCRI

Table 3.4   Catching–up regression, Korea, 1960–98

Dependent variable: Growth rate of REPCRI

	Coefficient	t–value	
Intercept	0.027	1.048	–
REPCRI	−0.002	−2.046	–
Openness	0.001	1.707	–
Adj. R Square	–	–	0.064
Observations	–	–	38

Note: REPCRI = relative per capita real income

Table 3.5   Catching–up regression, China, 1979–88

Dependent variable: Growth rate of REPCRI

	Coefficient	t–value	
Intercept	0.277	2.999	–
REPCRI	−0.040	−2.700	–
Adj. R Square	–	–	0.411
Observations	–	–	10

Note: REPCRI = relative per capita real income

coefficient is significant at the 5% level. All these confirm the Gerschenkron hypothesis that the gap between the North and the South represents a technology backlog for the less developed country to emulate.   The rate of gap–reduction slows down as the gap is reduced in size. Also as Kuznets (1982) stated and Coe, Helpman and Hoffmaister (1997) confirmed, openness is helpful for emulation.

For Japan, we can drop the openness index and plot out the scatter diagram between the catching up rate and the REPCRI in Figure 3.11, where the lower panel reproduces the time portrait of the REPCRI in a transposed form.   This shows, the observed slowing down of the Japanese economy in the 1990s may well mean its catching up process with America has reached a steady state, with the Japanese per capita real income at about 80% of that of America (or a steady state value of the gap at 20%).   For Korea, the openness index is far from settling down, so that nothing can be said yet about the steady state value of any Korean gap.

Can anything be said about the dynamics of China's catching up process? To this we now turn.   Figure 3.12 displays the time portrait of the catching up rate of China.

The recent slowing down of the Chinese economic growth has attracted much attention, coming at a time when the Japanese economy has a period of negligible growth.   Customarily, the Japanese difficulties are attributed to temporary setbacks and bad policy while the Chinese events invite doubts about the fundamental economic structure.   A word on what is happening to the economy of China is in order.

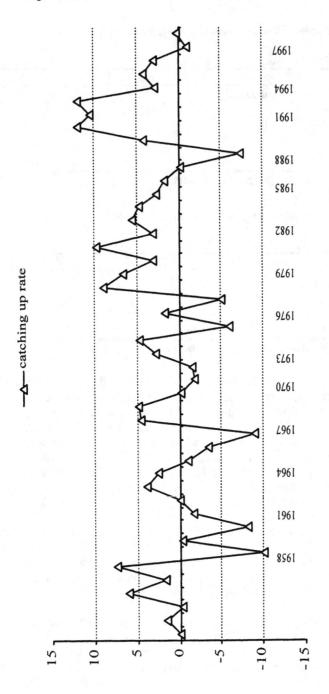

Figure 3.12   Time portrait of the catching up rates for China

Table 3.6   **Catching–up regression, China 1989–97**

Dependent variable: Growth rate of REPCRI

	Coefficient	t–value	
Intercept	0.258	3.345	–
REPCRI	–0.023	–2.695	–
Adj. R Square	–	–	–0.439
Observations	–	–	9

Note: REPCRI = relative per capita real income

In studying the recent past, we are interested in either the properties of a system (for example, how growth responds to openness) or its future outlook. For the latter purpose, some past record is to be excluded because of changed circumstances.   For example, most major Chinese economic initiatives were carried out by mass mobilization, before 1978, but not once afterwards.   The inclusion of a record that is no longer relevant only complicates the task of forecasting.   We thus concentrate on the post–1978 reform period which can be further divided into two sub–periods: 1979–1988 and 1989–1997. We regress the catching up rate against the REPCRI, for each sub–period and the entire post–1978 reform period. The results are reported in Tables 3.5–3.7 and Figures 3.13–3.14.

The intercept and the slope coefficients are significant at the 3% level for both sub–periods, but not for the entire post–reform period. To test the null hypothesis,

H_0: there is no structural change,

we compute the statistic,

$$F\text{–ratio} = \{(0.03815649 - 0.01924160)/2\}/[(0.01924169)/(18 - 4)]$$
$$= 0.009456105/0.0012026056$$
$$= 7.863 > 6.51,$$

so the null hypothesis is rejected at the 1% level.

The scatter plots for these two sub–periods are displayed as Figure 3.13 and Figure 3.14. What has taken place then is a pair of the 'boom–bust' reform cycles characteristic to the economy of China. The cyclical elements are strong, masking the catching up mechanism. Moreover, each cycle corresponds to such distinct and non–recurrent, institutional facts, like the rise and fall of the town and village industries.   An analogy is the economic effect of such non–economic events like the World Wars in the 20th century. These must be accepted as exogenous shocks. Any attempt to ignore or to predict such shocks on an econometric basis will not be helpful.

But at the very least, two qualitative conclusions can be drawn. First, at least in part, the Japanese difficulties today reflect deep–seated technological realities, namely, Japan has joined the older industrial countries like Britain and Germany, living in a world of rapid technological innovations implemented in America. Any

Table 3.7   Catching–up regression, China, 1979–97

Dependent variable: Growth rate of REPCRI

	Coefficient	t–value	
Intercept	0.084	1.555	–
REPCRI	–0.006	–0.852	–
Adj. R Square	–	–	–0.016
Observations	–	–	18

Note: REPCRI = relative per capita real income

reform in Japan will help, but unless the worldwide technological leadership is fundamentally shifted (like the overtaking of Britain by America), its situation is not going to change much. Specifically, its real per capita income will advance with America, with some lag.

Second, in its catching up, China has much further to go, before reaching a status like Japan. The precise course of advance is decided by many institutional factors, not predictable by traditional economic means. Paraphrasing Mark Twain, the rumors about the loss of steam in the Chinese catching up is certainly exaggerated.

At the same time, one cannot be complacent about the future. The thought experiment regarding car ownership in China reaching the Taiwanese level is a sobering thought. In today's technology, if that event happens overnight, then global warming, or resource depletion or both, will become an immediate concern, to Chinese and non–Chinese alike, with severe trade friction a distinct possibility. Today, the rest of the world is concerned about what China will export, especially in the area of manufactured goods. By that time, their concern would be what China will import, perceived as wreaking havoc to every oil–importing economy. Such events must be anticipated way in advance.

It is worthwhile to note that the average income is much higher in Hong Kong than in Taiwan, but the person/vehicle ratio is only 13:1, that is, only about one third of the ratio for Taiwan. Of course, every economy has its own conditions. Still, this comparison shows that the energy demand of high income societies is far from immutable. Thoughtful urban and regional design for the Chinese Mainland now can make a great deal of difference in future days.

Some more immediate matters

Under the current institutions, the economic growth of China has attracted huge amount of foreign investment and enjoyed an export boom. In turn, such foreign investment and export operations have used China as an export platform. Through transfer prices or the management of global supply chains, much of such exports were conducted by the foreign owned or foreign managed firms, with a large portion of the financial rewards going to those foreign interests. Much of the market gained by China in recent years represents industries migrated from Hong Kong and Taiwan, with part of the fabrication process done in China, but with the

Table 3.8   Capability to market abroad

Per capita GDP	Nominal (US $)	P.P.P. (US $)	Nominal/P.P.P.
Chinese Mainland	860	3,070	28%
Hong Kong	25,200	24,350	103%
Japan	38,160	24,400	156%

other parts (typically the more profitable segments) carried out elsewhere. Suppose Hong Kong and Taiwan form significant parts of the 'industrial pipeline' for China, and the recent investment from these two places implies the imminent depletion of the mobile portions of industries there, common sense argues that the pace of growth for China would have to take a breather. In short, the pace of rapid growth of China over the last dozen years may be hard to keep up.

In some sense, the current level of openness of China has served its purpose, but it is not likely to stay in the long run.[9] As a general rule, openness decreases with size. Figure 3.15 compares the openness indicator of Japan, Korea, Taiwan, Argentina and China, over the decades. Initially, data confirms this negative association between population size and the openness index. Japan provides an example where high growth does not call for very high level of openness. China is now more open than Japan, according to the index we used.

On the other hand, there is also much scope for growth for China, even though its nature has received scant notice. Table 3.8 reports the 1997 real and nominal per capita GDP of Hong Kong, China and Japan, from which we can measure the capability of market abroad for these three economies.

Thus, for each unit of GDP, measured by its ability to meet domestic needs, Chinese on the Mainland can receive no more than 30% of its worth in the world market, but Chinese in Hong Kong can get more worth abroad. The ability of Japanese to translate their own ware into international value is more than five times of the ability of China.

Now from (a) the current value of the 'openness' index of 40%, and (b) the fact that trade of China is approximately balanced (but with some surplus), export counts about 20% of the Chinese GDP. Should China match Japan in its ability of get its 'money's worth' in exporting to the world market, then China can double its GDP, without increasing its physical volume of export. Today, Koreans export large volumes of their Hyundai automobile or Samsung mobile phone under their own brands. In contrast, a large portion of Chinese exports are sold to, or through, multinational firms in globalized supply chains.

Now these multinational systems are far from being monopolies and monopsonists. As oligopolies they compete fiercely against each other, seeking to

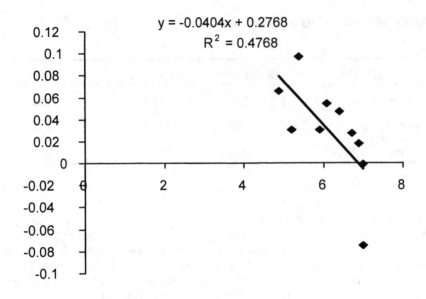

Figure 3.13   Catching–up scatter, China, 1979–88

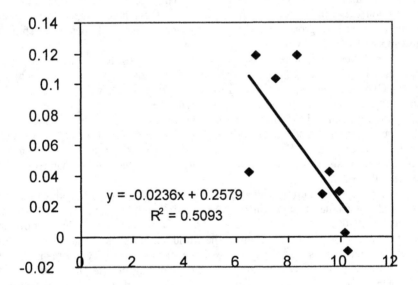

Figure 3.14   Catching–up scatter, China, 1989–97

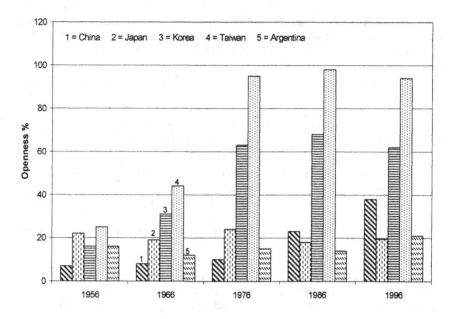

Figure 3.15 Openness: China in context

outflank rivals with supply sources of equal worth at the lowest cost, be it in China, Indonesia, Vietnam, or Lesotho. So by improving the 'worthiness' of their exports, Mainland Chinese exporters can win a far larger share of their goods' worth. This can be done, through better organization and stronger institutions, making product quality more stable or delivery time more punctual. Solid performance brings connections, then reputation and finally, in due time, reward. After all, that was how the Hong Kong Chinese gained their foothold on the world market, and they have not done badly now, according to Table 3.8. The force of the world market is certain and impartial, whether or not one deems it morally just.

For China, prowess for international marketing is valuable, but not indispensable. Once when Chinese suppliers have improved their quality or service on the world market, Chinese fabrication capacities would become highly in demand to the international managers of the rival supply chains. Additional growth can then be realized, not by exporting more of the same, but through better reward for essentially the same effort. Such bootstraps self–enrichment does not call for exporting physically more than today. No single foreign competitor of Chinese exports need be displaced from their current jobs. It will only mean a redistribution of the trade gains inside the supply chain.

Another main source for growth is through backward linkage. Today, the export industries of China depend heavily on manufactured imports from abroad, from machines, tools to parts, components and processed material. To make outputs competitive in the world market, such inputs must be of such high and reliable quality, and available just in time, so that they have to be procured abroad, at considerable cost. In fact, when a Taiwanese factory produced bicycles in Mainland China, initially 70% of the cost was for inputs from Japan and Taiwan. This was also the source of the earlier difficulties faced by the Beijing Jeep Corporation. Historically, the same type of problems was also present for Korea and Taiwan, until satellite industries there became mature. The local content of exports usually rises with the value–added for the exporting country and implies a lower 'openness' index.

Since Chinese customers have no 'economic chauvinism' (in fact, they have some preference for their imports over their import–substitutes), better earned Chinese means better clients for the non–Chinese. Certainly, such development–by–self improvement cannot be realized over night. Yet, judging by what the Chinese in Hong Kong have achieved, it is clearly within reach of the Mainland Chinese.

Returning to what is discussed in a previous section, here is where the long term Chinese economic interest is. The Chinese have considerable bargaining power inherent in their huge domestic market. It should be devoted to realize such capabilities, rather than to win market access of one good or another, for its own sake.

Postscript

Since the completion of the initial draft, two valuable sources have come to my notice.

First, a monograph on Immiserizing Growth: A Question of Changing Terms of Trade (*Pin Kun Hua Zeng Chang—Mao Yi Tiao Jian Bian Dong Zhong De Yi Wen*) by Ruzhong Wang (in Chinese ISBN7–80618–631–X) published by the Shanghai Academy of Social Science in 1999. This indicates the awareness of the issue of immiscrizing growth in China.

Second, the statement of Professor Lawrence Lau, before the Congressional–Executive Commission on China on Sept. 23, 2003. Based upon a study by Fung and Lau in *Asian Economic Journal* 14, pp. 489–96, 2003, this testimony provides an in–depth analysis of the position of China in the American supply chain, which provides huge profit to multinational firms but very little contribution to the GDP of China, since the Chinese workers mostly only do assembly jobs.

Notes

1   I appreciate greatly the comments by S. Clemhout, the editorial assistance of Andrea Williams–Wan, as well as the technical help by Jaehun Chung, but I take full responsibility for all the deficiencies in this chapter. Thanks are also due to the patient expert help of Paulette S. Carlisle.

2   Or else the oil boycott would never be an effective weapon.
3   In view of the Sonnenschein–Mantel–Debreu Theorem. See MasColell et al. (1995) and others.
4   This is particularly true, if domestic consumers are too poor to demand high standards. The practice of stringent quality control will then be alien to the society. See Morawetz (1981).
5   See Tan (1997).
6   By the year 2000, China had a total nominal GDP larger than Italy, and next to only France.
7   See Helpman and Krugman (1985).
8   The degree of this advantage is relative. It is conditioned on the assumption that the size of one player in the market would not pose perceived threat to other players to form a countervailing coalition against it. The exclusion of Japan from GATT membership—until Americans sponsored Japan—after World War II is an example of how such interactions work. The more export and foreign investment are regarded by developing economies today as key instrument for development, the more they become anxious that Chinese development would not hinder their own development agenda. It is not well understood in these countries that the success of China in export and attracting foreign investment comes partly from China's role as the export platform for other Sinitic economies, namely, Hong Kong and Taiwan, a role they could not play with the same effectiveness in any case, due to cultural distances.
9   The Chinese population is 27 times of Korea, and its openness index is about 2/3 of Korea. In the long run per capita incomes may equalize between these two countries. After all, currently all Sinitic economies, save Mainland China, has higher GDP per capita than the Korean. But then, the Chinese trade will be 18 times of the Korean trade. Currently Korean trade is about 2.5% of the world trade, then the Chinese trade will be 45% of the world total. So 90% of the world trade will involve the Chinese. This prospect is clearly absurd.

References

Coe, D.T., Helpman, E. and Hoffmaister, A.W. (1997) 'North South Spillovers', *Economic Journal* **107**, pp. 134–49.

Ernst, D. (2001), 'Catching Up and Post–crisis Industrial Upgrading: Searching for New Sources of Growth in Korea's Electronics Industry', in F.C. Deyo, R.F. Doner, and E. Hershberg (eds.) *Economic governance and the challenge of flexibility in East Asia* Rowman & Littlefield, Lanham, MD.

Helpman, E., and Krugman, P.R. (1985) *Market Structure and Foreign Trade: Increasing Returns, Monopolistic Competition and the International Economy*, MIT Press, Cambridge, MA.

Kuznets, S. (1982), 'Modern Economic Growth and the Less Developed Countries' in K.T. Li and T.S. Yu (eds.), *Experience and Lessons of Economic Development in Taiwan*, Academia Sinica, Taipei.

MasCollel, A., Whinston, M.D. and Green, J.R. (1995), *Microeconomic Theory*, Oxford University Press, New York.

Morawetz, D. (1981), *Why the Emperor's New Clothes Are Not Made in Columbia: A Case Study in Latin American and East Asian Manufactured Exports*, Oxford University Press, Washington, DC.

Tan, K.Y. (1997) 'China and the ASEAN: Competitive Industrialization through Foreign Investment', in B. Naughton ed., *The China Circle, Economics and Technology in the PRC, Taiwan and Hong Kong,* Brookings Institution Press, Washington, DC.

Interdependent Evolution: The North-South Interactions

Review of "Emulative Development through Trade Expansions: East Asian Evidence", jointly with P. H. Van[*]

Association transmits information Technology transfer is the mainstay for economic development, channeled through direct investment and trade among close associates. This Article cast the situation as a multi-stage game between an informed player and an uninformed player, and information gets gradually transferred over time. Players live in a world with unobservable states which are reflected imperfectly in messages observed by all, and elicit actions by players according to their respective interpretations. During their association, the uninformed takes note of how the informed acts when receiving various messages, updating his or her own message interpretation as the game goes along, in terms favoring the informed. That favor reflects the value of learning from the play, for the uninformed. In time, the uninformed gets enough information to quit and fend for himself or herself.

The Article further justifies the assumption that the true states are unobservable from the engineering literature. It also presents a list of case histories with different degrees of success in transferring technology.

Incentives sharpen observation The incentive scheme embedded in such joint operations of long association is essential to effective transfers. Transfer is highly successful only when the uninformed party is highly observant. This is a contact game. If the contacting party is a hired employee, then that person must have the incentive to observe closely. After all, relating the commonly observed message to the choice pattern of the informed party requires some sensitivity and imagination: it is not a job for the disinterested. Incentives may be built into the arrangement, for instance, if the person assigned to work for a term with the multinational firm in a joint venture is scheduled to serve at a position of responsibility after returning from the joint venture. The implication then is that whatever is learned from the multinational firm can be put into use, and personal rewards will follow from the effective application of this experience.

---

[*]The article first appeared in *International Trade Policy and the Pacific Rim*, J. Piggott and A. Woodland (eds.), pp. 348–366, 1999. The author is grateful to the publisher, Palgrave Macmillan, for granting the permit to reprint in this volume.

An extension on subcontracting The applicability of this analysis to the case of subcontracting also deserves some comments. Multinational firms often outsource some of their operations to their subcontractors in a developing economy. To save cost, the subcontractor is often chosen among the local firms with much potential but without a good deal of experience. To ensure that the assigned job can be completed satisfactorily, technical advice is often provided when the need arises. Several such cases on the bicycle and sewing machine industries of Taiwan are reported in Wan (2004).

Emulative Development through Trade Expansion: East Asian Evidence[1]

Pham Hoang Van and Henry Y. Wan, Jr
CORNELL UNIVERSITY

1 INTRODUCTION

This paper distils theory from the facts of development in East Asian countries: the government attracts foreign firms bringing technology. Local agents receive enough of it to achieve fast growth, but not enough to outcompete foreign firms or to deter their entry.

Currently, the East Asian economies have received much attention because of their sustained rapid growth (see World Bank, 1993), in spite of their lack of activity in research and development (R&D). Their mode of 'late industrialization' (Amsden, 1989) is characterized by an 'emulative process'. In this exploratory study, the mechanism of this process is analyzed, for two purposes. First, on the *normative* side, to design a policy regime that facilitates the acquisition of useful information and, second, on the *descriptive* side, to draw implications about the source and future of East Asian growth. Specifically, we consider:

(i)   the role of the state (see Amsden and Singh, 1994; and Bhagwati, 1996);
(ii)   the contribution of *trade, technical progress* and *accumulation* to growth (see Young, 1994); and
(iii) the prospect of a Soviet-style collapse (see Krugman, 1994)

In studying the process of emulation, we build upon the literature of 'New Growth Theory', 'New Trade Theory' and economic development. As in the theory of endogenous growth, the rate of technology diffusion is seen to depend on the intention and capability of the agents. It is the equilibrium outcome of an extensive game between the government of the developing country and some interacting agents: firms from the developed economy, who are initially better informed, and individuals in the developing economy, who may gain information by association.

This game-theoretic approach extends the literature on North–South trade (as surveyed by Grossman and Helpman, 1995), for example in several

163

directions. In contrast to the study of Rivera-Batiz and Romer (1992) on the informational interaction of two symmetrically similar economies, we focus on the interaction between a single, small developing economy and various developed countries.

The key is to capture, with a tractable model, additional realism in a complex world where the heterogenous interact strategically under the influence of competition among the similars. It is the South–South competition that keeps the North–South wage gap wide, and the North–North competition that quickens the pace of the product cycle.

Krugman (1979) and Grossman and Helpman (1991) have represented the North–South technology gap with a number of goods initially producible only by the North. At any instant, diffusion transfers the technology of a *constant fraction* of such products to the South. We continue this revealing line of analysis to address two questions which concern the developing countries most: (i) *What* decides that fraction? and (ii) *How* can the rate of diffusion be raised?

Alone, in the literature, Findlay (1978) has identified direct foreign investment as a catalyst for technology diffusion. We seek answers to two follow-up questions: (i) Does direct foreign investment play this role equally well under all policies? (ii) Can other forms of international economic relationships (for example, sub-contracting) serve as a catalyst?

With the exception of Findlay, the analytical literature has abstracted from the specifics of the North–South association, and left no role for trade and foreign investment to play in technology diffusion. It is silent on the reasons why many developing countries offer tax holidays to foreign firms using advanced technology. Nor does it explain why growth has accelerated in Chile and the Peoples' Republic of China (PRC) soon after their outward-oriented reforms. In fact, one cannot find in that literature the defects of inward-looking development, which has been the bane of China, Cuba, India and Egypt for more than 30 years.

To us, the heart of the emulation process is the information asymmetry and its reduction. We try to capture the *details* of real life: *who* learns *what* from *whom* and *how*? It is the details that explain *why* some developing economies outperform others, sometimes overtaking the latter after lagging behind. Such an analysis may also suggest *which* development policies work and *which* do not.

To pursue our specific goals, we draw insights from the literature on economic development and, in particular, studies of Japan, both as a recipient and as a source of technical information; for example, Komiya (1972) and Uchida (1991) on the former, and Kojima (1978) and Ozawa (1979) on the latter.[2]

But to distil insight from experiences in some situations, for other contexts differing in time and place, one needs a theory. Only a formal theory can organize facts to make inferences. This study is undertaken in an attempt to determine endogenously the rate of cross-national technological diffusion and, in particular, the role played by the policy regime of the developing economy. Accordingly, we simplify drastically the dynamics to incorporate the elements of mechanism design, as in Green and Laffont (1979), and the information-theoretic structure of Nermuth (1982). We set up a model more information-theoretic than usual (for example, as surveyed by Grossman and Helpman, 1991.). At that basic level we show that emulation depends on close association with the better-informed. Specifically, this is through the Bayesian updating of prior beliefs.

Ours is part of a broader study, which includes the conceptual frameworks in Wan (1993 and 1996), the empirical discussions in Lau and Wan (1994a) and Lin and Wan (1996), as well as the growth-theoretical inferences in Lau and Wan (1994b). Through a sequence of models like these, one hopes to gain insight into the nature of the catch-up process.

The justification for our unusual approach is its relevance to policy, especially for transitional economies like China, India and Russia, as well as certain African and South-American economies. Catch-up depends on rapid technology transfer; technology transfer requires an outward orientation (encouraging a closer relationship with the outside world). To illustrate this, we present a case related by Wong (1976) and commented on by Watanabe (1980) (from now on referred to as the Wong–Watanabe case).

In the next section, we summarize the Wong–Watanabe case along with six other selected cases related to East Asian growth, and draw from them a theoretical model. Section 3 presents a model where technology is specified as information-dependent, and information is acquired by rational agents in an environment decided by government policy. This exercise sheds light on the questions mentioned above and provides insights for the design of policy. Conclusions follow in the fourth section.

2 SOME SALIENT FACTS

The Wong–Watanabe Case in Brief [1]

An American firm assembled radios in Hong Kong from imported parts. The local supervisors learnt crucial lessons about the recruitment, training and supervision of indigenous labour, quality control, the scheduling of delivery and production layout. They then quit the US firm and started their own businesses assembling digital watches for export.

The above case is not an isolated incident, but a theme with many variations.

The General Instrument Variation [2]

The American firm General Instruments made certain simple products in Taiwan. The indigenous employees became so proficient that later many left to set up eleven new firms supplying similar items (Business Week, 3 March, 1986).

The Taiwanese Footwear Variation [3]

As Japanese wages rose, Mitsubishi, a supplier of plastic shoes to America, shifted its supply base from Kobe, Japan, to its Taiwanese sub-contractors. To reduce cost, it further encouraged Taiwanese skilled workers to spin off and act as new sub-contractors and many small firms arose (Levy, 1990). Then American chain stores came, sub-contracting and helping local firms to make leather shoes for them. Still later, Taiwanese firms, such as the Hongson Company, exported leather shoes to America under their own brand name (Seetoo, 1992).

The Taiwanese Bicycle Variation [4]

In the import substitution phase of policy in Taiwan, four major Taiwanese firms assembled low-grade bicycles from Japanese parts for local use. Many rivals then entered the market with cheaper products at even lower quality, and locally assembled motorcycles also appeared. All the 'big four' failed. After the outward-oriented policy reform in Taiwan, Schwinn, a popular American bicycle firm, contracted Giant, a local sporting-goods supplier, to hire the former employees of the 'big four' and import better Japanese parts to produce bicycles for the American market. Eventually, Taiwan became the world's largest bicycle exporter (by dollar value) with Giant shipping some outputs under its own brand name (Chu and Li, 1996).

The Mauritian Knitwear Variation [5]

Because of (i) quota restrictions under the Multi-fibre Agreements; (ii) the Lomé Convention which favours former European colonies in the *European Union* (EU) market; and (iii) the presence of a small Chinese community in Mauritius, the Hong Kong Chinese produced knitted woollen gloves for the European market under the institutions of an export zone which had been adapted from Taiwan to Mauritius. Even though there is not a single sheep in Mauritius, business boomed, surplus labour was absorbed and wages rose. Eventually non-Chinese local businesses joined the industry successfully (Findlay and Wellisz, 1993).

The Colombian Apparel Variation [6]

Colombians could export textiles to Venezuela behind the trade barriers of the Andean Plan, but not to the lucrative American market against East Asian competition. The stumbling block was apparently the bureaucratic Colombian trade regime, making it hard to deliver on time – while for the American fashion market punctual delivery is indispensable. Thus cut off from the American market, local firms also saw no need to be reliable in quality or well-informed about the sizes of American clients (Morawetz, 1981).

The Beijing Jeep Variation [7]

The American Motor Corporation (AMC) co-produced jeeps with the PRC in Beijing, aiming for the export market. But it was found that locally-produced parts were not of exportable quality and the cumbersome exchange control system made it impractical to import such inputs. The output was therefore reoriented towards the local market. Conflicts arose between the partners over issues of national prestige (Mann, 1989). In those days, Chinese employees served in a joint venture for only a fixed duration and on leaving foreign joint ventures, they had neither the opportunity to start businesses of their own, nor the chance to work as decision-makers elsewhere.

The seven cases can be summarized in the structured comparison in Table 16.1.

From the comparisons in Table 16.1, we can draw the following conclusions:

(a) Skill acquired may be either product-specific or not product-specific.
(b) The emulation process follows principles applicable in East Asia as well as elsewhere. In particular:

- goods for high income markets often contain characteristics hard to supply and hence are highly-valued;
- firms from the developed countries are better informed to supply such characteristics;
- by close association with those better-informed, individuals from a developing economy can become better-informed themselves; and,
- competition among the parties, which initially possessed better information, may prevent them from appropriating all the potential gains from the bargain.

(c) Both direct foreign investment and sub-contracting arrangements can facilitate emulation.
(d) Failure in emulation may be caused either by difficulties in importing required inputs or by lack of incentive for local individuals to learn.

Table 16.1   Selected cases related to East Asian growth

Case	Technology transferred	Relationship with foreign firm	The host economy	Remarks
[1]	Not product specific	Employee	East Asia	Temporal pattern: Foreign direct investment, Employment, Local entry
[2]	Product specific	Employee	East Asia	Temporal pattern: Foreign direct investment, Employment, Local entry
[3]	Product specific	Sub-contractor	East Asia	
[4]	Product specific	Employee of sub-contractor	East Asia	
[5]	Product specific	Bystanders	Not East Asia	Temporal–spatial pattern: Foreign direct investment, Local entry
[6]	?	Sub-contractor	Not East Asia	Problem: Input control
[7]	?	Joint venture	East Asia	Problems: Input control; No incentives for Employees

(e)   What is worth noting is not that General Instruments shifted production to Taiwan to cut labour cost (as trade theory predicts), but that many local Taiwanese producers of the same items entered the market after General Instruments, and that these local producers were former employees of General Instruments.

(f)   Again, what is remarkable is not the initial 'quota-jumping' into the EU by the Hong Kong investors but that the subsequent entries came from Mauritian South Asians and not from South Asians from Bombay or Karachi. The opportunity to observe the Hong Kong investors at close range clearly gave the former group an advantage. Thus, the emulation process is alive and well in variations [3] and [5].

3   A THEORETICAL EXAMPLE OF TECHNOLOGY TRANSFER

In a 'stylized fashion', the Wong–Watanabe case is now modelled as a three-period, three-player game: Player 1 represents the government of a developing economy; Player 2 the representative foreign firm in a developing economy; and Player 3 the representative individual in the developing economy in question.

The evolution of the game is described in Table 16.2.

Table 16.2   The evolution of a three-period, three-player game

Period 1	Period 2	Period 3
Government of LDC chooses policy regime.	Representative foreign firm chooses good for production. Representative individual from the LDC chooses learning effort.	Representative individual from the LDC chooses whether to start own business with the information gained in period 2, or to continue working for the foreign firm.

In period 1, the policy regime is chosen by player 1, the government of the less developed country (LDC). This decides the production possibilities of player 2, the representative foreign firm, and the information structures available to player 3, the representative local individual, in subsequent periods. The government maximizes the payoffs of its constituents, as represented by wages earned and the information acquired for future production, perhaps at some cost of effort.

The foreign firm maximizes the present value of its profit stream. At the beginning of period 2, it decides which good to produce in the LDC. Endowed with one unit of entrepreneurial input, the foreign entrepreneur has full information on the possible production of every product. The entrepreneur makes certain key decisions for the firm, to maximize the residual revenue from the enterprise, after all other inputs have been rewarded.

The representative individual in the LDC may work for wages at the foreign firm. Meanwhile, production information may be gained by observing both the (imperfect) signals about the production process and the concurrent actions of the foreign firm. With such acquired information, the local individual may either continue to work for the foreigner in period 3, or start a business of his/her own with the acquired expertise.

The developing economy can produce food, the numeraire, or three different manufactured goods for which it assembles imported inputs. The world prices for goods x (radios for the world market) and z (digital watches for the world market) are given (the developing country is small). Good y is a lower-quality variant of good x and is used only for domestic consumption. For simplicity, good y is assumed to be a perfect substitute for 'food'.

The individuals in the developing economy may gain production information in period 2 that is useful in period 3. In contrast, we assume, for simplicity, that firms from the developed economy face the same opportunities in period 3, regardless of what happens in period 2. In case history [1], this means the demand for high-quality radios is neutral relative to demand for watches; in case history [2], the foreign investor sells at competitive prices in period 3, where the entry of the spin-off firms matters little.

The manufactured goods are made with a Leontief technology, using imported inputs α, local labour β, and entrepreneurial service γ. Imported inputs include materials and tools/equipment. Labour is divided into direct and supervisory types, in fixed proportions. For simplicity, they are assumed to command the same wage. The production condition is random and not perfectly observable. For example, the climate may make the plant 'too hot' or 'too wet', rendering the product quality unacceptable. Based on the available information signal, decisions must be made to apply specific preventive preparations to the material: 'COOLING' when 'hot'; 'DRYING' when 'wet'.[3] Imperfect information may be refined by testing, at some cost.

The interactions between information, decisions and incentives make the development problem non-trivial. The government acts to maximize the payoff of its constituents. Government matters because its constituents cannot select the policy regime; only the government can do this.

We now construct an example to capture the essence of the Wong–Watanabe case. Recall that the condition of production is assumed to be random and not directly observable. It may be represented by any one of the six states in:

$$E = \{1, 2, 3, 4, 5, 6\} \tag{16.1}$$

with equal probability: the probability of e in E is $h(e) = 1/6$ for all e.

What is observed is signal s in some finite signal space S. The probability of observing signal s in state e is:

$$q(s,e) = Pr[s \mid e]; \quad \sum_{s \in S} q(s,e) = 1 \tag{16.2}$$

Information is a stochastic matrix $Q = [q(s,e)]$, and the ordered pair (S, Q) is player-specific, updated by experience.

In the present context, the signal space available depends on the initial knowledge and experience of the individual in question. In particular, we assume the following. Firms from developed countries always have perfect information:

$$S = E, \; q(s,e) = 1, \text{ if and only if, } e = s \tag{16.3}$$

The individuals of the LDC initially have null information:

$$S' = \{0\}, \; q'(0,e) = 1, \text{ for all } e \in E \tag{16.4}$$

The individuals of the LDC may acquire imperfect information after working with the foreign firm:

$$S'' = \{LOW, HIGH\}, \; LOW = \{1, 2, 3\} \text{ and } HIGH = \{4, 5, 6\} \tag{16.5}$$

under the *assumption* that if the state of the environment *e* is in a particular subset of *E* then the individual will receive *with certainty* a signal denoting that subset. Thus,

$$q''(LOW, e) = 1, \text{ if and only if, } e \in LOW$$
$$q''(HIGH, e) = 1, \text{ if and only if, } e \in HIGH \tag{16.6}$$

The imperfectness of information here is a 'coarsening' of the perfect information case.

Table 16.3 summarizes the signal space and information map for each player, with:

$$Q = \begin{bmatrix} 1 & 0 & 0 & 0 & 0 & 0 \\ 0 & 1 & 0 & 0 & 0 & 0 \\ 0 & 0 & 1 & 0 & 0 & 0 \\ 0 & 0 & 0 & 1 & 0 & 0 \\ 0 & 0 & 0 & 0 & 1 & 0 \\ 0 & 0 & 0 & 0 & 0 & 1 \end{bmatrix} ; \ Q' = \begin{bmatrix} 1 \\ 1 \\ 1 \\ 1 \\ 1 \\ 1 \end{bmatrix} ; \ Q'' = \begin{bmatrix} 1 & 0 \\ 1 & 0 \\ 1 & 0 \\ 0 & 1 \\ 0 & 1 \\ 0 & 1 \end{bmatrix} \tag{16.7}$$

Table 16.3   Signal space and information map for each player

	Signal space	Information map
Player 2 (foreign firm)	S	Q
Player 3 (local employee)		
Inexperienced	S'	Q'
Experienced	S''	Q''

Once the production condition signal is received, the firm will select one of the alternatives; 'drying' or 'cooling', for the input. The alternatives are denoted, respectively,

$$a \in A = \{DRYING, COOLING\} \tag{16.8}$$

The portion of acceptable outputs for production process *i* is the yield value, $u_i(a, e)$ (for the same (a, e) pair the yield may be product dependent). Writing:

$$ODD = \{1, 3, 5\} \quad \text{and} \quad EVEN = \{2, 4, 6\} \tag{16.9}$$

where 'ODD' signals a wet condition and 'EVEN' signals a hot condition, we assume that for goods *x* and *y* (high- and low-quality radios, respectively),

$$u_x(a,e) = u_y(a,e) = 1, \text{ if, } e \in a$$
$$u_x(a,e) = u_y(a,e) = 0, \text{ if } e \notin a \tag{16.10}$$

with

$$x = u_x(a,e) \, \min[\alpha/a_{\alpha x}, \beta/a_{\beta x}, \gamma/a_{\gamma x}]$$
$$y = u_y(a,e) \, \min[\alpha/a_{\alpha y}, \beta/a_{\beta y}, \gamma/a_{\gamma y}] \tag{16.11}$$

where a_{ij} is the requirement of input i for one unit of output j.

Good y is produced for the domestic market of the developing economy. By assumption, it is a perfect substitute for food, with a constant relative price in 'food', $p_y < p_x$, the world relative price for x. Moreover, the relative input contents are assumed to be such that:

$$a_{\alpha x}/p_x < a_{\alpha y}/p_y \quad \text{and} \quad a_{\beta x}/p_x < a_{\beta y}/p_y \tag{16.12}$$

implying that such 'localized' products are not very attractive for the foreign producer.

Good z (a digital watch) is a relatively simpler product than x and y, so that:

$$u_z(a,e) = 1, \qquad \text{if } e \in a$$
$$u_z(a,e) \in (0,1), \text{ if } e \notin a \tag{16.13}$$

The last statement indicates that although the 'actions' taken may not be the best, the output need not be a total loss for the simpler products. For good z, the production function is now

$$z = u_z(a,e) \, \min[\alpha/a_{\alpha z}, \beta/a_{\beta z}, \gamma/a_{\gamma z}] \tag{16.14}$$

All players share the following information as common knowledge:

- State space: $E \equiv \{1,2,3,4,5,6\}$; ODD $\equiv \{1,3,5\}$; EVEN $\equiv \{2,4,6\}$.
- Prior probability: $h(e) = 1/6, \forall e \in E; h(\text{ODD}) = 1/2 = h(\text{EVEN})$.
- Action space: $A \equiv \{\text{DRYING, COOLING}\}$.
- Yield (reward) index: $u_i(a,e) \in (0,1), u_i(a,e) = 1$ if $e \in a$ for $i = x,y,z$.
- The optimal rule with perfect information, χ:
  'COOLING if e is EVEN; DRYING if e is ODD'.
- Player 2 is perfectly informed.

Player 2 (the foreign entrepreneur) has perfect information (Q), and so will always take the optimal action.

On receiving a signal of LOW or HIGH, the inexperienced player 3 (the local individual) does not know how this signal relates to the true state. Thus receiving a LOW signal does not allow him/her then to assign higher probability to any state than before. Null information (Q') essentially remains, and there is only a 50–50 chance of taking the proper action.

The experience of working inside a foreign firm makes all the difference. During that period the local worker observes both an imperfect signal, and the actions taken by the foreign entrepreneur. Since the foreigner is known always to take the optimal action, it is known that DRYING reflects the ODD signal; and COOLING reflects the EVEN signal:

$$\Pr[s \in \{1,3,5\} \mid a = DRYING] = 1 = \Pr[s \in \{2,4,6\} \mid a = COOLING] \quad (16.15)$$

Further, by knowing that the foreigner has perfect information (about the state of nature), the worker can then deduce that DRYING action reflects the ODD state:

$$\Pr[e \in \{1,3,5\} \mid a = DRYING] = 1 = \Pr[e \in \{2,4,6\} \mid a = COOLING] \quad (16.16)$$

By repetitively observing the frequency of the actions of the foreign entrepreneur and their correlation with those signals received by himself:[4]

(i) $h''(ODD) = \Pr[a = DRYING] = 1/2 = \Pr[a = COOLING] = h''(EVEN)$; and
(ii) $\Pr[LOW \mid a = DRYING] = 2/3$; $\Pr[LOW \mid a = COOLING] = 1/3$ (16.17)
  $\Pr[HIGH \mid a = DRYING] = 2/3$; $\Pr[HIGH \mid a = COOLING] = 1/3$

With this information, the local employees can spin off and start operating on their own in period 3. By then, without the benefit of observing the actions of the former employer, they must fall back on their own received signals. However, the updated beliefs about the signals promise better actions. Using Bayes' rule and the probabilities in (16.15) to (16.17), the conditional probability of a state belonging to a particular subset, given the local individuals' own imperfect signals, becomes:

$$\Pr[e \in \{1,3,5\} \mid s'' = LOW] = \Pr[a = DRYING \mid s'' = LOW]$$

$$= \frac{\Pr[LOW] \mid [a = DRYING] \times \Pr[ODD]}{\Pr[LOW \mid a = DRYING] \times \Pr[ODD] + \Pr[LOW \mid a = COOLING] \times \Pr[EVEN]}$$

$$= \frac{(2/3)(1/2)}{(2/3)(1/2) + (1/3)(1/2)} = 2/3$$

$$\Pr[e \in \{2,4,6\} \mid s'' = LOW] = \Pr[a = COOLING \mid s'' = LOW] = 1/3$$
$$\Pr[e \in \{1,3,5\} \mid s'' = HIGH] = \Pr[a = DRYING \mid s'' = HIGH] = 1/3 \quad (16.8)$$
$$\Pr[e \in \{2,4,6\} \mid s'' = HIGH] = \Pr[a = COOLING \mid s'' = HIGH] = 2/3$$

From these, the local entrepreneur can adopt the rule: 'COOLING if the signal is HIGH; DRYING when the signal is LOW'.

The above notation may make this outcome seem trivial, but one should recognize that, without the benefit of observing the foreigner in the previous period, the local entrepreneur would have no way to relate the LOW (or HIGH) signal to the states, and the probability of taking the proper action would have been 1/2. With the benefit of observing the foreigner, the local entrepreneur can now take correct action two-thirds of the time.

To illustrate the outcomes in choosing different policy regimes, we assign numerical values to various parameters. Suppose the three output prices are:

$$p_x = 5; \quad p_y = 1; \quad p_z = 3 \tag{16.19}$$

and the prices of the inputs α and β are,

$$p_\alpha = p_\beta = 1 \tag{16.20}$$

where p_α, the price of imported inputs, is the CIF price (taxes included). The unit input requirements for the three outputs are:

$$
\begin{aligned}
x &: a_{\alpha x} = a_{\beta x} = a_{\gamma x} = 1 \\
y &: a_{\alpha y} = a_{\beta y} = a_{\gamma y} = 2/9 \\
z &: a_{\alpha z} = a_{\beta z} = a_{\gamma z} = 3/4
\end{aligned}
\tag{16.21}
$$

Further, assume that the yield for good z is 1/2 if the 'proper' action is not taken:

$$u_z(a, e) = 1/2 \text{ if } e \notin a \tag{16.22}$$

The expected yields of x, y and z for the three information structures are:

x : $\begin{cases} \text{with null information :} \\ \text{with perfect information :} \\ \text{with imperfect information :} \end{cases}$ $\begin{aligned} &Eu_x(a,e) = (6)(1/6)[(1/2)(0) + (1/2)(1)] = 1/2 \\ &Eu_x(a,e) = (6)(1/6) = 1 \\ &Eu_x(a,e) = (1/6)[1 + 0 + 1] + (1/6)[1 + 0 + 1] = 2/3 \end{aligned}$

y : $\begin{cases} \text{with null information :} \\ \text{with perfect information :} \\ \text{with imperfect information :} \end{cases}$ $\begin{aligned} &Eu_y(a,e) = (6)(1/6)[(1/2)(0) + (1/2)(1)] = 1/2 \\ &Eu_y(a,e) = (6)(1/6) = 1 \\ &Eu_y(a,e) = (1/6)[1 + 0 + 1] + (1/6)[1 + 0 + 1] = 2/3 \end{aligned}$

z : $\begin{cases} \text{with null information :} \\ \text{with perfect information :} \\ \text{with imperfect information :} \end{cases}$ $\begin{aligned} &Eu_z(a,e) = (6)(1/6)[(1/2)(1/2) + (1/2)(1)] = 3/4 \\ &Eu_z(a,e) = (6)(1/6) = 1 \\ &Eu_z(a,e) = (1/6)[1 + 1/2 + 1] + 1/6[1 + 1/2 + 1] \\ &\qquad = 5/6 \end{aligned}$

In period 2, the foreign firm would compute the residual return for each of the three goods. In period 3, the local individual would do the same and

Table 16.4   Reward in the three industries using the optimal rule under different information structures

	I *Null information* *(Local-inexperienced)*	II *Imperfect information* *(Local-experienced)*	III *Perfect information* *(Foreign firm)*
Supervisory return			
Good x	1/2	1/3	3
Good y	1/4	1	5/2
Good z	1	4/3	2
Local worker wage			
	1	1	—

Note: Boxed figures denote the maximum reward in each column.

compare them to the opportunity wage of working for the foreign firm. These are shown in Table 16.4.[5]

With the information in Table 16.4, we can determine the equilibrium evolution for our extensive game. To save space, we shall sketch it with the following game tree (the equilibrium choices are marked with thick lines). Player 1 will choose an outward-oriented strategy, g_0 (marked with a thick line in Figure 16.1), rather than other policy options such as g_1, the avoidance of 'export dependence' as practised by the Indian government with respect to the machine tool industry (see Lin and Wan 1996).[6] By column III of Table 16.4, player 2 would produce good x (rather than y, z or ϕ – no entry) and adopt the full information optimum decision rule, χ. By column II in Table 16.4, player 3, who has already been in close association with player 2 in period 2, will acquire imperfect information, and then choose to apply this in the production of good z (rather than x, y or ϕ – continue working for wages) using the imperfect information rule, χ''.

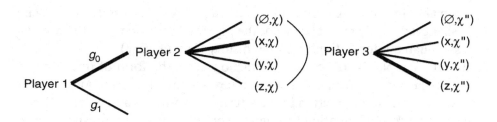

Figure 16.1   Game tree, showing equilibrium choices

Note that the acquisition of information by player 3 in period 2 is itself a purposeful choice. Such an option is preferred when one compares column I to column II. If the institutional environment does not favour certain entrepreneurial activities, then any ε cost of information acquisition will deter player 3 from making this choice.[7] Furthermore, the fact that player 3 only acquires imperfect information prevents him/her from competing with player 2 in producing good x during period 3.[8] This assures that those in the position of player 2 will reveal their expertise in period 2.

The above simple example has captured the essence of a plausible scenario. We now summarize some of the lessons gained from the exercise as follows:

Proposition
In the context of the case studied, we found the following:
1. By closely associating with better-informed (foreign) individuals, less-informed persons from a developing economy can:

   (a) improve their own probability estimates about the state, based on imperfect signals (that is, $(S', Q') \rightarrow (S'', Q'')$);
   (b) modify their decision rules accordingly (that is, $\chi' \rightarrow \chi''$, where χ' is a completely random decision rule); and
   (c) improve their payoff (from 1 to 4/3 in period 3) as a consequence.

2. The technology transfer that favours the developing economy poses no threat to the interests of the initial foreign investors (because x and z are different goods).
3. The operation of an 'export platform'[9] may benefit all parties concerned (see item 1(c) above for the host country, and even without any information about the opportunity cost for the foreign firm, the fact that they come to invest reveals that they benefit).

Remarks
1. To include an import substitution regime, our example must be extended to include a process of producing inputs at home. In real life, one may learn about producing inputs under such a policy. But a foreign firm facing a 'sheltered' home market and not the highly competitive world may reveal less valuable information (see case history [6] on p. 352).
2. In our example, North–South interaction takes the form of direct investment: the foreign firm–local worker nexus conveys production information. In contrast, interaction in the alternative form of sub-contracting may convey market information through the observed pattern of response from the foreign buyers to market signals (see case history [3] on p. 351).
3. Our example may also be modified to study information propagation among persons in the developing economy (see case history [5] on

p. 351), though more periods must be added. Our analysis is equally applicable to technology acquisition between developed economies. With threatened quotas, the US government induced Toyota to co-produce cars in Fremont, California; it was the American car makers' opportunity to observe Japanese managerial expertise.

4   CONCLUSION

We have proposed an approach that is more explicit where information is concerned than the development literature.[10] We specify the content of, and channel for, information transmission in the emulative process. By capturing selected aspects of real life in our example, this study offers an information-theoretic approach for the fine-tuning of policy design.

Specifically, we distinguish 'lacking information' between (i) a coarse partition of information; and (ii) the inability to assess such information. Partitions can be associated with (possibly costly) actions of information-gathering (that is, a 'test'). How costly the test is may again depend upon how well- informed is the agent.

In the above example, to generate $S' = \{\{1,2,3\},\{4,5,6\}\}$, one may apply the test:

$$T(S') = e > \#(E)/2?$$

where $\#(E)$ = number of elements in set E. A negative (affirmative) answer corresponds to the set $\{1, 2, 3\}$ ($\{4, 5, 6\}$). The test comes with a cost $C[T(S')]$.

The alternative test:

$$T'' = |e - 7/2| = 5/2?$$

partitions E into $\{\{2,5\},\{1,3,4,6\}\}$. The application of both T'' and $T(S')$ generates the four-member partition, $\{\{1,3\},\{5\},\{2\},\{4,6\}\}$. By a union operation, we get a 'sufficient' partition: $\{\{1,3,5\},\{2,4,6\}\}$, which offers the maximum information value – as high as full information.

In a multi-period context, our approach identifies 'path-dependence'. It shows that it matters whether $T(S')$ or T'' is applied first. When used alone, $T(S')$ improves the value of information, but T'' does not. This cannot be shown with a numerical representation of information. Some industrialization policies (for example, export-led growth) may both acquire useful information and pay their own way. Others (for example, import substitution) may not do so.

Future extensions may elaborate on the fact that technical progress may involve the production of goods with 'more demanding characteristics', which are typically afforded only by the more affluent developed world. Manufacturing export to the North is therefore especially important. This may be studied using insights from Engel's Law, captured, for example, in Basu and Van (1998), with the Geary–Stone preference.

Returning to the descriptive issues mentioned in the Introduction above, the case studies presented and our subsequent analysis suggest certain points.

First, trade is essential in the emulative process because it is trade that induces technology transfer, which may induce another round of trade. However, it should be noted that the initial spark comes from trade and not from technology transfer. The foreign investment that brings technology is attracted to the sites of export platforms. One should also note that, as in the Wong–Watanabe case, the assembly of digital watches may require different equipment from that needed for the assembly of radios. Therefore, in the putty-clay context, gross investment will rise because of trade-induced technology progress.

Second, as wages rise, labour shortage may make the equipment underutilized in industries which arose during an early cheap-labour phase. Therefore, net capital accumulation may be seriously overstated, which could lead to the conclusions drawn by Young (1994) and Kim and Lau (1994).[11]

Third, both *laissez-faire* Hong Kong and state-guided Korea have benefited from similar outward-looking orientation. Hence the difference in the role played by the state may not matter all that much.

Fourth, the investment in all four Asian NIEs is largely market-driven. Unlike the Soviet Union, their consumption forgone has never been directed to outmoded equipment for outdated products. They cannot fail in the Soviet way.

Finally, from Lau and Wan (1994a), the technology transfer from Hong Kong has spurred growth across the border inside the PRC.[12] The phenomenon is clear-cut, since the growth rates are higher in locations closer to Hong Kong. This seems to indicate that Krugman (1994) may be too complacent about the Asian challenge. The slowing down of growth within the four NIEs does not necessarily imply the slowing-down of growth in Asia as a whole. Problems such as trade adjustment, resource shortage and environmental pressure, as discussed in Wan (1996), could become very serious.

Notes

1.   We appreciate the helpful comments received when earlier versions of this chapter were presented at Cornell University; the National Chengchi University, Taipei; the Institute of Economics, Academia Sinica, Nankang, Taiwan; and the Hong Kong University of Science and Technology. Special thanks are due

(chronologically) to our discussant Professor Peter Warr, Miss Nita Watts, an anonymous referee, and Professor Alan Woodland. Their advice enabled us to make great improvements. All remaining imperfections are our responsibility.

2. The role of direct foreign investment in technology diffusion is neither new nor an East Asian phenomenon. The English businessman, John Cockerill, was instrumental in spreading the Industrial Revolution to continental Europe via his Belgian investment (Henderson, 1954).

3. To simplify exposition, 'code words' *hot* and *wet* as well as *cooling* and *drying* are used for actual events and corresponding actions in our stylized example. The following quotations on machining and welding are cited to show that our example does capture the essence. On machining: 'Many decisions may be arrived at seemingly by "gut feeling". For instance, a machinist may be able to tell when a cutting tool is dull simply by looking at it...the general shape of wear scars on the top face, corner, and flank face of the tool, and in addition [s/he is able to] relate these features to events in the last machining pass. Changes in chip color, vibrations of the machine tool, and the surface finish obtained on the component are the first signs that the tool is becoming worn and should be checked at the end of the machining pass' (Wright and Bourne, 1988, p. 19); and on welding: 'Of interest are the effects of current, voltage, and travel speed on the quality of the weld. Because of the extremely large number of materials, electrodes, shielding gases, and other variables; an experimental design to determine the interaction effects is prohibitively large...Experienced welding engineers have encountered many of the interaction effects of these variables throughout their careers. They use this knowledge whenever they estimate the values for the welding situation they have not previously encountered. This knowledge, in the form of experience, was coupled with the knowledge of the steps they use to solve the problem' (Tonkay and Knott, 1989, pp. 647–8).

4. The transfer of knowledge by repeated observation is pervasive and manufacturing is no exception. This notion is implied in the following quotation: 'It takes many years for a person to acquire enough information to be called an expert. It usually takes a long time...to get the information out of the expert person... but hopefully not as long as it took the expert to acquire the information in the first place' (Wright and Bourne, 1988, p. 19).

5. The rate of return to supervisory effort, r_i is calculated as follows:

$$r_i = \frac{p_i E u_i(a,e) - a_{\alpha i} p_\alpha - a_{\beta i} p_\beta}{a_{\gamma i}}, \quad i = x, y, z$$

6. If this developing economy was intending to consume y it must import α and pay for it with 'food' export.

7. See case study [7].

8. In case history [2] the former employees of General Instruments did establish eleven firms to produce their product, which apparently contradicts the above discussion. In private communication, a former officer of General Instruments informed the second author that spin-off firms only entered when that product no longer commanded any innovators' profits. Thus the delayed competition does not offset the initial gain from wage-saving.

9. That is, an 'offshore' production basis.

10. See Easley and Kiefer (1988) for references on an alternative approach to such problems.

11. For a more detailed argument, see Van and Wan (1997).

12.   Hong Kong itself, however, does not exhibit a growth rate higher than its neighbours. That is because the rise of the ability to emulate is more than offset by the exhaustion of available technology that is easy to emulate. This is precisely why Verspagen (1991) derived a hat-shaped growth profile over time (see Lau and Wan, 1994b).

References

Amsden, A. H. (1989) *Asia's Next Giant: South Korea And Late Industrialization* (New York: Oxford University Press).

Amsden, A. H. and A. Singh (1994) 'The Optimal Degree of Competition and Dynamic Efficiency in Japan and Korea', *European Economic Review*, vol. 38, no. 3–4, pp. 941–51.

Basu, K. and P. H. Van (1998) 'The Economics of Child Labor', *American Economic Review* forthcoming.

Bhagwati, J. (1996) 'The "Miracle" that did not happen: Understanding East Asia in Comparative Perspective', in E. Thorbecke and H. Y. Wan (eds), *Government and Market: The Relevance of the Taiwanese Performance 1945–95* (Ithaca, NY: Cornell University Press).

Chu W. W. and J. J. Li (1996) 'Growth and Industrial Organization: A Comparative Study of the Bicycle Industry in Taiwan and Korea', *Journal of Industry Studies*, vol. 3, no. 1, pp. 35–52.

Easley, D. and N. Kiefer (1988) 'Controlling a Stochastic Process with Unknown Parameters', *Econometrica*, vol. 56, no. 5, pp. 1045–64.

Findlay, R. (1978) 'Some Aspects of Technology Transfer and Direct Foreign Investment', *American Economic Review*, vol. 68, no. 2, pp. 275–9.

Findlay, R. and S. Wellisz (1993) (eds), *The Political Economy of Poverty, Equity, and Growth: Five Open Economies* (New York: Oxford University Press).

Green, J. R. and J. J. Laffont (1979) *Incentives in Public Decision-Making* (New York: Elsevier North-Holland).

Grossman, G. M. and E. Helpman (1991) *Innovation and Growth in the Global Economy* (Cambridge, Mass: MIT Press).

Grossman, G. M. and E. Helpman (1995) 'Technology and Trade', in G. M. Grossman and K. Rogoff (eds), *Handbook of International Economics: Volume III* (Amsterdam: Elsevier).

Henderson, W. O. (1954) *Britain and Industrial Europe, 1750–1870: Studies in British Influence on the Industrial Revolution in Western Europe* (Liverpool: Liverpool University Press).

Kim, J.-I. and L. J. Lau (1994) 'The Sources of Economic Growth of East Asian Newly Industrialized Countries', *Journal of the Japanese and International Economies*, vol. 8, no. 3, pp. 235–71.

Komiya, R. (1972) 'Direct Foreign Investment in Post War Japan', in P. Drysdale (ed.), *Foreign Investment in Asia and the Pacific* (Toronto: University of Toronto Press).

Kojima, K. (1978) *Direct Foreign Investment: A Japanese Model, Multinational Business Operations* (London: Croom Helm).

Krugman, P. (1979) 'A Model of Innovation, Technology Transfer, and the World Distribution of Income', *Journal of Political Economy*, vol. 87, no. 2, pp. 253–66.

Krugman, P. (1994) 'The Myth of Asia's Miracle', *Foreign Affairs*, vol. 73, no. 6, pp. 62–78.

Lau M.-L. and H. Y. Wan Jr (1994a) 'The Hong Kong–Guangdong Nexus', mimeo, Cornell University, Ithaca, New York.

Lau M.-L. and H. Y. Wan Jr (1994b) 'On The Mechanism of Catching Up', *European Economic Review*, vol. 38, no. 3–4, pp. 952–63.

Levy, B. (1990) 'Transaction Costs, the Size of Firms and Industrial Policy: Lessons from a Comparative Case Study of the Footwear Industry in Korea and Taiwan', *Journal of Development Economics*, vol. 34, no. 1–2, pp. 151–78.

Lin, Y. and H. Y. Wan Jr (1996) 'Laissez Faire as a Source of Comparative Advantage – Experiences from the Taiwanese Machine Tool Industry', mimeo, Cornell University, Ithaca, New York.

Lucas, R. E. Jr (1988) 'On the Mechanics of Economic Development', *Journal of Monetary Economics*, vol. 22, no. 1, pp. 3–42.

Mann, J. (1989) *Beijing Jeep* (New York: Simon & Schuster).

Morawetz, D. (1981) *Why the Emperor's New Clothes Are Not Made in Colombia: A Case Study in Latin American and East Asian Manufacturing Export* (Oxford: Oxford University Press).

Nermuth, M. (1982) *Information Structures in Economics* (Berlin: Springer-Verlag).

Ozawa, T. (1979) *Multinationalism, Japanese Style: The Political Economy of Outward Dependency* (Princeton, NJ: Princeton University Press), esp. ch. 3.

Rivera-Batiz, L. and P. Romer (1992) 'Economic Integration and Endogenous Growth', in G. M. Grossman (ed.), *Imperfect Competition and International Trade* (Cambridge; Mass.: MIT Press), pp. 347–66.

Seetoo, D. H. (1992) 'Globalisation with Self-Owned Brands: The Case of Hongson', in N. T. Wang (ed.), *Taiwan's Enterprises in Global Perspective* (New York: M. E. Sharpe), pp. 327–41.

Tonkay, G. L. and K. Knott (1989) 'An Expert System for Welding', in S. T. Kumara, R. L. Kashyap and A. L. Soyster (eds), *Artificial Intelligence: Manufacturing Theory and Practice* (USA: The Institute of Industrial Engineers).

Uchida, H. (1991) 'The Transfer of Electrical Technologies from the U.S. and Europe to Japan: 1869–1914', in D. J. Jeremy (ed.), *International Technology Transfer: Europe, Japan and the U.S.A., 1700–1914* (Aldershot: Edward Elgar).

Van, P. H. and H. Y. Wan Jr (1997) 'Interpreting East Asian Growth', in B. S. Jensen and K. Y. Wong (eds), *Dynamics, Economic Growth and International Trade* (Ann Arbor, Mich.: University of Michigan Press).

Verspagen, B. (1991) 'A New Empirical Approach to Catching Up or Falling Behind', *Structural Change and Economic Dynamics*, vol. 2, no. 2, pp. 359–80.

Wan, H. Y. Jr (1993) 'Trade, Development and Inventions', in H. Herberg and N. V. Long (eds), *Current Issues in International Trade Theory* (Ann Arbor, Mich.: University of Michigan Press), pp. 239–54.

Wan, H. Y. Jr (1996) 'Six Challenges Facing the Chinese Economies', in L. F.-Y. Ng, and C. Tuan (eds), *Three Chinese Economies: China, Hong Kong, and Taiwan: Challenges and Opportunities* (Hong Kong: Chinese University Press), pp. 11–27.

Watanabe, S. (1980) 'Multinational Enterprises and Employment Oriented Appropriate Technologies in Developing Countries', *ILO Working Papers* (Multinational Enterprise Programme), no. 14.

Wong, F.-T. (1976) 'Country Paper, Hong Kong' in *Intra-national Transfer of Technology* (Tokyo: Asian Productivity Organization), pp. 2–3.

World Bank (1993) *The East Asian Miracle: Economic Growth and Public Policy* (New York: Oxford University Press).

Wright, P. K. and D. A. Bourne (1988) *Manufacturing Intelligence* (Reading, Mass.: Addison Wesley).

Young, A. (1994) 'Lessons from the East Asian NICS: A Contrarian View', *European Economic Review*, vol. 38, no. 3–4, pp. 964–73.

PART II
East Asia in Context

Contrast Among the Chinese Economies

Review of "Six Challenges Facing the Chinese Economies"*

Overview This Article cross-classifies economies by their size, and also their stage of development, to focus on issues to be faced by the economies of Hong Kong, Taiwan and Mainland China in their aspiration to become fully developed.

Four challenges face China, two of which are relevant in her aspiration to become "quasi-developed" like Hong Kong and Taiwan, and two more when China progresses further, towards full development.

To become quasi-developed, the tasks outlined in the Article are to induce a "reverse brain drain": from the Chinese staying overseas and to nurture private firms which alone have the vitality to spur the economy into sustained rapid growth on its own. To a great extent, these have been done by the government in the past decade, even though the record is not yet a complete success. The issue remains institutional. China is still operating under the rule of man, rather than the rule of law. But even then, progress has been made.

To develop further, China must take into full consideration the resource scarcity and environmental fragility of the economy. Actually, China has faced such issues, even before reaching the stage of full development. In recent years, it seems the challenges have arrived earlier than it was predicted in the Article. See Diamond (2005) for a related discussion.

Hong Kong and Taiwan face different problems: how to keep their wage rates higher than the Chinese, when all these economies can produce essentially the same set of goods. The two challenges most applicable for them are: to nurture professionalism in management and to be innovative in product design, etc. On such issues, neither of the economies has gained full success. Taiwan is slightly better off in that de-industrialization has gone less far than Hong Kong.

Some detailed facts The evolution of and interaction between Hong Kong, Taiwan and Mainland China and the comparison among these three economies are very instructive about what takes for successful development. As late comers in industrialization, one must utilize all advantages coming one's way — low

---

*The article first appeared in *Three Chinese Economies — China, Hong Kong and Taiwan: Challenges and Prospects*, Linda F. Y. Ng and Chyau Tuan (eds.), pp. 11–27, 1996. Permission has been obtained from The Chinese University of Press for reprint in this volume.

labor cost, opportunities to acquire technology from abroad, market discipline, and a sufficiently transparent body of the rules of game are all important so that one can attract the most number of the talented and nurture the local industrial base. The case histories of three successful firms are illuminating.

(a) The Taiwan Semiconductor Manufacturing Company (TSMC) in Taiwan is the world's first and the largest "dedicated chip foundry". It was founded by Morris Chang, who was born in Mainland China, studied in Hong Kong, and went from there to America to study and work for 37 years, only to be attracted to Taiwan in 1985 to launch TSMC, a firm with government stocks but managed like any private firm.

(b) Hon Hai Precision Industry Company is the largest manufacturing firm in Taiwan founded by Terry Gou who — born in Taiwan to a family from Mainland China — started his private firm in Taiwan, serving American, Japanese and Finnish clients in electronics parts and assembly, with his principal production base located in Mainland China, on the border of Hong Kong and under a Taiwanese management team.

(c) The Netac Technology Co. of Shenzhen, China, near Hong Kong, is a pioneering firm in mobile storage, started by a Chinese entrepreneur educated in America, and had successfully established its intellectual property right in American courts.

Two elements can be discerned from these firms:

(i) Some of the common elements from the three cases above are the source of technology which comes from America, the manpower from Taiwan or Mainland China, and the transportation/communication infrastructure of Hong Kong. All of them have thrived in the free wheeling world market in a manner like the private enterprises.

(ii) The apparent improvement of the regulatory environment has taken place over time in Mainland China. In the early days, the environment was not friendly to the market force so that firms like the TSMC did not arise in Mainland China, notwithstanding the presence of low cost labor. Later, official discretion was necessary to interpret the laws and regulations to allow private firms to compete, according to Hsing (1998). This is the time firms like Hon Hai can be attracted to operate its fabrication operations there. More recently, start-up firms like Netac can blossom in China. This corroborates the view of Fung et al. (2005) that transparent institutions and a "deeper" reform are most effective in attracting foreign investment to China. The latter in turn is the key to technology acquisition.

Six Challenges Facing the Chinese Economies

Henry Wan, Jr.
Cornell University, U.S.A.

I. INTRODUCTION

At present, the three Chinese economies of Hong Kong, Taiwan and mainland China share two characteristics. In terms of growth rates, all these three enjoy respectable sustained performances which are impressive to Westerners. But in terms of per capita output, none of these three is "fully developed" in the sense of America, Japan or the Scandinavian states. Thus, continued growth is their common goal. To achieve their aspirations, these economies must identify and overcome the challenges facing them. This is not an easy task since these economies are all in transition, economically, sociologically and politically, heading toward unchartered waters. Their future cannot possibly be a simple extrapolation of their past. Moreover, the economic literature contains no well-developed theories for guidance.

It is important that we recognize at the outset that the best one can offer is educated speculation.

To make the discussion policy-relevant, one must draw insights from both economic theory and the historical record. History rarely repeats itself. To apply lessons from the past to issues facing the present, *mutatis mutandis*, one needs some theoretical framework. Theoretical analysis deduces sharp conclusions from simple, tractable scenarios, under a host of *ceteris paribus* assumptions. To make such results practically helpful, one also needs the historical perspective.

For illustration, let us consider the following important example. The industrialization of Hong Kong and Taiwan depended upon a labour force with high efficiency and low wage rates. Hourly wages in Hong Kong and Taiwan have never been low, compared to less developed lands like Bangladesh. Labour cost is low, only because the output per worker is quite high. The important question is then, how do these East Asian labour forces become so efficient, compared to those workers elsewhere, with comparable educational, social and perhaps ethno-cultural backgrounds? The issue is not just a matter of incentives. The labour forces in Hong Kong and Taiwan still perform better under similar reward systems. In many instances, an immediate answer is in on-the-job training programmes, which train the workers to produce outputs of high quality. Some economists therefore would attribute such human capital formation to "education", an interpretation which is certainly not wrong, yet for the sake of policy, it is also not entirely right. Unless there were an immediate payoff, no one would finance such highly job-specific programmes, certainly not as part of general, formal schooling.

Such labour skill may also be viewed as acquired through learning-by-doing. This interpretation is again quite correct descriptively, as such training is on an on-the-job basis, but as we shall see, unless such a conscious training programme is explicitly recognized, one omits the Danish prince from *Hamlet*. Such a programme is typically well-focused, training labour skills for outputs of a quality higher than is affordable on the local market, in view of the low local wage, and hence income. Thus, only in outward-oriented economies can such a training programme justify itself. This perhaps explains why in Hong Kong and Taiwan, labour is trained to produce high quality output, while in the insular market of India, the indigenous management of joint ventures often argues that the insistence of foreign partners for high product quality is rather pointless.

Again, on-the-job training programmes in Hong Kong and Taiwan are cost-effective, perhaps only because they are not reinvented on the spur of the moment. They often represent the tried-and-true systems transplanted by Japanese (or U.S.) multinationals (Watanabe 1980) which were forced by rising Japanese wages to relocate their factories. In this sense, the product cycle theory is highly relevant. On the other hand, the reason why Japanese firms invest in Hong Kong and Taiwan but not elsewhere may be related to a host of factors, from a hospitable policy of the host government to certain Sino-Japanese historical-cultural ties which economize the transaction cost (Kojima 1978).

The above example is important. It illustrates that, based upon simplistic interpretations of any current theory, one cannot formulate a policy to replicate the economic performance of Hong Kong and Taiwan.

The industrialization of Hong Kong and Taiwan bears some family resemblance to that of Japan, yet there are many differences. Much Japanese industrial competence was acquired either during the desperate and futile efforts in war during World War II, or because of the offshore procurement policies of the U.S. during the Korean conflict (for example, Morishima 1982). Foreign investment in pre-World War II days also helped, but perhaps to a lesser degree. The Japanese established their world-wide market channels and brand names on their own, but these were also utilized by them later to market goods made in Hong Kong and Taiwan, at least in the early phases (Levy 1990). In many ways, Hong Kong and Taiwan had an easier time than Japan in breaking into the world market, but they now also have a harder time becoming operationally independent, as well as establishing niches in the up-scale markets. Thus for policy purposes, reliance on historical analogy alone may again lead to misleading forecasts.

In many ways, the current development of mainland China resembles the earlier development of Taiwan and Hong Kong. Yet, in other aspects, it has its own rhythm and challenges. These will be discussed below, in due course.

II. PRELIMINARY CONSIDERATIONS

Broadly speaking, the developmental problems facing an economy depend upon both the "size" of its population and the "phase" of its development. The population of an economy can be "large", as for mainland China, "medium", as for Japan, and "small" as for Taiwan and Hong Kong. Economies can also be classified as "developing", like mainland China's, "quasi-developed", like Taiwan's and Hong Kong's and "developed" like Japan's. To proceed from a "developing" to a "quasi-developed" phase, an economy faces certain problems and needs certain policies. These are different from those of an economy proceeding from a "quasi-developed" to a "developed" phase.

It also matters whether an economy is a technology leader or follower, and whether an economy is culturally or geographically distant from the developed world.

India, Japan and the three Chinese economies are non-western societies. They all industrialize at a time when the West enjoys technological leadership. This is a fact one cannot ignore. It is a historical lesson that cross-fertilization is crucial to technological progress. Historically, Chinese culture stagnated after the Tang dynasty perhaps partly because of its geographical isolation from all the other centres of high culture, from Western Europe to the Indus-Ganges plain. The collapse of the Soviet economy has many causes. Its failure to interact with the non-communist world has certainly played a major role, causing its technical backwardness in the Electronic Age.

What confronts a backward and non-western economy is a two-fold problem, first, to develop its own economy by utilizing all that western technology can offer, and then, to continue to interact with the West so as to become a full partner. The former is a task which has been handled successfully by Hong Kong and Taiwan. Their record serves as a useful reference to mainland China. The latter is an area where Japan has risen up to the challenge. The Japanese experience is clearly relevant to both Hong Kong and Taiwan.

But neither Japan, Taiwan nor Hong Kong has a population so large that by the very act of becoming fully developed can it affect the world economy much. In this aspect mainland China belongs to a separate category. Whether and how mainland China will fully develop poses resource and environmental problems of a global scale. One cannot possibly dismiss them in any serious discussion.

The next three sections are devoted to the various specific challenges:

(a) in becoming quasi-developed, and
(b) in becoming (fully) developed, as well as
(c) the consequences of having a large population.

In each of these three challenges, we focus upon the two most important aspects, making six in total. Some concluding remarks follow, concerning the interactions among these three.

To summarize, we present Table 2.1.

Section III discusses how the mainland Chinese economy can become *quasi-developed*. The principal issue is ideological, and the main challenges are:

Table 2.1 Economies and Theories

Types of Economies	Population Sizes			Theories
	Small	Medium	Large	
Development Phases: Fully Developed	Switzerland Benelux The "Nordics" ↑	*Japan Germany, France, Italy, U.K.*	U.S. ↑	New Growth Theory
	—— (b) —— ↑	————	—— (c) —— ↑	———— New Trade
Quasi-developed	*Hong Kong Taiwan*	——	↑	Theory
	————	————	—— (a) —— ↑	————
Less Developed	——	——	**Mainland China**	Ditto Institutional Economics Economic Demography Environmental Economics

Note: Italics for non-western societies; Bold for planned economy.

(a) to induce a "reversed brain drain" and

(b) to nurture private firms into well-established efficient enterprises.

Section IV discusses how Hong Kong and Taiwan can become (fully) developed. The issue is socio-cultural, and the main challenges are:

(a) the cultivation of professionally managed enterprises, and

(b) the acquisition of industrial niches, specifically, to market products of innovative design.

Section V discusses additional issues for the mainland Chinese economy to become (fully) developed. The issue is technological, and the challenges are:

(a) to achieve growth without being hampered by resource constraints, and

(b) to achieve growth without causing undue global environmental stress.

On these questions, the literature on economic theory offers much insight, but no concrete conclusions. It is for us to apply the available tools selectively and appropriately.

For the ideological issues facing mainland China today, one may refer to various writings in Institutional Economics, which are applicable to the current market transition of China. For the acquisition of market niches by Hong Kong and Taiwan, one may benefit from the extensive literature on the New Trade Theory, where product differentiation, innovation and product cycles are considered. Broadly speaking, goods with a high value-added ratio are often the fruits of the innovative process, produced under increasing returns and facing monopolistic competition. Such products typically are "skill intensive". The acquisition of such skill is a matter of human (or "knowledge") capital formation, as studied in the extensive literature on the New Growth Theory. The prospect of a fully developed China raises issues of both Resource Economics and Environmental Economics, as well as Economic Demography.

III. THE ROAD TO QUASI-DEVELOPMENT: THE ECONOMIC CONSEQUENCES OF IDEOLOGY

Among the non-western World, economies in both East Asia and South Asia share a common characteristic: the scarcity of resources per capita. Contrary to the popular view, the saving/income ratios of these economies are not low relative to Great Britain and America, however their per capita real income is low in absolute terms. In such an economy, the improvement of real income per capita depends on the capacity for the formation and the utilization of human capital. The key is often not how to produce more of the same goods, but to attain a higher value of outputs with the same inputs. In the New Trade Theory, what distinguishes a developing economy from a developed economy is that whatever the former can produce, so can the latter, and whatever the latter alone can produce is demanded by all (for example, Krugman 1979). These factors decide whether one can afford imported resources and goods which are needed to support a high standard of living.

Nowadays, many such developing economies export manufactured goods to Europe and America. For example, apparel made in Bangladesh is widely marketed in the U.S. Typically, foreign direct investment and sub-contracting relationships are fruitful means of acquiring foreign technology at the early stage of industrialization. According to Uchida (1991) and Lall (1987), Japan in the late nineteenth century and India in the twentieth century have both experimented with import substitution as well as the limitation of foreign direct investment, both with unsatisfactory outcomes. As pointed out by Komiya (1972), in the first decades of the twentieth century, Japan welcomed foreign direct investment and this laid the foundations of both its automobile and its electric appliance industries. Significantly, once a sufficient level of industrial competence was acquired, Japan had no more need for the return of foreign direct investment after World War II.

What sets Hong Kong and Taiwan apart from the more recently industrialized economies (say, Cyprus and Mauritius) is their ability to shift their export mix from perfectly competitive commodities like shirts, to imperfectly competitive goods, like personal computers. For the former, all that is needed is a hardy, effective labour force. For the latter, one needs a labour force with creativity and expertise, and a well-established network of sub-supplier chains.

To be specific, according to Uchida (1991), a "reversed brain drain" occurred in Japan as early as in the late Meiji era, when people working in the West brought home technology on their return. This contributed to the acquisition of industrial competence. After World War II, with Japan already possessing the critical mass of technical manpower, firms like Sony refused to produce under foreign trademarks, but marketed products under their own brand name (Morita 1986).

A similar development has begun in Taiwan. Especially in the electronics industry, a sizeable number of experienced engineers and scientists have returned from America, helping to build up an information industry around the Hsinchu Science-based Industrial Park. More recently, firms like Acer have also begun to ship products of their own design and under their own brand name.

These need not be the only channels for acquiring foreign technology and competing in the world market, but history suggests that these are effective ones. Based upon tried-and-true acumen acquired inside the environment of industrially advanced societies, repatriate technical manpower can help firms to seize business opportunities as they see fit. It is a cost-effective option when compared to the alternative of competing for world market niches with purely domestically launched efforts. This is different from working under subcontracts, licensed production, or joint ventures, where the foreign partners have both the ability and the motive to keep local firms from becoming a rival in their favoured market. The mark of the genuine maturation of an industrial society is the growth of domestic private firms without government sheltering. Those firms who succeed under the baptism of competitive fire are more likely to be fitter than those which arise under state assistance. Significantly, according to Morishima (1982), Meiji Japan quickly privatized its state-owned heavy industry, when such firms piled up loss after loss. Recently, Taiwan was also forced to modify its protectionist policy on automobiles as the heavily protected Yueloon Motors failed to compete well, notwithstanding decades of government sheltering.

In fact, by such standards, the self-propelled rise of the Evergreen Marine Line is more indicative of the vigour of the Taiwanese economy than the growth of the government nurtured *chaebuls* are of the Korean economy's strength.

In assessing the long-term performance of the mainland Chinese economy, especially regarding its attempt to catch up with the Asian Newly Industrialized Economies (NIEs), these remain to be the only valid standards to apply.

Both in inducing a "reversed brain drain" and in cultivating private businesses, the current mainland Chinese economy suffers from ideological constraints of its own making.

Legally, private enterprises can operate either in rather limited spheres (like taxi operators), or in the guise of rural co-operatives, an arrangement which provides "political correctness". Yet, due to past history, from the "Anti-Rightist Campaign" to the more recent sporadic crack-downs in the aftermath of 1989, such local entrepreneurs perceive that they do not share the same *de facto* legitimacy enjoyed by their counterparts (and rivals!) in Hong Kong and Taiwan.

In contrast, firms in Taiwan operate under a stable but well understood *modus operandi*. According to Chu (1990), a great majority of firms under-report their taxes to a certain extent, with corrupt tax officials acquiescing. Those which "exceed certain limits" are prosecuted and punished. But by no stretch of imagination would any future government on that island suddenly condemn more than 90% of all private firms for tax evasion, by the full severity of the existing laws. *De jure*, that could be and perhaps should be done, but *de facto*, it will never be. The state continues to receive a diminished but largely adequate revenue, rarely running a budget deficit of a size comparable to that of OECD economies. Businessmen continue to operate in full legitimacy with a great sense of security. The working class enjoys a rapidly rising wage level under a continuing labour shortage. According to Chen *et al.* (1991), the state sector in Taiwan remains quite sizeable and inefficient, yet these industries are held in ridicule, not enshrined in the constitution as in mainland China. It is far from Utopia, but the complaints are far from serious.

Likewise, repatriate technical manpower is among those who lived for decades under western democracy where racism, crime and income inequality coexist with a high degree of personal and press freedom. Dissent may not always be effective, but it is tolerated in the society. Justice is not always done in the snarled courts with wrong-doers being defended by the best legal brains money can buy. When they return to Taiwan, repatriates find an environment less ideal in many ways, but not that strikingly unfamiliar. They can concentrate on their work, no longer under the incipient socio-cultural disadvantages of western societies. Their foreign-reared children may come back with rather radical views not deemed fully acceptable locally. Yet they would not get into immediate trouble.

In contrast, the environment in mainland China, even today, poses an entirely different set of problems. "Spiritual pollution" is still officially warned as dangerous. "Peaceful evolution" by any means is deemed an evil plot. Bourgeois democracy is the original sin in that land of Marxism-Leninism. Would-be repatriate engineers and scientists are largely apolitical. Yet, they perceive that in mainland China they may easily blunder into a political minefield, right and left, if they pull up their stakes in the West.

It is often argued in mainland China today that political ideology does not affect economic performance. Recent events make such a view dubious. It is in Taiwan and *not* in mainland China that the "reversed brain drain" has brought back many experienced former employees of foreign high-tech firms. It is in mainland China and *not* in Taiwan that entrepreneurs indulge in "short-term behaviour," rushing to emigrate after making a fast buck.

As a show case, the Rong family may enjoy political prominence, but do not head a lean-and-mean operation rivalling Acer or the Evergreen Marine Line, let alone Sony or Kyocera.

The future of the mainland Chinese economy is inseparable from the future of the mainland's political development. Various papers in Xu (1990) provide the institutional facts of this complex topic. The situation can best be understood by approaching it from the New Institutional

Economics — an emerging theory based upon the twin concepts of incomplete markets and incomplete contracts (for example, Kreps 1990). The essence of the theory is that the production process involves uninsurable risks, and no enforceable contract can encompass all those specific details crucial to the interpersonal relationships underpinning the modern economy. For production efficiency, the private ownership system assigns shares of profit stream to motivate decision-makers within the production system.

The insistence on the system of *ownership by the entire people* is enshrined in the current constitution of the People's Republic of China, along with the *leading role* of the Chinese Communist Party. The abandonment of the former is perceived as eroding the prestige of the latter. Yet, short of affirming the full political correctness of private ownership of Chinese firms by Chinese citizens, all expediencies devised so far appear to be problematical.

The "responsibility contract" system may motivate the manager to fulfil production quotas with apparent efficiency. Whether equipment and facilities are well maintained is not assured, in practice, let alone such issues like product development, brand reputation or institution-building.

The "profit-loss accountability" of state firms may promote efficient operations, but employees have no interest in reporting large taxable profit rather than spending the revenue on themselves and claiming that as a necessary expense.

The need for entrepreneurs to purchase "political correctness" in the guise of "local co-operatives" or "foreign-related joint ventures" makes their position vulnerable to extortion of every kind.

Attempts to control various irregularities have created a plethora of regulations, constraints, and opportunities for another host of civil servants to abuse their discretion for personal gain.

Even the increase in competitive pressure leads to difficulties. Many state firms fail to be competitive, not because of their inefficiency, but because they are saddled with responsibilities towards their retired employees. Those who survive may not be the fittest.

The above discussion does not argue that one should adopt one ideology or another on non-economic grounds. But ideologies, have their economic consequences. One can only ignore such facts at one's own peril.

IV. THE ROAD TO DEVELOPMENT:
THE ECONOMICS OF INSTITUTIONS AND CULTURE

The economic challenges facing Hong Kong and Taiwan are of a different sort. At present, the industrial competence of mainland China has been rising. Yet in dollar terms, the wage cost there has not. Paradoxically, the more desperate the state finance in mainland China is, the more likely the regime is to opt for inflation and hence devaluation. Hence, the more competitive its exports will be. To fend off competition and to take advantage of the difference in wage costs, many firms in both Hong Kong and Taiwan have moved their downstream production operations to mainland China. The reduction of wage cost allows the expansion of the downstream operations at the new site. The added demand for upstream inputs helps to absorb the reassigned labour force in Hong Kong and Taiwan, often into higher-paid jobs. What is retained is often a type of production process demanding more skill. But this process will end with the reallocation of the entire production process. This situation has been experienced by Japan before, when parts of its own industry were relocated to Hong Kong and Taiwan, a couple of decades ago. The countermeasure for Japan then was to produce goods with even higher quality and skill requirements, often by marketing commodities which had first been introduced to Japan, such as artificial fibre and electronic products. The threat facing both Hong Kong and Taiwan (as well as Singapore and South Korea) now is their inability, thus far, to market high quality, locally designed products, competing against Japan and other advanced economies.

Their inability to compete against Japan in upscale markets appears to be quite natural, since the latter is an economy with both a larger home market and a longer history of industrialization. But this is not so. In Europe, certain small economies like the four Scandinavian states, the three Benelux states, Austria and Switzerland, do not seem to share the same difficulties. They produce top-of-the-line products competing against firms in Italy, the U.K., France and Germany. Each of these small economies succeeds in capturing a set of niches on its own. By that token, Hong Kong and Taiwan today have not yet realized their true market potentials. The true nature of such shortcomings remains elusive. Our discussion below is necessarily speculative.

There is much similarity between firms in these small European states and firms in Hong Kong and Taiwan: they are flexible in identifying and seizing opportunities in the world market and they often enter into joint ventures and subcontracting arrangements with foreign firms. But the differences are also marked. These European firms usually enjoy a reputation for producing top-of-the-line specialty goods and services. In contrast, firms in Hong Kong and Taiwan are often regarded as imitators who can only compete on price. The vicious circle of low reputation, thus low quality, and thus low reputation is discussed in Chiang and Masson (1988).

To move upscale, the challenges facing firms in Hong Kong and Taiwan are many, but among these two seem to be the most important. First, the Chinese enterprises are overly "person-based": they rarely employ professional management teams, and they have difficulties in retaining their best employees. At the present stage of development, productivity and wages rise rapidly. As a consequence, output-mixes also change in quick succession. The present high rate of personnel turnover may actually facilitate the diffusion of technology. But this is not helpful in developing proprietary technology and brand reputation, which are essential for high quality products. In the European context, the excellence of an outfit does not depend upon continued management under the original founder. Second, the Chinese enterprises have not developed marketing skills comparable to that of their European counterparts. They can offer goods and services of a relatively simple nature, such as ocean transportation, but not complex products, involving intricate design, such as upscale cameras, watches, and cars. These goods are what the Japanese succeeded in producing and marketing decades ago. Paradoxically, as a people, the Chinese do have design talents (e.g. in architecture), marketing experience (e.g. in shipping), and global connections in science and technology (e.g. the network which has given rise to the Hsinchu Science-based Industrial Park), as well as the traditional high regard for established brand names (e.g. in traditional businesses such as restaurants, liquor, herbal medicine, etc.). Yet, they have not been able to "get their act together" in offering top-of-the-line goods and services on the world market.

It would be simple to attribute all this to political uncertainties, such as Beijing's political claims over both Hong Kong and Taiwan. Since the current regime in mainland China does not have a long pro-business record, the firms in Hong Kong and Taiwan may not take the long view. But the matter seems to be more complex. After all, Singapore also has a Chinese society. It enjoys a perceived political stability which Hong Kong and

Taiwan lack. Up to now, Singapore has not done any better than Hong Kong and Taiwan in introducing upscale products of its own in the world market.

It would also be simple to assert that Chinese firms, wherever they are, suffer daunting cultural barriers in carving out highly coveted product niches in the world market. However, similarly located in a non-western society, Japanese firms do not seem to find such handicaps insurmountable.

All one can say now is that the challenges exist. They are not insurmountable, but can be overcome with conscious effort and time.

V. THE PROBLEMS OF A POPULOUS COUNTRY

We must now face some most intractable facts of life, which work against mainland China's aspiration of becoming fully developed. Currently, mainland China has more than four times the population of America. Whatever could reasonably be done in population policy, the Chinese population would not fall for many decades. Given the fact that the United States has the lion's share in the worldwide consumption of several key commodities, like petroleum, the arrival of China as a fully developed economy would cause havoc in the world market for such goods.

Broadly speaking, the challenges confronting mainland China are of two types:

First, the living standard of a developed economy requires a very high level of resource usage. Some of these like water, arable land as well as residential land must be supplied locally, and an "adequate" supply may not be possible. Others, like petroleum and natural gas, can be imported, in principle. But given the need to satisfy a population exceeding a billion, world trade can only transform the shortage of one economy to the shortage for the entire world. Worsening terms of trade and an export gap may be in store.

Secondly, even if enough resources can be obtained for the economy, one must still contend with the possibility of environmental degradation through acid rain, global warming or waste disposal, for example.

The practical implications are three-fold. All avenues for conservation must be explored, and an aggressive policy for population control must be preserved. Furthermore, if it is at all necessary, per capita consumption must be kept in check, until the population size has been greatly reduced.

This also imposes some delicate requirements in political development.

Further economic development requires democratization as well as a firm, long-term policy on demography, resources and the environment. These two requirements may well not mix.

VI. SOME CONCLUDING OBSERVATIONS

So far, we have considered the separate development of the three Chinese economies. We must now shift to issues of their economic integration and, in particular, how that process would influence their future development.

Recently, both laymen and economists have been excited by the implications of the economic integration of Hong Kong, Taiwan and China. This topic has aroused so much interest simply because first, the mainland Chinese economy, despite its scale advantages, has been lagging far behind the economies of Hong Kong and Taiwan in per capita terms, and second, the process of economic integration is viewed as a means to revitalize its performance. In contrast, if the economies of Sri Lanka and India were to merge into one, that would create much less excitement, not just because the populations of India and Sri Lanka are respectively somewhat smaller than those of mainland China and Hong Kong/Taiwan, but principally because the Sri Lankan economy is not expected to affect the post-integration aggregate economy much. Thus, quantitatively speaking, the integrated economy would not be appreciably different from a pre-integration Indian economy.

The situation is expected to be quite different for the three Chinese economies, and such expectations are in fact anchored in recent events.

The current economic reform in mainland China and the increased trade-cum-investment flow among the three Chinese economies have had a pronounced impact. Productivity, output, trade and export surplus have all grown in mainland China while profits have also risen for firms in Hong Kong and Taiwan. In fact, these three economies have become an island of prosperity within a world in recession. Western observers extrapolate such trends and predict that these, in turn, will smoothly bring these three economies to further growth.

Neo-classic economic theory also provides optimistic predictions of economic integration. It concludes that when barriers to the movement of productive factors and goods are removed, productive efficiency should rise so that those who gain can afford to compensate for those who lose, and everyone can be better off. Such predictions are made on assumptions of perfect information and complete markets.

However, we know for a fact that the neo-classic analysis is largely beside the point. What matters to the development of mainland China, and in particular to Guangdong Province, is not so much the flow of physical capital, but the human capital which has come with direct foreign investment. Jacob Viner has shown that to benefit from the inflow of foreign physical capital, an economy must run an import surplus, but mainland China enjoys an export surplus instead. Likewise, the fact that no important segment of the economies of Hong Kong and Taiwan is suffering is due to the "backward linkage" of the South China boom, and not to any side payment. The situation fits the product cycle theory well, yet that theory has so far not been exhaustively studied. One must turn to recent economic history for insight.

Two scenarios may be sketched for reference:

(a) The East Asian model, where the prosperity of Japan spills over to the Asian NIEs and the next NIEs of Thailand, Malaysia and Indonesia. As long as the advanced member, Japan, continues its advance, all ends well.

(b) The Eastern Europe-Soviet Union model, where post-World War II economic integration under Council for Mutual Economic Assistance (CMEA) provided both a supply of high quality products to the Soviets without requiring any hard currency payment, and unopposed market expansion for East German, Czechoslovak and Hungarian industries. However, by concentrating on such easy conquests, the technically more advanced industries in Eastern Europe eventually lost their vitality. Their industries eventually ended in stagnation, backwardness and collapse. This is a case of "united we fail."

For Hong Kong and Taiwan, much may also be learnt from the post-World War II Finnish economy. The latter prospered on Soviet trade and then suffered with the Soviet collapse. Symbiosis with a large, inefficient and potentially unstable neighbour is always a calculated risk. But the choices facing Hong Kong and Taiwan may be even tougher than those for Finland. In certain export markets, the combination of mainland wages and the technology and market access of Hong Kong can outcompete Taiwan, left by itself, and the same holds for PRC-Taiwan coalition against Hong

Kong. Likewise, a PRC-South Korea combination can undercut Hong Kong as well as Taiwan, should both refrain from working with PRC. The challenges are not insurmountable. But it takes the public airing of issues and the goodwill of various interest groups to devise an optimal course of action, and to implement it by sharing possible sacrifices.

This perhaps supplies us with a cautionary note: for Hong Kong and Taiwan to prosper in the long run, and in fact to be of any long-term use to the mainland Chinese economy, they must continue to compete in the world market for product niches of higher and higher quality, just as the Japanese have been doing all along. This is not an "easy way out" at all. In fact, there is no true "easy way out" in the long run, within our world of continuous technological dynamism.

REFERENCES

Chen, Shih-Meng, et al. (1991). *Disintegrating KMT-State Capitalism, A Closer Look at Privatizing Taiwan's State-and-Party-Owned Enterprises* (Text in Chinese). Taipei: Taipei Society.

Chiang, Shih-Chen and Robert T. Masson (1988). "Domestic Industrial Structure and Export Quality." *International Economic Review*, 29, pp. 262–270.

Chu, Cyrus (1990). "A Model of Income Tax Evasion with Venal Tax Officials." *Public Finance*, 45, pp. 392–408.

Kojima, Kiyoshi (1978). *Direct Foreign Investment: A Japanese Model, Multinational Business Operations*. London: Croom Helm.

Komiya, Ryutaro (1972). "Direct Foreign Investment in Post War Japan." In *Foreign Investment in Asia and the Pacific*, edited by Peter Drysdale. Toronto: University of Toronto Press.

Kreps, David (1990). *A Course in Micro-economic Theory*. Princeton, New Jersy: Princeton University Press.

Krugman, Paul (1979). "A Model of Innovation, Technology Transfer, and the World Distribution of Income." *Journal of Political Economy*, 87, pp. 253–266.

Lall, Sanjaya (1987). *Learning to Industrialize: The Acquisition of Technological Capability by India*. Hampshire: Macmillan.

Levy, Brian (1990). "Transaction Costs, the Size of Firms and the Industrial Policy: Lessons from a Comparative Case Study of the Footwear Industry in Korea and Taiwan." *Journal of Development Economics*, 34, pp. 151–178.

Morishima, Michio (1982). *Why Has Japan "Succeeded"? Western Technology and Japanese Ethos*. Cambridge: Cambridge University Press.

Morita, Akio (1986). *Made in Japan: Morita, Akio and Sony*. New York: Dutton.

Uchida, Hoshimi (1991). "The Transfer of Electrical Technologies from the U.S. and Europe to Japan: 1869–1914." In *International Technology Transfer: Europe, Japan and the U.S.A., 1700–1914*, edited by David J. Jeremy. Aldershot: E. Elgar.

Watanabe, Susumu (1980). "Multinational Enterprises and Employment Oriented Appropriate Technologies in Developing Countries." *ILO Working Papers* (Multinational Enterprise Programme), No. 14.

Xu, Dianjing, *et al.*, eds. (1990). *China's Economic Reform: Analysis, Reflections and Prospects* (Text in Chinese). Hong Kong: The Chinese University Press.

Alternative Approaches for the Industrial Structure

Review of "Specialization Pattern and Multistaged Growth: The Korea-Taiwan Comparison", jointly with Toshiyahu Kato[*]

Overview This Article has a novel emphasis: the transformation of the industrial structure is the byproduct of globalization. Before the taking-off of industrialization, firms in all societies are perfectly competitive. Goods they supply are more-of-the-same: offering neither specialty nor expertise. While whether there will be a transformation is decided by globalization, what form the transformation will take is dependent on development strategy. Thus, Korea and Taiwan differ in their own transformation trajectories. This is so even though the ultimate goal for all developing economies is to achieve high value-added per capita, with firms having their own product design, brand name, and so on.

Consider Japan and China which are very special in their historical preconditions; and Hong Kong and Singapore which are atypical for their small size. Within East Asia where profound transformations took place, the Korea-Taiwan comparison provides much insight for development studies.

Some salient features At the beginning of Korean industrialization, the government supported business groups massively to achieve scale economy (Stern, et al 1995). Currently, oligopolistic Korean firms may not yet have that much specialized R&D, but they excel in the fabrication process. In contrast, the small and medium Taiwanese firms target niche markets. As monopolistically competitive enterprises, they rely on specialized expertise, such as "first to market", but not sophisticated technology.

Both economies have their successes, but their lag behind both Japan and Western Europe becomes increasingly conspicuous. In the face of the 1997 Crisis and later the adjustments to the massive Chinese export expansion, the average growth rates of both Korea and Taiwan have slowed down. Measured by the ratio of their per capita income to that of the world's leading economy (namely, America), the slowing down of their growth happens at a much earlier phase than Japan.

---

[*]The article is reprinted from the *Review of Development Economics*, Vol. 5, No. 2, pp. 256–265, 2001, published by Blackwell.

At present, quite a few of the most successful firms in both economies either have a fair portion of foreign-owned stock shares, or enjoy some brand name recognition worldwide, or both, like cars from Hyundai Motors and cell phones from Samsung in Korea, as well as personal computers from Acer in Taiwan. Both economies also produce intermediate goods, such as memory chips from Samsung and mother boards from Asustek. These are sold to a few industrial clients with long association, like Dell and Hewlett-Packard. The need for mass marketing is bypassed, along with sales promotion and after-sales services.

Which is the superior choice? Different economists apparently favor different strategies. Mody (1990), for example, is an early observer predicting Korean supremacy in electronics. Others like Aw, Chung and Roberts (2003) are more impressed by the competitive selection among firms in Taiwan. The evidence from the latter is summarized in their own words:

> "Taiwanese industries are characterized by less concentrated market structure, more producer turnover, smaller within-industry productivity dispersion across producers, a smaller percentage of plants operating at low productivity levels, and smaller productivity differentials between surviving and failing producers."

Specific industrial examples At the industry level, Kuo and Wang (2001) found that for products with infrequent change, like the black and white or color television, Korean firms would commit more capital and perfect their fabrication technology to guarantee lower cost and better quality, until they eventually trounce their Taiwanese rivals. So the Taiwanese firms would gravitate to products of frequent change, like the monitor for personal computers, where the Korean firms would decline to compete. Operating in the usual Korean way, with heavy fixed investment at every change, is too costly.

In memory chips, Fuller, Akinwande and Sodini (2005) found that after receiving technology transfers from foreign firms (who unload their less profitable technology), it takes "patient capital" to innovate and keep up. Due to the high fixed cost for both R&D and the production facilities, three of the seven Taiwanese firms left the sector, and the remaining four find it hard to get foreign sources of technology in join ventures. Among the Korean firms, Samsung built up its competence over a long period, and Hyundai had to sustain losses for 10 years, before becoming a major supplier. By the opinion of Taiwanese firms, viability for a firm requires at least 15% share of the world market.

Cause and effect For what *cause* did Taiwan deny its businesses the "patient capital" enjoyed by their Korean rivals? The popular explanation is that Taiwan's former Mainland rulers viewed the empowering of the local Taiwanese capitalists as a political threat. Facts do not support this *politicized* view. TSMC, Taiwan's flagship in information technology (IT), was founded by Morris Chang, a Mainlander. He did not get "patient capital" from the Mainland leaders to compete against Samsung in DRAMs and gave up. After the local Taiwanese took power, no local firms got massive government backing either. The truth is, lacking access to international organizations like the IMF and the World Bank, it would be politically suicidal for Taiwan to adopt the financially risky policy that landed Korea in the Crisis of 1997–1998 .

In financing development, to what *effect* would Taiwan's policy lead to in the long run? Maybe the effect is quite limited. Historically Samsung, as part of a Korean business group, entered the DRAMs field, under government support against the then dominant Japanese firms. Presently Nanya, part of a Taiwanese business group, is currently expanding its facilities for DRAMs, by floating new equity issues *in Europe*, against Samsung. Europe and Japan have the interest to back Taiwanese firms with technology, but without much cash, just to preserve alternative sources to Korea's. Historically, Taiwanese business groups, like Formosa Plastics and Chi Mei, made their fortunes by producing commoditized chemicals, using "cheap engineers" and mature technology unloaded by Japan. So their current ventures in IT is a familiar game. Whether they can and will sustain the "trial by ordeal", only the future can tell.

Benefit and cost The Korean market success relies on "patient capital" not raised by owners who would demand a decent return, but loaned by government dominated banks. This was first due to policy, and subsequently because the debtors became "too big to fail". This has allowed Korean firms to accumulate the expertise in fabricating "commoditized" goods, with thin profit margins, heavy initial cost and high excess capacities due to cyclical demand. Inflation spells, debt crisis (like 1997), and a weakened small and medium enterprise sector are the required costs which Taiwan declined to pay in the past. Holding large shares in the world market did not give the Korean firms monopoly profit but complaints from America and Europe, for bailing out Hynix and price-fixing with the Japanese firms. According to McKinnon (2004), the Korean reform has alleviated much of the problems, but not entirely.

In contrast and according to Sturgeon and Lee (2005), for information technology (IT) goods, the Taiwanese firms export a lopsided portion of their exports to a few American and Japanese firms. In 2003, the top five clients took 71%. With such high buyers' concentration, the value-added earned by the seller remains relatively meager. Any attempt to develop one's own brand often alienates the major clients.

Success in development is measured in high-paid jobs and innovative profits which reward human capital formation and not the number of billionaires and the market share in goods produced with mature technology. On those scores, the lead of Japan over Korea and Taiwan remains huge.

A prisoner's dilemma? Beyond the events in particular sectors, and the current evolution of Korea and Taiwan, we now turn to the choice of other developing economies today, seeking a role model for replication. Even if one asseses the historical record and prefers the Korean approach, its wide replication may have unexpected consequences. So far, much of the Korean development is concentrated in several integrated industries such as steel, automobiles and shipbuilding. Replicating such a strategy by other developing countries may cause serious trade friction and excess capacity within particular sectors of the world economy. As it is, Hyundai Motors had a 40% utilization ratio of their factory in 1998. In contrast, the Taiwanese approach of development is spread over various niche products. It is far less likely to cause imbalance in the world economy.

Review of Development Economics, 5(2), 256–265, 2001

Specialization Pattern and Multistaged Growth: Korea and Taiwan Compared

Toshiyasu Kato and Henry Wan, Jr*

Abstract

The sustained rapid growth of Korea and Taiwan represent two alternative paths of successful development. The difference between these two paths is reflected in industrial concentration, macroeconomic management, and export mix. During the 1997 crisis, Korea absorbed severe shocks and then scored a quick recovery, while Taiwan proceeded at a more or less constant pace. Taiwan has followed a "usual progression" experienced by Netherlands or Switzerland before; Korea has struck out on a different path, under a more active government policy. Before the current, ongoing reform, the development policy of Korea dates back to President Park, and fits his style of personal management over the economy. It has its own rationale, but also entails greater financial risks. The different roles played by the small and medium enterprises in the two economies provide food for thought in development economics.

1. Introduction

In recent decades, both Korea and Taiwan have been lauded as models for economic development (Lau, 1990). Their exports have also grown at rates much faster than the world average (Noland, 1997). Yet, in spite of their shared rapid growth in output as well as trade, there are well noted differences between the two, in industrial concentration (Feenstra et al., 1999) and in macroeconomic management (Adelman, 1999). Korea has promoted business groups and occasionally relied on foreign borrowing and inflationary finance; Taiwan has engaged in neither practice but has provided a policy environment in which small and medium enterprises thrive. The two economies also differ in their export contents: Korea focuses on scale economy and Taiwan benefits from niche markets. When the financial crisis of 1997 came, Korea absorbed severe setbacks, then scored a quick recovery; by and large, Taiwan maintained its pace of growth. The similarities and dissimilarities between these two economies should provide many insights into the development process in general. Yet although the literature is replete with facts (various chapters in Ito and Krueger, 1993; Rodrik, 1995), it is relatively sparse on the patterns behind the facts. Hopefully our own interpretations can help in understanding the process of development.

To complete this agenda, ideally one should offer a detailed model that is relevant to policy, tractable in analysis, and sufficiently succinct in exposition. When the last requirement becomes too hard to meet, a possible alternative is simulation. Although no such exercise will be carried out here, our discussion may facilitate future research in this direction. Above all, if the topic is important and the approach addresses the essence of the matter, then a researcher has to present the findings as well as is possible. This study is organized around two propositions. First, between Korea and

* Wan: Department of Economics, Cornell University, Ithaca, NY 14853-7601, USA. Tel: 607-255-6211; Fax: 607-255-2818; E-mail: hyw1@cornell.edu. We are thankful for the very helpful comments from Professors Bjarne Jensen and Ping Wang, two anonymous reviewers, and Ms Andrea Williams-Wan. All remaining shortcomings are the responsibility of the authors.

Taiwan, the various differences in their pattern of international specialization, their industrial concentration, and their macroeconomic performance are neither random nor isolated occurrences. Instead, they are the manifestations of two alternative development paths. In a broad sense, the growth of Taiwan has followed the "usual progression" of many advanced economies, while Korea has pursued a variation under strong government guidance. The Korean effort has been successful in many aspects, but has not been without costs. This is reflected in its record of growth rate: a high average, accompanied by a high variance.

Second, in a world with increasing returns, Korea has searched for and attained internal economy of scale, with their more vertically integrated industries geared for mass production. In contrast, Taiwan has enjoyed external economies, with a network of clustered small and medium enterprises (SMEs). Under an "open system," these firms freely associate and form a dense interfirm system which harks back to the "industrial districts" of Lancaster and Sheffield, in the days of Alfred Marshall. Their adaptability to changing markets accounts for the relatively smooth growth of Taiwan. Their far-reaching contacts are instrumental to the acquisition of technology (Wan, 2000a,b) and the attainment of an average growth rate not less than that of Korea, when computed over a long period as in Ranis (1999). These two topics will be presented in turn.

In a trading world, the alternative paths of development are reflected in the different sequences of trade patterns. What an economy exports reveals where its comparative advantage lies: for example, is it low-wage or high-skill? The level of skill is associated with the industrial structure. In *perfectly competitive industries*, firms lack distinction and produce more of the same. In *monopolistically competitive industries*, each firm has some specialty to offer. In *industries with contestable markets*, firms need the capability to manage factories with scale economy. The patent system rewards innovators in *oligopolistic industries*. The above four industry types in trade theory (Helpman and Krugman, 1985) serve well as building blocks for us. Thus, the process of development is accompanied by the transformation of the export mix, corresponding to the industry types which produce such outputs.

We identify below the historical transformations undergone by many nations which are fully developed today, such as Switzerland and The Netherlands. In both direction and pace, Taiwan is advancing in their footsteps. In contrast to this "usual progression," there is an alternative path. Its hallmarks include the Heavy Chemical Industry (HCI) Drive, accomplished by a forced march under strong government guidance. Thus we call it "the Korean variation," since among all those economies which have accepted inflation for accelerated development,[1] Korea is the most successful. We shall review what the policy objective of Korea is, how that objective is pursued, and what the consequences of such efforts are. One of the consequences appears to be the increased risk of financial crises.

To be complete, any comparison between Korea and Taiwan should explain why it is that, until now, the mean growth rate of Taiwan equals or even slightly exceeds that of Korea. After all, Korea has the advantage of size in population, in total GNP, and in outputs of most goods that Korea produces, from cars and steel to ships and DRAM chips. One might try to explain Taiwan's relative strength in terms of the "external economy *of scale*." But this cannot be the familiar type of "Marshallian externality," where for each firm, the cost of a homogeneous product decreases with the total industry output. After all, in industries like auto-making or shipbuilding, Korea dominates Taiwan in industry output no less than in firm output. In various industry studies,

Taiwan has been described as adaptable to market variability. Yet, that literature contains no *analytic* explanation how such adaptability comes about. Since to many economists today, anything that cannot be framed in analytic terms is suspect, we shall offer our interpretation to such findings from the descriptive studies. For additional discussion, see Jensen (2000).

Summing up, we maintain that in enjoying a rapid and stable growth rate, Taiwan has benefited from its thriving small and medium enterprises. It is not just because when compared with Korea, the Taiwanese industrial structure is less concentrated both in output and in employment, or because the average Taiwanese firm is smaller in size. The critical fact is that with government backing, large Korean business groups have assumed a more dominant position *vis-à-vis* the SMEs than their counterparts in either Taiwan or Japan. Their dominance appears to have critically weakened the Korean small and medium enterprises (Kim, 1997).

2. Industrial Types, Pattern of Specialization, and the "Usual Progression"

To recapitulate, for our analysis we recognize four types of industries: (A) perfect competition, (B) monopolistic competition, (C) contestable market, and (D) differentiated oligopoly.

Both A and B have large numbers of small firms. The difference between the two is that the former is composed of firms that are largely undistinguished in their fields, while the latter is composed of firms each of which has some specialty to offer. Both C and D contain a small number of large firms. The difference between these two is that, in the former, the "barrier to entry" is based only upon the internal return to scale, while in the latter, patent protection or a trade secret is the source of brand loyalty among its clientele.

In our usage, an industry is a collection of firms which produce goods with comparable technical requirements. By this definition, we recognize many industries in the electronics sector. For illustration, Table 1 includes one representative electronics industry of each type. Since transportation cost is neither zero nor infinity, firms in type C industries—like the producers of cement and fertilizer—enjoy internal returns to scale, operate in economies at various stages of development, and compete against each other. In terms of the skill level, type A industries require the least and type D the most, with types B and C in between.

Broadly speaking, one may have a "product ladder" model which matches the comparative advantage of an economy with its export-mix, which is classified by industry types. This is shown in Table 2.

Table 1. Selected Outputs and Industry Types—Example from the Electronics Sector

Industry type	Representative output
A. Perfect competition	Assembly of radios and digital watches
B. Monopolistic competition	Application-specific ICs (ASIC)
C. Contestable market	Memory chips
D. Differentiated oligopoly	Central processing units (CPUs)

Table 2. Development Phase and Specialization

Phase of development	Export mix
I. Less-developed	A (perfect competition) and C (contestable market)
II. Mid-level	B (monopolistic competition) and C (contestable market)
III. Developed	D (differentiated oligopoly) and C (contestable market)

We can now describe a "law of motion" in this model. In a trading world, consider a "small country" with a fixed labor supply and no influence over world prices. The current value of output can be (a) consumed, (b) invested in physical capital, or (c) allocated to provide social overheads like infrastructure and education.

Technology, or human capital in the broader sense, is what ultimately decides the pace of development. To be sure, physical capital plays an important role, with new techniques embodied in new equipment. But capital formation is certainly not exogenous. For forward-looking rational agents in a market economy, the rate of investment is decided by the schedule of expected marginal productivity of capital, as Ramsey taught us. That schedule shifts upward with skill acquisition through education, imitation, and learning-by-doing; see Van and Wan (1997). Without technical progress, growth may not last for long on the strength of investment alone: Soviet forced saving did not help. Thus, the system dynamics are driven by the accumulation of capital and the progress in technology.

Labor and capital are used in various types of industries as inputs for production. The output level of a firm depends on the input levels and a "technical progress index"[2] which stands for the level of productivity. For industries of types C and D, internal economy of scale also matters. Firms in industries of types A and B require much lower capital intensity than those in industries of types C and D. For simplicity, the technical progress index is assumed to increase as output accumulates in industries of types B, C, and D (but not necessarily type A, where the technology may be mature), though the rate of increase may vary from one sector to another. These rates can also be affected by the social overhead provided by the government. In a globalized economy, the export mix can also be influenced by government policy.

There are two phase transitions in Table 2: the first is from phases I to II, and the second is from phases II to III. In spite of their crucial importance, there has been no analytic treatment of either phase transition in the literature. Consider first the transition from phases I to II. Over time, both skill and wages rise naturally as experience accumulates through learning by doing. In a developing economy, this process is greatly reinforced by the spillover of technology through trade (Coe et al., 1997). Participation in the global subcontract networks is the catalyst for this phase transition. Export content shifts from the products of industries of the perfectly competitive type to those of the monopolistically competitive type (Meyanathan and Munter, 1994). Interfirm linkages develop so that together they can compete better in the world market in cost, quality, and punctuality of delivery. See also Shieh (1992).

Coming now to the second transition, we first take note that in advanced economies, SMEs like those in the Swiss engineering industries are highly respected worldwide for their expertise. They provide well-paid jobs. At the same time, with the rise of the skill level, large firms may emerge from the ranks of SMEs over time owing to their successful innovations. An example is Philips of Eindhoven, The Netherlands. No sectoral industrial policy of the government is involved in either country. In short, judging from European experience, the rise of large firms is not indispensable for successful economic development. Likewise, government intervention is not necessary for the emergence of large firms.

By now, the question of whether non-Western economies can develop in the same manner has perhaps also been settled in the affirmative. In many (though not all) export sectors, from garments (Shieh, 1992) and footwear to bicycles (Chu and Li, 1996) and machine tools (Fransman, 1986), Taiwan has been developing according to this same pattern. In electronics—the mainstay of the Taiwanese economy today—the fair and careful study of Hobday (1995, p. 98) deserves to be cited here: "few studies systematically examine the cost, benefit, successes, and failures of state policies. In electronics, it is likely that direct technological and industrial interventions had little effect during the 1960s and 1970s. . . . Many small Taiwanese businesses mistrusted the government, feared officialdom and kept distance from state agencies." Although the government set up several public firms upstream, such firms have charged world market prices and hence had no impact on the export mix (Chen and Ku, 1999). In more recent years, the government has been more involved with the high-tech industries. Still, the aim has never been to back an enterprise with such financial muscle, until it can overwhelm its foreign rivals with internal economy of scale.[3] For a careful analysis of how Taiwan's policy works, see the case study of Tung (2001).

Together, the two transitions characterize what we call the "usual progression." Note that among those which adopt this development path, various economies may progress at different paces. This is attributable to factors such as the initial conditions, the supply of social overhead, and macroeconomic management by the government.

3. The Korean Variation

Lasting imprints have been left on the Korean economy by its 18 years under President Park. In his view, economics has precedence over democracy, mammoth enterprises are indispensable for development, and a strong state is justified for their supervision (Park, 1962). Business groups were both nurtured and governed with "directed credit." Short-term "policy loans" were granted by banks under State control, at interest rates below the rate of inflation (Sakong, 1993). Any time, any heavily indebted firm can be bankrupted by the state. Backed by the state, the business groups excluded most SMEs from export, and reduced them to supplicants to the large businesses which act as sales outlets. Concentrating on mass-produced goods, Korean firms in capital-intensive industries have captured the lions' share in the world markets of DRAMs, oil tankers, etc., but have made little profit (Kim, 1997). They have faced sharp price swings and often excess capacities. By 1997, business groups had grown "too big to fail," and the long-repressed labor force had become radicalized and intractable.

Unlike Taiwan, where in the role of international subcontractors, the SMEs supply an export mix which spreads over a wide range of niche products, Korea has the industrial structure and export content which are dominated by large firms in contestable markets. In a greenhouse environment, most Korean large firms have grown under inflationary finance and foreign borrowing rather than natural market forces.

The development path taken by Korea should also be compared against the record of Japan, the supposed template of Korea under Park. There are subtle but significant differences. First, in Japan, directed credit to businesses carries positive real interest rates. The government encourages firms to enter new industries by overcoming coordination failure rather than forcing them to act against their own best judgement. Indeed, without the bait of loans at negative real interest rates, the Japanese MITI never had that much leverage as the Korean government against the Japanese firms. Second, in dealing with the SMEs, large Japanese firms look for support in quality improvement, not direct financial gain (Kato, 1999). The implication is that their products have much brand loyalty to build upon. Third, from transistor radios to computer numerically controlled (CNC) machine tools, to reliable fuel-efficient small cars, Japanese exports have won market shares by product design and quality control as much as by cost advantage. The presence of a perennial trade surplus implies that, unlike Korea, Japan has no need for foreign borrowing to invest in capacities, or to boost exports on the strength of internal scale economy alone. By the criterion of export profitability, the Japanese government seems to have compensated for the market failure only to some degree, but never to the extent of overshooting the target of the first best. By anecdote, Korea under President Park forced Hyundai to enter shipbuilding against the company's wish (Jones and Sakong, 1980).

Of course, for historic reasons, Japan in 1945 had both more human capital than Korea and the first-mover's advantage since Japanese recovery was due to the Korean War. One can also argue that the outcome of a "patent race" is uncertain in any event. Japan might have been lucky in launching profitable new goods. The fact remains that in Japan's export expansion after World War II, foreign borrowing and inflationary finance played no part. Year after year, trade surpluses and high foreign exchange reserves have been the rule for Japan, but not for Korea. In addition, more Korean exporters seem to rely on scale economy in contestable markets than do their Japanese counterparts. These are industries with high fixed costs, and hence low supply elasticity. In our scheme, efforts of the Japanese government have helped to launch the type D industries and speed up the movement of the economy along the "usual progression." In contrast, the Korean Heavy Chancel Industry Drive might have rushed business groups into the type C industries, and the economy off the well-trodden path.

Figure 1 categorizes, by their phase of development, four West Pacific economies, associated with their characteristic industry types as well as the source of competitive strength. The *theme* of usual progression is then:

"Indonesia"   to   "Taiwan"   to   "Japan,"

and the (Korean) *variation* is:

"Indonesia"   to   "Korea"   to   "Japan,"

where the quotation marks indicate that we are dealing with a stylized world in which the name of an economy in real life is only meant to represent an archetype. The merit of the "variation" in comparison with the "theme" is supposed to be faster growth. So far, this has yet to be justified by the observed performance.

To be sure, nothing said above implies that development by the "usual progression" is efficient, or that the Korean "variation" is unwise. Certainly, the pace at which Korea has caught up has often been startling to the Japanese. Apart from some measurement problems, few can deny that, in many areas, Korea has achieved a rate of technology acquisition faster than the PRC, or Taiwan, or Singapore, or Hong Kong. Still, in

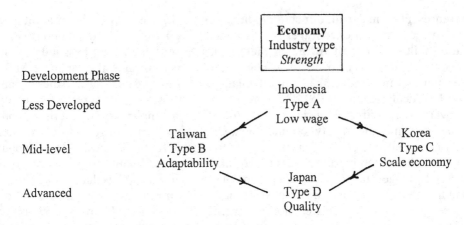

Figure 1. Four Patterns of Specialization in the West Pacific

keeping low foreign exchange reserves, incurring much foreign debt, and opting for an output mix with highly volatile terms of trade, the pre-1997 Korean mode of development was inherently highly risky (Thorbecke and Wan, 1999).

The 1997 crisis caught Korea in a three-fold trap: a low foreign exchange reserve which could not stand much drain, an acute trade deficit which threatened to exhaust the reserves if there was no devaluation, and a high level of private, foreign debt with short duration, which would force many firms into insolvency if there was a devaluation which inflated the obligation to pay. This was not an unexpected misfortune either, since the crisis came only because the economy could not repeat the narrow escape from the near debt crisis during the second oil shock. In the end, it was Korean patriotism in donating personal heirlooms and the IMF-led loans that saved the day.

4. The Contribution of SMEs to Adaptability—Theoretically Considered

In many industrial studies, thriving SMEs have been viewed as the source of Taiwan's rapid and stable growth. The broad contact between Taiwan's SMEs and their clients provides a channel for technology transfer in various industries, such as bicycles according to Chu and Li, garments according to Shieh, electronics according to Hobday (1995), and machine tools (Amsden, 1985). For further discussion, see Wan (2000c). For a late-comer in industrialization, such interaction clearly helps to achieve rapid growth. We now turn attention to the relationship between the SMEs and the stability of growth. A satisfactory analysis must account for the random shocks inherent in the market equilibrium. It is no surprise that no formal analysis has been conducted in the literature. Again, simulation seems to be an attractive approach for such an important issue. We shall suggest below how such a model might be constructed.

The questions involved here are: Why is it that, as time goes on, mass production methods seem to become less and less profitable, in comparison with the technology for "flexible production"? Why do the clustered small and medium enterprises seem to have some advantage in adapting to the market fluctuations? What causes more and more developing economies to participate in the global supply chain?

To get some insight into such problems, one should first consider a fixed commodity space, with a large but finite number of types of potentially producible final goods meeting some particular human want, say, for breakfast cereal. For simplicity, one may visualize that each type is represented by a point, where all points are evenly distributed around a circle.[4] Next, assume that there is a large but finite number of individuals, that each has the same income in every period, and that each devotes the same portion to a single kind of this type of final good. At the beginning of each period, Nature assigns to each individual one kind as the current personal favorite. Again for simplicity, assume that in each period, the distribution of individuals over commodity types has a smooth, symmetric profile with a single peak. The location of this peak is random. It is also identically and independently distributed over time. This completes the basic specification of the demand conditions.

In addition, one might assume that if unit prices are equal, any individual with a particular income has a "proximity preference," preferring an actually produced good close to that kind which is the current personal favorite. This proximity preference is balanced by the commodity price, since one always prefers more than less. It is also intuitive that individuals have "steeper" preference gradients at higher incomes (the rich are more "choosy" than the poor).

Next, we turn to the supply side. Each good is supposed to be produced by a large but fixed number of steps, which may be carried out under a single management, or by a number of firms, each carrying out a number of steps. Again we may assume for simplicity that steps handled by any one firm form a "segment." Any final product is made by joining segments. Since interfirm coordination is not cost-free, the cost of production rises with the number of "joints," even though, over time, technical progress can reduce the cost of "joining." The production process requires some fixed equipment and common labor. Thus, "fragmented" production has the advantage that different final products may share certain segments so that, on average, firms producing shorter segments are likely to have a higher utilization rate of their equipment.

When properly formulated, the model suggested above seems to go quite far in explaining how the progress in communication and transportation enlarges the trading world, and how the affluence of consumers and the "fragmentation" of production are mutually supporting tendencies in modern life.

5. Concluding Remarks

On the eve of the 1997 crisis, the Korean government had already decided to promote the SME sector. The crisis has caused some temporary delay of this initiative, but it further strengthened the resolve for a thorough reform. At the present, the economies of both Korea and Taiwan are booming. So all our discussion thus far is not about the future prospect of these two economies. Instead, what we try to do is to distill useful insight out of the past records for development policy.

References

Adelman, Irma, "State and Market in the Economic Development of Korea and Taiwan," in Erik Thorbecke and Henry Y. Wan (eds.), *Taiwan's Development Experience: Lessons on Roles of Government and Markets*, Boston, MA: Kluwer Academic (1999):289–326.

Amsden, Alice, "The Division of Labor is Limited by the Rate of Growth of the Market: The Taiwan Machine Tool Industry in the 1970s," *Cambridge Journal of Economics* 9 (1985): 271–84.

Chen, Tain-Jy and Ying-Hua Ku, "Second-Stage Import Substitution: The Taiwan Experience," in Gustav Ranis, Sheng-Cheng Hu, and Yun-Peng Chu (eds.), *The Political Economy of Taiwan's Development into the 21st Century*, Vol. 2, Cheltenham, UK: Edward Elgar (1999): 79–108.

Chu, Wan-Wen and Jia-Jing Li, "Growth and Industrial Organization: a Comparative Study of the Bicycle Industry in Taiwan and South Korea," *Journal of Industrial Studies* 3(1) (1996): 35–52.

Coe, David T., Elhanan Helpman, and Alexander W. Hoffmaister, "North–South Spillovers," *Economic Journal* 107 (1997):134–49.

Feenstra, Robert C., Tzu-HanYang, and Gary G. Hamilton, "Business Groups and Product Variety in Trade: Evidence from South Korea, Taiwan and Japan," *Journal of International Economics* 48 (1997):71–100.

Glaeser, Edward L., José A. Scheinkman, and Andrei Shleifer, "Economic Growth in a Cross-Section of Cities," *Journal of Monetary Economics* 36 (1995):117–43.

Helpman, Elhanan and Paul R. Krugman, *Market Structure and Foreign Trade: Increasing Returns, Monopolistic Competition, and the International Economy*, Cambridge, MA: MIT Press (1985).

Hobday, Michael, *Innovation in East Asia: The Challenge to Japan*, Aldershot: Edward Elgar (1995).

Ito, Takahashi and Anne O. Krueger (eds.), *Trade and Protectionism*, Chicago, IL: University of Chicago Press (1993).

Jensen, B. S., "Homogeneous Dynamics, Exogeneity, Human Capital, and Increasing Returns to Scale," (2000).

Jones, LeRoy P. and Il Sakong, *Government, Business and Entrepreneurship in Economic Development: The Korean Case*, Cambridge, MA: Harvard University Press (1980).

Kato, Yoshiyasu, "Ownership Structure of Vertically Related Firms and Production Efficiency: An Analysis of Keretsu Group in Japan," unpublished paper presented at the Far Eastern Meeting of the Econometric Society Meeting, Singapore (1999).

Kim, Linsu, *Imitation to Innovation: The Dynamics of Korea's Technological Learning*, Boston: Harvard Business School Press (1997).

Lau, Lawrence J., *Models of Development* (revised and expanded), San Francisco, CA: ICI Press (1990).

Meyanathan, Saha Dhevan and Roger Munter, "Industrial Structures and the Development of Small and Medium Enterprise Linkages: An Overview," in S. D. Meyanathan (ed.), *Industrial Structures and the Development of Small and Medium Enterprise Linkages: Examples from East Asia*, Washington, DC: World Bank (1994).

Noland, Marcus, "Has Asian Export Performance been Unique?" *Journal of International Economics* 43 (1997):79–101.

Park, Chung-Hee, *Our Nation's Path*, Seoul: Dong-A (1962).

Ranis, Gustav, "Reflections on the Economics and Political Economy of Development at the Turn of the Century," in Gustav Ranis, Sheng-Cheng Hu, and Yun-Peng Chu (eds.), *The Political Economy of Taiwan's Development into the 21st Century*, Vol. 2, Cheltenham, UK: Edward Elgar (1999):3–30.

Rodrik, Dani, "Getting Interventions Right: How South Korea and Taiwan Grew Rich," *Economic Policy* (April 1995):53–108.

Sakong, Il, *Korea in the World Economy*, Washington, DC: Institute for International Economics (1993).

Shieh, G. S., *"Boss" Island: The Subcontracting Network and Microentrepreneurship in Taiwan's Development*, New York: P. Lang (1992).

Thorbecke, Erik and Henry Wan, "How did Taiwan Withstand the Asian Financial Crisis?" in Erik Thorbecke and Henry Y. Wan (eds.), *Taiwan's Development Experience: Lessons on Roles of Government and Markets*, Boston, MA: Kluwer Academic (1999):433–45.

Tung, An-Chi, "Taiwan's Semiconductor Industry: What the State Did and Did Not," *Review of Development Economies* 5(2) (2001):266–88.

Van, Pham Hoang and Henry Y. Wan, "Emulative Development through Trade Expansion: East Asian Evidence," in J. Piggott and A. Woodland (eds.), *International Trade Policy and the Pacific Rim*, Basingstoke, UK: Macmillan (1999):348–66.

Wan, Henry Y., "Function vs. Form in the Fragmented Industrial Structure: Three Examples from Asia Pacific Experience," in Leonard Cheng and Henryk Kierzkowski (eds.), *Global Production and Trade in East Asia* (yet decided) (2000a).

———, "Why Trade Matters to Development: A Learning Model," in Alan D. Woodland (ed.), *Economic Theory and International Trade: Essays in Honour of Murray C. Kemp*, Cheltenham, UK: Edward Elgar (2000b).

———, "SMEs in the Globalized Developing Economies: Some Asia–Pacific Examples," in Charles Harvie and Boon-Chye Lee (eds.), *SMEs in East Asia in the Aftermath of the Asian Financial and Economic Crisis*, Cheltenham, UK: Edward Elgar (2000c).

Notes

1. Japan, supposedly the template for Korea, has never financed investment with inflation. On the other hand, inflationary finance in Latin America has never created genuine competitiveness.

2. Like the output-augmenting technical progress index.

3. Given the size of Taiwan's foreign exchange reserves, that sort of option might be quite tempting to policymakers in other developing economies. But that would be against the government's guiding principle of "seeking growth within stability."

4. For similar specifications, see Glaeser et al. (1995).

Comparative Worldwide Development Records

Review of "Towards a Unified Theory of the Growth Process", jointly with Erik Thorbecke[*]

This paper continues the line of research in Wan (2004). It introduces an axle-and-spokes view about the world economic development since World War II, with America as the incumbent technological leader and engine for growth. It differs from most of the growth theories (both the neoclassical as well as the endogenous strains) surveyed in Aghion and Howitt (1998) by its emphasis for interdependence. It also differs from the models of convergence, from Baumol (1986) to Barro and Sala-i-Martin (1995), in that it explains the recalcitrant gap setting American per capita real GDP apart from all other economies. It also differs from other research on catching up by emphasizing the key role played by trade and foreign direct investment as the catalyst for technological transmission.

In fact, the same world distribution of real per capita incomes which Quah (1996) called the twin-peak phenomenon is shown as a necessary result of this theory. Basically, the catching-up mechanism implies a law of motion for the relative per capita real income, measured on the basis of purchasing power parity, treating concurrent America level as 100%. There are three equilibria, including: (1) a boundary stable equilibrium "at 0"; (2) an interior stable equilibrium which falls short of the American level; and (3), an interior unstable equilibrium between the above two. From (3), any upward movement would start a motion which gravitates to a limiting path of partial catching-up, converging towards (2). In contrast, any downward movement would lead to a path "towards zero", which is (1), formally a boundary stable equilibrium. Actually, this last possibillity does not necessarily mean falling income levels, etc., but falling behind America with an ever-widening gap.

Data suggest that income polarization is taking place, making the twin peaks steeper. (Actually, America forms a one-country pinnacle, which seems not taken into consideration by Quah, *ibid.*)

---

[*]The article is reprinted from *WIDER Angle*, No. 1, pp. 5–8, 2004, published by World Institute for Development Economics Research.

Towards a Unified Theory of the Growth Process

by Erik Thorbecke and Henry Y. Wan

Comparing the rate of growth of real per capita income of an economy with the level of real per capita income of the same economy and taking a cross-section of such paired data, Lucas, (in the late 1980s) concluded that 'the mid-income countries grow the fastest, next the high-income countries, with the low-income countries growing the slowest'. While this finding is, of course, correct on average it begs the question of why certain very poor countries were able to escape the poverty trap while others continued to stagnate and why some mature economies continue to grow while others retrogressed.

Most East and South East Asian countries displayed a real per capita income in 1950 around or less than one-tenth that of the US. By the end of the 20th century Japan, Hong Kong, and Singapore had reached per capita real income levels between 70 and 80 per cent of that of the US, while Taiwan and South Korea enjoyed levels of incomes around half of that of the US. Although the growth performances of Thailand and Malaysia were somewhat less spectacular they reached a relative income level between a fourth and a third of that of the US.

In contrast, practically every sub-Saharan nation – starting from a very low initial level comparable to that of Taiwan and South Korea – saw its relative income gap with the US augment *not* fall. Likewise most Latin American and South Asian economies had fallen behind relative to the American standard of living over the second half of the 20th century.

We observe a similar divergent growth pattern in the second half of the 20th century among groups of developed countries. A number of Western European countries managed to improve their relative income position vis-à-vis America, while such economies as Australia, New Zealand and Argentina retrogressed.

The objectives of this paper are two-fold: first, to review the relative growth pattern of a large sample of countries and derive distinct clusters-based on initial conditions and differential growth performances; and second, to provide a possible theoretical explanation of the observed divergent growth patterns.

Before turning to the empirical evidence a few concepts need to be defined. Let x be the per capita real income of an economy with $y = (dx/dt)/x$ as the growth rate of x. In turn let z stand for the per capita real income of the US (assumed to be the leading economy and techno-logical leader over the period with which we are concerned). It is further assumed that the American economy is growing at a constant rate, c. A useful concept, v, is that of the ratio of a given country's per capita real income to that of the US, i.e. $v = x/z$. For example, in 1961 (three-year average) both South Korea and Taiwan had similar v's, the ratio of their per capita real incomes to that of the US was between .11 and .12. By 1997 (three-year average), the corresponding ratios were .54 and .46, respectively.

A key concept that follows directly from the above discussion is that of the income gap, i.e., $g = (1-v)$. Returning to the previous example, Taiwan's income gap (with respect to the US) in 1961 fell from 88% to 46% and South Korea's income gap was reduced from 89% to 54%, by

1997. Note that since the growth rate of the US economy is taken as constant (=c), a country growing at a rate faster than c would see its relative gap vis-à-vis the US shrink, and *vice versa*. Subsequently, we shall assume that the technological gap depends on the relative per capita real income ratio.

Next, we explore the empirical evidence. We used the *relative per capita real income* series of the Penn World Table, version 6.1, in which the per capita real income (expressed in constant purchasing power parity) of all economies is given as a percentage of the concurrent American figure. We computed the relative per capita real income ratio, v, and the gap = $(1-v)$ for 106 countries for which continuous time series were available over the period 1960 to 1998. Four different groups of countries following distinct growth patterns could be identified based on initial conditions and growth performance. Table 1 gives the relative incomes (v), and relative income gaps (g) for twenty countries (five representative countries in each of the four categories), in both the beginning year and final year. It also shows the ratio of the gap reduction (or increase) to the initial gap (in column 5) and the corresponding rank.

The four growth patterns captured in Table 1 are: 1. *Poor and Stagnating* (Group I): initially poor countries that continued to stagnate (essentially sub-Saharan Africa); 2. *High Growth* (Group II): initially poor countries that grew at a fast rate; 3. *Mature and Decelerating* (Group IIB): relatively rich countries that achieved to reduce their income gaps with the US slightly (mainly Western Europe); 4. *Mature and Retrogressing* (Group III): rich

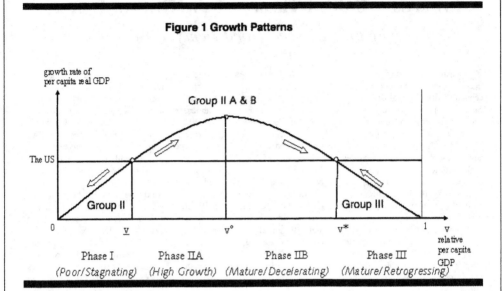

Figure 1 Growth Patterns

growth rate of
per capita real GDP

Group II A & B

The US

Group II

Group III

0   v̲   v°   v*   1   v

relative
per capita
GDP

Phase I   Phase IIA   Phase IIB   Phase III
(Poor/Stagnating) (High Growth) (Mature/Decelerating) (Mature/Retrogressing)

countries with incomes almost comparable to that of the US at the outset that fell relatively behind in terms of per capita real income (Australia, New Zealand, Argentina and a few Western European economies). It can be seen from Table 1 that Group I countries are characterized by very large initial relative gaps and increasing gaps over time. In contrast, Group II, starting from a slightly higher level of relative income managed to shrink their relative gaps drastically. The relative gap reduction ranges from a high of .81 for Hong Kong to a low -6.65 in New Zealand. The first observation that jumps out is how successfully East Asia has performed in terms of relative gap reduction. Five of the first six countries out of the full sample of 106 countries are from East Asia (see column 6 of Table 1). Conversely, the five countries in Group III (Mature/ Retrogressing) underwent major increases in the size of their relative gaps and are ranked at the bottom (102-106).

A phase diagram can be used to explain the very different growth

patterns discussed above. Figure 1 captures the distinct patterns exhibited by the four groups of countries. The rate of growth of per capita real income, y, is plotted on the vertical axis and the relative ratio of a given country's per capita real income to that of the economic and technological leader (the US), v , is shown on the horizontal axis. Note that, c, represents the assumed constant growth rate of the leader. There is a stable equilibrium at v* and an unstable equilibrium at v (both equilibria can be thought of as steady states). The direction of the arrows indicates that any v near v* must gravitate toward v* and any v lower than v must move away and down from v.

The intuition behind this diagram is that every country has the *potential* to grow in a quasi-logistical fashion. A very poor economy may typically grow at a very low rate and essentially stagnate. The few economies that achieve to take off will see their growth rates accelerate up to a maximum (the peak of the parabola in Figure 1) before decelerating. The

diagram in Figure 1 reflects a number of simplifying hypotheses. For those economies with a relative per capita real income, v, they will tend to lag increasingly behind the leading economies. East Asia and some South Eastern Asian countries were among the few cases that managed to escape the poverty trap. One can conceive of, v, as the take-off point, i.e. the threshold relative income ratio required to start the process of self-sustained growth. Depending on the specific initial conditions of a country, v, might range between 5 and 10 per cent. For those economies with a relative per capita real income ratio between, v, and v*, their growth rates will tend to exceed that of the leader, i.e., c and the catching up process is underway. As the diagram indicates, a phase of growth acceleration is followed by one of deceleration. Finally, it is postulated that, v, may approach some steady state value less than 1 (v = 1, represents the per capita real income of the US) so that the catching up process will never be fully completed (it is interesting to note that throughout the whole period, from 1961 to 1997, only two countries enjoyed temporarily higher per capita real incomes than the US – Luxembourg and Switzerland). Since the initial conditions differ, as do the policies and institutions adopted by a given country over time, so does the shape of the parabola in Figure 1, as will be discussed shortly.

Each of the four prototype groups can be thought to operate within a distinct phase of development. Sub-Saharan Africa is clearly within phase I- the pre-take-off phase and is mired in a poverty trap as long as it does not reach the take-off point (v). In the last half century, the 'High Growth' economies of East Asia, after taking off, went through phase IIA (the sub-phase during which their growth rates accelerated up to the peak of the parabola (v^0) and are presently engaged in phase IIB displaying falling growth rates still higher than that of the US. The 'Mature' economies (essentially Continental Western Europe) fall within phase IIB – the phase of decelerating growth rates. Finally, the regions of recent settlement in the south and Great Britain are retrogressing in Phase III.

The growth pattern depends crucially on initial conditions and on the specific nature of the policy and institutional regime in place. Perhaps the most important mechanism influencing the growth pattern is through the acquisition of technology. The rate at which countries can reduce their relative gaps with the leader (the US) can be approximated as the product of two terms, 'the ability to learn' (which can be taken as depending on v) and the 'opportunity to learn' which increases with the income (technological) gap, g.

In order to demonstrate the key role played by policies and institutions in shaping a path of growth and relative equity, we revisit briefly the East Asian development model. The fundamental role of the government in East Asia after the Second World War can be distinguished into the

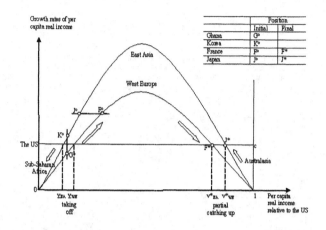

Figure 2 Alternative Growth Paths

first two phases shown on Figure 1. In the first (pre take-off) phase the government sets up the institutional and policy foundations required for the growth of agriculture and the spread of primary education to allow a take-off from a poor agrarian economy and traditional society into a path of sustainable development and modernization. The transfer of the agricultural surplus and the building up of a pool of educated workers provided the resources needed outside of agriculture to enter the second phase, characterized by a continuous and careful shepherding of the economy to acquire technology, upgrade and modernize the economy and ultimately catch up with the Western World.

In the 'High Growth', phase IIA, East Asia (and a few South East Asian economies) adopted an essentially common core of policies characterized by the following elements (for details see Thorbecke and Wan, 2004); 1. Reliance on Macroeconomic Stability through the maintenance of relatively balanced budgets and equilibrium exchange rates; 2. Openness and

Outward Orientation provided the major catalyst in the acquisition of technology with trade and foreign investment acting as conveyor belts in the transfer of state of the art technology; 3. Emulation of the United States as the Technological Leader – entering into a variety of transactions with American firms and penetrating the US market provided invaluable sources of technological information; 4. Intra-East and South East Connections – taking advantage of strategic complementarities with Japanese firms (the neighborhood effect) and within ethnic Chinese majorities and minorities.

Figure 2 illustrates the fundamental importance of policies and institutions. The upper parabola tracks approximately the growth pattern of East Asia while the lower parabola reflects the path followed by Western Europe. It can be seen that at the outset (1961) France enjoyed a significantly higher relative income (see point F^0 in Figure 2) than Japan (J^0). Yet at the end of period (1997), Japan's relative income (J^*) was above that of France (F^*). Figure 2 also includes a

Table 1 Four Distinct Growth Patterns: Per Capita Real Incomes and Gaps with the US, 1961-1997*

Twenty economies in 4 groups	Three year average over 1960-1962		Three year average over 1996-1998		Relative gap reduction	
	Relative per capita real income v_{61}	Relative gap in per capita real income g_{61}	Relative per capita real income v_{97}	Relative gap in per capita real income g_{97}	Ratio $(g_{61}-g_{97})/g_{61}$	Rank*
Group I *Poor/Stagnating*						
Uganda	4.3	95.7	2.9	97.1	-0.01	45
Tanzania	3.7	96.3	1.5	98.5	-0.02	51
Ethiopia	4.3	95.7	1.9	98.1	-0.02	54
Ghana	13.4	86.6	4.3	95.7	-0.11	82
Senegal	15.9	84.1	5.0	95.0	-0.13	86
Group II *High-Growth*						
Hong Kong	23.9	76.1	85.5	14.5	0.81	1
Singapore	21.0	79.0	84.7	15.3	0.81	2
Japan	41.3	58.7	79.7	20.3	0.65	3
Taiwan	11.3	88.7	54.4	45.6	0.49	4
Korea	11.6	88.4	46.4	53.6	0.39	6
Group IIB *Mature/Decelerating*						
Italy	59.1	40.9	69.0	31.0	0.24	11
Belgium	64.9	35.1	71.8	28.2	0.19	13
Finland	63.9	36.1	67.8	32.2	0.11	20
France	65.8	34.2	68.3	31.7	0.07	22
Norway	74.9	25.1	84.9	15.1	0.38	7
Group III *Mature/Retrogressing*						
Great Britain	77.8	22.2	69.0	31.0	-0.39	102
Argentina	59.0	41.0	37.0	63.0	-0.54	103
Australia	86.6	13.4	77.9	22.1	-0.65	104
Sweden	86.8	13.2	70.4	29.6	-1.24	105
N. Zealand	94.6	5.4	58.3	41.7	-6.65	106

*Rank in terms of relative reduction in gap out of a total sample of 106 countries from best (Hong Kong, ranked 1) to worst (New Zealand, ranked 106). A positive ratio denotes a relative gap reduction with the US and a negative ratio denotes an increasing gap with the US Out of the total sample of 106 countries, 36 reduced their relative gaps with the US and 70 increased their relative gaps.

comparison of South Korea and Ghana. Both countries had approximately the same per capita real incomes at the outset but followed very divergent paths subsequently. South Korea embarked on a high growth path while Ghana was not able to reach the take-off point and stagnated within phase I. Finally, Figure 2 shows the retrogression of Australasia in phase III.

Erik Thorbecke is Graduate School Professor and Professor of Economics at Cornell University and Henry Y. Wan is Professor of Economics at Cornell University.

The article draws on an earlier work by the authors titled 'Revisiting East (and South East) Asia's Development Model', paper prepared for the conference on 75 Years of Development, Cornell University, May 7-9, 2004, and, Henry Y. Wan (2004) 'Economic Development in a Globalized Environment: East Asian Evidences', Norwell MA: Kluwer Academic Publishers.

PART III

Some Debates in Development Theory

Must Trade Retard Growth for the Developing Economies?

Review of "Why Trade Matters to Development: A Learning Model"[*]

This Article addresses the issue whether trade driven by comparative advantage would deprive developing economies the opportunity to improve productivity through learning-by-doing, under an import-substitution program. The short answer is: most likely not so. There are two reasons.

Even if the initial exports are such low technology goods like sandals, plastic flowers and stuffed toys, to participate in world trade usually allows the developing economies to improve gradually the services needed for trading. This is, in the long run, useful for developing such exports like electronics offering high learning potentials.

Furthermore, there is the Engel's Law, under which poor societies excluded from world trade may not consume nor produce certain goods requiring high technology. The record from East Asia clearly shows that outward-oriented policy is more conducive to growth, starting from the revival of Japan after World War II, where supplying the military needs of America in the Korean War was an indispensable step. The transformation of Hong Kong during the same Korean War had launched the former entrepôt down the road of industrialization. Taiwan 1958 and Korea 1962 were the dates for trade liberalization that ushered in high growth. The separation of Singapore from Malaysia had a similar effect. The end of its dream to be the major industrial center over a sizable customs union forced Singapore to trade extensively with the high income trade partners. The effect of the 1978 reform to the Chinese economy today is self-evident.

---

[*]The article first appeared in *Economic Theory and International Trade: Essays in Honor of Murray C. Kemp*, A. Woodland (ed.), pp. 295–310, 2002. The author is grateful to the publisher, Edward Elgar, for granting the permit to reprint in this volume.

Why Trade Matters to Development: A Learning Model

Henry Wan Jr

1. INTRODUCTION

By conventional wisdom, trade is conducive to development. For example, according to Lucas (1988, p. 41), 'The dramatic...success stories... have all been associated with increase in exports ... [of]... goods not formerly produced in these countries'. For more formal statistical corroboration, see Lau and Wan (1994). Bhagwati (1999) summarises the main arguments for such a conclusion.

The importance of the role of trade may be seen in a highly aggregative analysis of Clark (1993), in which both the downfall of the centrally planned economies and the success of the East Asian economies are traced to the failure and success in harnessing trade for technical progress, in the face of Western advances in research and development (R&D).

But although circumstantial evidence suggest that trade benefits development, the analytic findings of Young (1991, 1993) showed that the theory of learning-by-doing may actually imply the exact opposite. The conclusion is seconded by Stokey (1991, p. 79): 'Suppose that human capital is acquired through learning-by-doing and so is stimulated by the production of high quality goods, then, free trade will speed up human capital accumulation in the North and slows it down in the South'. The elegance of such logic appears persuasive among most theorists, judging from the treatment in Aghion and Howitt (1998). Thus the plot thickens.

In principle, trade may benefit development through channels other than learning (see Van and Wan 1997), such as:
1. The pro-competitive effect. Trade brings competitive pressure against oligopolists and monopolists and hence improves allocative efficiency.
2. The scale effect. Trade may allow a fuller exploitation of scale economies; the opposite can also happen under the Graham Paradox (Helpman and Krugman 1985).
3. The accumulative effect. Trade enhances the marginal product of capital and stimulates investment, which increases output.

4. The technological spill-over effect. Trade facilitates the information flow and allows developing economies to emulate the best practice in production and management.

Young and Stokey have never denied that trade may benefit development through non-learning channels. Chuang (1998) – a student of Stokey – showed the spill-over benefit may dominate the negative influence of trade through learning. Young himself also showed that with three or more countries, trade might benefit one developing country through learning, at the expense of an even less developed economy. We believe that the topic deserves further analysis, because, while Young's three-country case is analytically valid, it is not what drives the episodes of the East Asian economies cited by Lucas. Their trade expansion reflects *trade creation* with the developed economies, not *trade diversion* from other developing areas, like South Asia or Africa. To leave matters as they are will lead readers to believe that, for developing countries, trade tends to be beneficial for non-learning reasons, but harmful through learning. That ambivalent general impression is not warranted.

It will be shown that the conclusions of Young and Stokey come from two crucial assumptions, namely, (a) all economies – rich and poor – share consumption patterns that are sufficiently similar for the present purpose, and (b) their production requires no imported or domestic input. In significant aspects, both (a) and (b) differ from the facts of life. In East Asia, a developing economy may thrive by supplying outputs its home market cannot absorb, using inputs it cannot yet efficiently produce. Experience may be gained in supplying services for one export today, which helps to export others later. Once (a) and (b) are relaxed, the same reasoning in the contributions of Young and Stokey can be extended to reach the policy assessment of Lucas and Bhagwati, that is, trade may benefit developing economies through learning, even in the (two-country) North-South context.

In the next section, we present a simple model, to be followed by three examples. The first example captures the essence of the special assumptions of Stokey and Young. Unsurprisingly, one reaches their conclusion that trade harms development. Once those special assumptions are relaxed, the next two examples show the opposite result that trade benefits development. Final comments are offered in the Conclusion.

2. A SIMPLE MODEL

Learning-by-doing is intrinsically a dynamic effect, and the international division of labour is inherently an issue of general equilibrium. In comparing different trade regimes under the impact of learning, it is understandable that Stokey and Young have adopted their simplifying assumptions. On the other hand, development policy is concerned with the welfare of the world's least fortunate. On such issues, one must hope that tractability of the analysis can be balanced against the veracity of the policy assessment. We cut the analytic Gordian knot by considering a very simple model of our own. Insight and not generality is our present goal.

Consider the choice of policy regimes of a small, developing economy, taking as given certain initial conditions at the time of choice. For simplicity, we adopt the following simplifying assumptions.

2.1 Assumptions

(1) *Policy regimes:* There are two policy choices $C=A$ for autarky and $C=T$ for free trade.

(2) *Primary input:* There is a single primary input labour, x_0, supplied in the fixed amount of unity.

(3) *Technology:* There are $N>1$ goods, each producible in the economy with a no-joint-output technology, and representable as a fixed coefficient (Leontief) production function given by

$$x_i = \min\{x_{ji}/a_{ji}\}, \quad 1 \le i \le N, \quad 0 \le j \le N,$$

where x_i stands for output i, x_{ji} stands for input j used to produce output i ($j=0$ stands for labour) and a_{ji} stands for input j required to produce 1 unit of output i.

(4) *Learning:* The input-output coefficient $a_{ji} = f_{ji}(X_1,...,X_N)$ is a non-increasing function for all $1 \le i \le N$, $0 \le j \le N$, where X_k is the cumulated amount of output k, $1 \le k \le N$.

(5) *Bounded learning:*

$$\partial f_{ji}/\partial X_k = 0 \quad if \quad either \quad X_k \ge X_k^* \quad or \quad X_i \ge X_i^*,$$

where X_k^* and X_i^* are respectively the 'learning ceilings' for industries k and i, in that once the cumulative output reaches the ceiling, the technology of this industry is called 'mature'. Further output accumulation in this industry provides no useful experience, and experience from any other industry can no longer reduce input requirements for this industry.

(6) *The non-triviality of learning:* If $X_i < X_i^*$ then $\partial f_{0i}/\partial X_i < 0$, in that for any industry not using mature technology, output accumulation at least reduces labour requirement.

(7) *Preferences:* All agents in this economy share both the input endowment and Geary-Stone preferences representable by the utility index

$$u = \sum_{i=1}^{N} b_i \log(c_i + \delta_i), \quad b_i \geq 0, \quad \sum_{i=1}^{N} b_i = 1 > b_1 \; ; \quad \delta_i \geq 0,$$

where c_i stands for the consumption of good i. If good i is not for consumption, $b_i = 0$.

Remark: An intuitive interpretation of (7) is that the representative agent consumes not commodity c_i, but 'characteristic' $(c_i + \delta_i)$, in the sense of Lancaster (1971), with δ_i being the latent endowment of the characteristic. Let the i-th characteristic denote 'mobility' then any person who walks is endowed with a quantity δ_i of that characteristic. This may be augmented by renting a bicycle, a car, or purchasing an air ticket, provided the price is right.

(8) *Given world prices:* The country being *small*, one can always normalise by selecting the units for goods and set the unit world prices of all goods to unity.

(9) *Balance of trade:* Each period, the aggregate consumption must equal the aggregate value-added

$$\sum_{i>0} c_i = \sum_{i>0} \left(x_i - \sum_{j>0} x_{ji} \right).$$

2.2 Definitions

I now introduce some definitions.

Definition 1: *The set of industries with mature technology is*

$$M = \{i \in \{1, N\}: \; X_i \geq X_i^* \}.$$

Definition 2: *Policy* $C (= A \; or \; T)$ *causes the economy to be shut-out (or stagnation) if:*

$$\forall i, \; x_i^C > 0 \; then \; i \in M,$$

where x_i^C is the value for output i under policy C.

Remarks:
1. In this model, a *shut-out* means no progress in technology for the present.
2. Further, a *shut-out* under autarky is permanent.
3. Since *no shut-out* dominates *shut-out*, one can rank policies in a situation if one policy causes a *shut-out* but the other does not.

For our purpose, we find the concept *shut-out* very useful (Wan and Weisman 1999). In each situation, our attention can now be focused upon the pair of policy-dependent current output vectors given by

$$x^A = (x_i^A)_{\forall i} \quad and \quad x^T = (x_i^T)_{\forall i}.$$

By short-circuiting the need for a fully dynamic analysis, we can retain tractability, even after relaxing the special assumptions of Stokey and Young.

We now have all the building blocks for our three examples, with the result of a double *shut-out*. For Example 1, *shut-out* is the outcome under free trade but not under autarky; for Examples 2 and 3, *shut-out* is the outcome under autarky but not under free trade. Further, Example 1 has the special assumptions similar to Stokey and Young. These are relaxed in Examples 2 and 3.

3. EXAMPLE 1 (INTERNATIONAL SUBSTITUTABILITY)

We now adopt four more assumptions, in the spirit of Stokey and Young. The first two establish why their conclusions rest in a very special case, and the second two lie at the heart of their reasoning.

(3') *Ricardian technology:* There is no intermediate input, traded or produced:

$$a_{ji} = 0, \quad \forall j > 0, \quad \forall i.$$

(7') *Mill-Graham preferences:* There is no Engel effect:

$$\delta_i = 0, \quad \forall i.$$

Remark: One implication of (7') is that no matter how rich or poor, everyone consumes every good in positive amounts and must produce every good under autarky.

It is now clear that Assumptions (3) and (7) of the Leontief technology (a generalisation of the Ricardian) and the Geary-Stone preference (a generalisation of the Mill-Graham) not only provide computational convenience but also highlight the special nature of Assumptions (3') and (7'), which underlie the conclusions of Stokey and Young.

Next we adopt the simplest specifications sufficient to portray the reasoning of Stokey and Young.

(10) *Comparative advantage:* $a_{01} = 1 < a_{0i}, \quad \forall i > 1.$

(11) *Maturity of technology:* (a) $1 \in M$, (b) $N \notin M$.

Assumptions (10) and (11a) together capture the reservation of Stokey and Young against free trade: the force of comparative advantage drives the developing economy to a production pattern that provides no useful experience. In contrast, (7), (7') and (11b) jointly imply that, under autarky, the developing economy – however poor it is – will consume every good, including some that will yield valuable learning.

This establishes the following proposition.

Proposition 1: *For Example 1, the economy is* **shut-out** *under free trade, but not under autarky.*

Proof. For free trade, $\forall i \notin M$, $i > 1$. Thus, for such a good, the value of marginal product of labour $= 1/a_{0i} < 1/a_{0i} = 1 =$ the value of marginal product of labour in good 1 and hence, $x_{0i}^T = 0$. For autarky, $x_N^A = c_N = (b_N)(1)/a_N > 0$ (by routine computation) where, by (11b), $N \notin M$.

4. EXAMPLE 2 (INTERNATIONAL COMPLEMENTARITY)

In this section and the next we show that the mere relaxation of the special assumptions (3') and (7') may yield results diametrically opposite to Example 1. Briefly, this is accomplished by constructing special examples with chosen numerical values. Two examples are given, each representing a case important in real life.

We first consider the effect of internationally traded inputs. There are two consumption goods, the traditional good 1 (abacus or sandals), which is produced directly and the modern good 2 (calculator or plastic shoes) which is costlessly fabricated from good 3 (simple parts) and good 4 (sophisticated material such as silicon chips or petrochemical powder) each requiring half a unit for each unit of output. Both intermediate inputs are produced by labour alone. The processes yielding both final goods 1 and 2 use *mature technology*; the processes producing the intermediate inputs, goods 3 and 4, do not.

The economy has a comparative advantage in good 3, but not in good 4, nor in good 2, which may be viewed as a mixture of goods 3 and 4. In fact, under Engel's effect, good 2 will be neither consumed nor produced in autarky. More specifically, we adopt the following assumptions.
(3") *Production functions:*

$$x_1 = x_{01}/a_{01}, x_2 = 2\min\{x_{32}, x_{42}\}, x_3 = x_{03}/a_{03}, x_4 = x_{04}/a_{04}.$$

(7") *Utility index:*

$$u = (1/2)[\log c_1 + \log(c_2 + 1)] \quad (b_1 = 1/2 = b_2; \quad \delta_1 = 0, \quad \delta_2 = 1).$$

(10") *Comparative advantage:* Input coefficients satisfy the inequalities $a_{03} < a_{01} = 1 < a_{02} < a_{04}$, where $a_{02} = (1/2)(a_{03} + a_{04})$ is the domestic unit labour required for good 2.

(11") *Mature technology:* $M = \{1, 2\}$.

We can now establish the following proposition.

Proposition 2: *For Example 2, the economy is* **shut-out** *under autarky, but not under free trade.*

Proof. For free trade,

$$1/a_{03} = \max \ \{1/a_{0i} : \forall i\}, \quad [\text{Assumption} \ (10")]$$

so that to attain the highest value of the marginal product of labour, all labour will be allocated to produce good 3, using a technology which is not mature. Thus the economy is not shut-out. For autarky all we need to verify is that $x^A = (1, \ 0, \ 0, \ 0)$ or, equivalently, that $(c_1, \ c_2) = (1, \ 0)$ is a *corner solution* for the consumer's equilibrium under the constraint that $(c_1, \ c_2)$ must be non-negative. Now, at $(1,0)$, the marginal utilities per unit value of labour are

$$(1/2)(1)/(a_{01}) = 1/2 \quad \text{for good} \ 1,$$
$$(1/2)(1)/(a_{02}) < 1/2 \quad \text{for good} \ 2,$$

proving what we desired. Thus $x_i^A > 0$, only for $i = 1 \in M$, so the economy is *shut-out* under autarky.

In the world of globalised production of today, those developing economies with sustained rapid growth either export parts under subcontract or import sophisticated components from the advanced economies (see Hobday 1995). In such context, the logic of Stokey and Young implies that trade plays the indispensable role for the developing economies to gain useful experience in production. Due to Engel's effect, an autarkic economy can scarcely afford those sophisticated goods, which alone provide their producers with valuable experience.

Remarks:
1. Nothing is changed if one assumes that the process producing good 2 uses some labour.

2. By the above analysis, customs unions among the developing economies may not bestow much benefit in providing valuable production experience. At best, one may replicate the domestic markets of an India or a China, which in themselves have never provided much benefit: most of what is sold there is produced with *mature technology* and generates no valuable experience.
3. It is also clear why the insistence on requirements of a 'high local content' (like Brazil used to demand for computer-related products) does not always benefit development.

5. A GRAPHIC ILLUSTRATION OF EXAMPLES 1 AND 2

Consider a small developing economy in a world with two final goods: good 1 for an abacus and good 2 for a calculator, with $c = (c_1, c_2)$ denoting the consumption bundle for the representative agent who has a fixed supply of one unit of labour. By normalisation, each unit of every good, whether or not it is for final consumption, is worth the same value on the world market. Both goods are produced with labour under constant returns: abacus is produced with mature technology; calculator consists of mechanical and electronic components, the technology of producing neither is mature. Presently, the unit labour requirements of these are as specified in Table 19.1.

In Table 19.1, each calculator uses half a unit of mechanical component as well as half a unit of electronic component, where each unit of the former requires half a unit of labour and each unit of the latter requires seven half units of labour. Thus, within each unit of calculator, the labour requirement is one-quarter unit for the mechanical part and seven quarters for the electronic part. So the total is 2 units of labour for each calculator.

Table 19.1 Unit Labour Requirements

(1)	(2)	(3)	(4)=(2)×(3)	(5)
	Component /Unit	Labour/ Component	Product	Labour /Unit
Abacus				1
Calculator				
Mechanical	½	½	¼	
Electronic	½	3 ½	1 ¾	
Sum				2

Now consider the following two examples specified in Table 19.2. Intermediate inputs are traded in Example 2, but not traded in Example 1. Thus, under free trade, the developing country specialises to produce the good in which it enjoys a comparative advantage. This is abacus in Example 1, yielding a per capita income of $1/1 = 1$ and mechanical components in Example 2, yielding per capital income of $1/(1/2) = 2$. Thus the free-trade budget line in the consumption space will always have a negative 45 degrees slope, with intercepts 1 and 1, or 2 and 2 under Example 1 and Example 2, respectively.

Table 19.2 Comparison of Examples

	Example 1	Example 2
Production	Integrated	Fragmented
Utility	$\log c_1 + \log c_2$	$\log c_1 + \log (1 + c_2)$

As shown in Figures 19.1 and 19.2, the production possibility frontier under autarky is always linear, with intercepts $c_1 = (1, \ 0)$ and $c_2 = (0, \ 1/2)$.

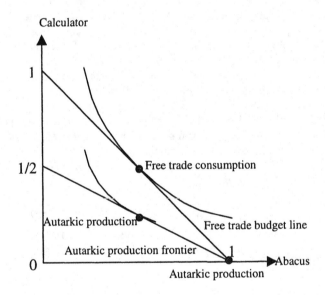

Figure 19.1 Example 1

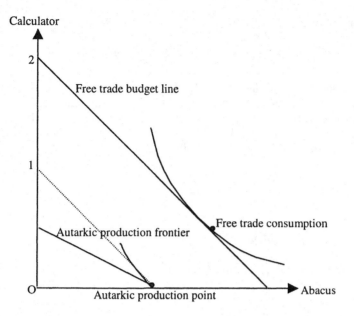

Figure 19.2 Example 2

6. EXAMPLE 3 (DOMESTIC COMPLEMENTARITY)

To demonstrate the versatility of our general formulation, we include a further example, which appears relevant in view of the economic development literature. This is a variant of Example 2 above, with the introduction of a non-traded intermediate input, 'service' (quality control, production scheduling, etc.), which is produced domestically in sector $N = 4$. We identify sectors 1, 2 and 3 respectively as 'traditional', 'light' (wigs, toys, parasols, etc.) and 'heavy' (electronics, transportation equipment, etc.) industry sectors.

For illustration, we adapt from Example 2 the relevant assumptions as follows:

(3''') *Production functions:*

$$x_1 = x_{01}, \ x_2 = (3/a_{02})\min\{x_{02}, 2x_{42}\},$$
$$x_3 = (3/a_{03})\min\{2x_{03}, x_{43}\}, \ x_4 = x_{04}/a_{04}.$$

Remark: One may reinterpret x_0 and x_4 as direct and indirect labour respectively.

(7''') *Utility index:*

$$u = (1/2)[\log c_1 + \log(c_3 + 1)], \quad (b_1 = 1/2 = b_3; \ \delta_1 = 0, \ \delta_3 = 1).$$

Remark: Noticeably, at the early phase, the light industry exports of developing economies are not much demanded in their home markets.

(8''') *Given world prices:* The unit price of all *traded* goods 1, 2 and 3 are normalised to 1.

(9''') *Balance of trade:* Each period, the following must hold:

$$\sum_{i=1}^{N} c_i = \sum_{i<N} \left(x_i - \sum_{0<j<N} x_{ji} \right).$$

(10''') *Comparative advantage:*

$$a_{01} = 1 = a_{04}, \ a_{02} < 1 < a_{03},$$

but,

$$(1/3)a_{03} < (2/3)a_{02} < 1.$$

To complete our example, we retain the following assumption.

(11'') *Mature technology:* $M = \{1, \ 2\}$.

Thus, under free trade, current learning takes place in sector N.

By routine computation, similar to that employed for Example 2, we can establish that

$$x^A = (1,0,0,0,0) \quad \text{and} \quad x^T = (0,1/a_{02},0,1/3).$$

In view of Assumption (11''), we have proved the following proposition.

Proposition 3: *For Example 3, the economy is **shut-out** under autarky, but not under free trade.*

Corollary: *The comparative advantage of the economy will shift to good 3 (the product of 'heavy industry') when a_{04} has been reduced sufficiently.*

Observation: By Assumption (11''), a_{01} remains at unity, but a_{04} declines with learning. The comparative advantage of the economy lies with good 2 (the 'light industry' product) only if

$$[(2/3)a_{01} + (1/3)a_{04}]a_{02} < 1 < [(1/3)a_{01} + (2/3)a_{04}]a_{03}.$$

Remarks:
1. In the modern world, there are two types of jobs: the skilled and the unskilled. Only for the former type does experience improve productivity and reduce manpower requirement.
2. In modern industries, there are two types of products. For one type, relatively more skilled work is required; the accumulation of output makes the production more efficient; the operations are yet not standardised, making it difficult for less developed economies to compete; the output satisfies the sophisticated needs of the people. These are often classified as 'heavy industries' as distinct from the others, which are referred to as 'light'.
3. In developing economies, there are two types of trade regimes. For one type, the heavy industries are promoted by trade restrictions so that their output may be absorbed by the domestic market and not the world market. This is the import substitution regime, with autarky as its idealisation. The other is called outward-oriented, with free trade as its ideal form.
4. In centrally planned economies, the trade regime is consciously designed to serve the long-term goal of an economy. Understandably, import substitution policy is usually pursued to promote the heavy industries.
5. Historically, many East Asian economies started their development program under severe balance of trade pressure. They exported whatever they could: toys for Hong Kong, wigs for Korea and parasols, etc. for Taiwan.
6. Four decades after World War II, central planning is abandoned by most economies as a dead end, in New Delhi no less than in Beijing, in Moscow no less than in Brasilia. Foreign technology and foreign investment are universally welcome with tax holidays, etc. At the same time, East Asian economies have become competitive over time in automobiles, computers and consumer electronics.
7. Part of the explanation may lie in the need for imported key parts and components (engines for cars, central processing chips for computers) when developing economies embark on industrialisation. That is where Example 2 comes in. But the other part is the gradual building up of human capital (for management and marketing) in 'light industries' to lay the foundation of heavy industrialisation. In business literature, the availability of satellitic industries for industrial suppliers are repeatedly cited nowadays as an advantage of East Asia as industrial sites. Example 3 is an attempt to explain such a mechanism in analytic terms. For related trade literature, see Jones and Kierzkowski (1990).

7. CONCLUSION

On policy issues that affect the world's least developed countries, this chapter has studied how trade influences learning with three examples and has come up with conflicting conclusions. As researchers in trade theory, when perplexed, we seek guidance from the life work of Murray Kemp, the trade theorist *par excellence* of our day, and ask how he might have handled it when conflicting theoretical possibilities coexist on issues of significant welfare consequence.

Two points soon become clear.

1. Economics is an empirical field. Economists discipline arguments with theory, yet policy assessment must still be anchored on evidence, a task no different from what faces the trial lawyer or the historian. Kemp (1964) ended the first edition of his trade theory with an unwritten chapter, reserved especially for econometric evidence. It is his methodological statement for all ages.

2. Econometrics is not merely applied statistics. Structures are drawn from economic analysis to form specifications and help the processing and assessment of evidence. For example in his joint study (Hadley and Kemp 1966) on transportation cost and trade, Kemp arrived at the most comprehensive and realistic formulation of the topic, even to this day.

In short, thoughtful empirical work should be made on the trade-learning nexus, in proportion to its policy relevance.

We now turn to two lines of empirical research on learning. First, Backus, Kehoe and Kehoe (1992) found significant learning effects only with disaggregated, manufacturing data. Also a high index of intra-industry trade (a situation closer to free trade) is seen to benefit growth performance. This is to be expected. By our Examples 2 and 3, any productive activity using mature technology (like making sandals) yields output value but not valuable experience. Thus, significant learning effects can hardly be found from aggregate data.

Second, Krugman (1994) cited econometric studies that attributed East Asian high growth to investment, and not to trade or productivity gain. Now such results involve both the East Asian economies where, by Lucas, launching new export industries is a signal characteristic, and the aggregate production function, about which one should quote Solow (1966, pp. 1259-60) in full:

> I have never thought of the macroeconomic production function as a rigorously justifiable concept... It is either an illustrating parable, or else a mere device to handle data, to be used so long as it gives good empirical results, and to be abandoned as soon as it doesn't, or as soon as something better comes along.

Thus, by his criterion, we can conclude that the aggregate production function no longer 'gives good results' in identifying the cause for growth, if in launching new industries, the importance of learning and trade can be independently established by other means.

An informative example is well documented in Stern et al. (1995): the 1986 entry of Hyundai Motors into the American car market. Believing that the expected learning from its US sales would be crucial to its viability, Hyundai both (a) invested heavily to meet the US emission standard, and (b) prepared for an initial loss of US $1000 per car. The gambit paid off after efforts over the period 1974-1986, when its first sales happened to incur no loss. Since the project may benefit any firm in the industry beyond the one making the first sales, this justifies the generous loans from Korean government banks, by the Kemp (1960) criterion.

Here, the expected productivity gain, investment, export sales and realised gain are indispensable links which form a virtuous circle. Exports must be an integral part of the investment plan, or else spending would never be targeted on a specific foreign emission standard. There must be expected benefit from learning, but not from scale economies or else there would never be the need nor the rationale to prepare for losses on initial sales. History proved that the expectations were rational. The gambit paid off. To analyse the cause for growth, the aggregate production function approach claims that investment is all-important, which we accept, but dismisses as unimportant the causes of investment in the first place, namely, learning and trade. That is certainly not giving good results.

In real life, each investment project involves a flow input and flow output model, with the anticipated productivity gain built into the output stream. The closest approximation in the growth literature is the putty-clay model, like that of Kemp and Thanh (1966).

We present below some further observations, which are both tentative and second-hand.

First, exporting to the most 'demanding' markets is essential to learning. According to Morawetz (1981), style is crucial for garments sold in America, but not inside the Andean Group. Catering to American fashion, East Asian suppliers have acquired the capability for punctual delivery, which their Columbian counterparts cannot match. Thus, autarky would be ineffective for learning.

Second, the import of key components is essential to the sales of up-scale goods. According to Chu (1997), when Taiwan's exports of bicycles expanded, its local content percentage fell. Thus, internationally traded inputs help learning.

Third, the skill developed in exporting certain products appears to be transferable to other, more valuable, products. According to Kim and Leipziger (1993), Handok, a Korean firm, moved from exporting wigs to computer parts in just a few short years. Thus, domestically supplied (export) services help learning, irrespective of what is initially exported.

As such, these are certainly inconclusive in themselves, but they may offer a basis in the future to organise a search for systematic evidence.

It is apropos to note that the focus of the present study is on the policy implications of the learning mechanism and trade regimes, as a response to the work of Young and Stokey. Time and space do not allow a full exploration here into the analytic relationship between the models used here and the gains from trade literature covered in Kemp (1995).

ACKNOWLEDGEMENTS

I would like to acknowledge the helpful comments of Simone Clemhout, the useful advice of an anonymous referee and the stimulation gained from reading the forthcoming paper 'Learning-by-doing, trade in capital goods and growth' by Goh Ai-ting and Jacques Olivier. I am thankful for Mrs Paulette Calisle's patient assistance in preparing this paper. All remaining errors are my responsibility.

REFERENCES

Aghion, Philippe and Peter Howitt (1998), *Endogenous Growth Theory*, Cambridge MA: MIT Press.

Backus, David K., Kehoe, Patrick J. and Timothy J. Kehoe (1992), 'In search of scale effects in trade and growth', *Journal of Economic Theory*, **58**, 377-409.

Bhagwati, Jagdish (1999), 'The miracle that did happen: understanding East Asia in comparative perspective', in Erik Thorbecke and Henry Wan, Jr (eds), *Taiwan's Development Experience: Lessons on Roles of Government and Market*, Norwell, MA: Kluwer Academic Publishers.

Chu, Wan-wen (1997), 'Causes of growth: a study of Taiwan's bicycle industry', *Cambridge Journal of Economics*, **21**, 55-72.

Chuang, Yih-Chiy (1998), 'Learning-by-doing, the technology gap and growth', *International Economic Review*, **39**, 697-721.

Clark, Carol (1993), 'Relative backwardness in Eastern Europe: an application of the technological gap hypothesis', *Economic Systems*, **17**, 167-93.

Goh, Ai-ting and Jacques Olivier (2002), 'Learning-by-doing, trade in capital goods and growth', *Journal of International Economics*, **56**, 411-44.

Hadley, George and Murray C. Kemp (1966), 'Equilibrium and efficiency in international trade', *Metroeconomica*, **18**, 125-41.

Helpman, Elhanan and Paul Krugman (1985), *Market Structure and Foreign Trade: Increasing Returns, Monopolistic Competition and the International Economy*, Cambridge MA: MIT Press.

Hobday, Michael (1995), *Innovation in Asia: A Challenge to Japan*, Aldershot: Edward Elgar.

Jones, Ronald W. and Henryk Kierzkowski (1990), 'The role of services in production and international trade: a theoretical framework', in R.W. Jones and A.O. Krueger (eds), *The Political Economy of International Trade: Essays in Honor of Robert E. Baldwin*, Oxford: Blackwell.

Kemp, Murray C. (1960), 'The Mill-Bastable dogma', *Journal of Political Economy*,

68, 65-67.

Kemp, Murray C. (1964), *The Pure Theory of International Trade*, Englewood Cliffs, NJ: Prentice-Hall.

Kemp, Murray C. (1995), *The Gains from Trade and the Gains from Aid*, London: Routlege.

Kemp, Murray C. and Pham Chih Thanh (1966), 'On a class of growth models', *Econometrica*, **34**, 257-82.

Kim, Kihwan and Danny Leipziger (1993), *Korea: A Case of Government-led Development*, Washington, DC: World Bank.

Krugman, Paul (1994), 'The myth of Asia's miracle', *Foreign Affairs*, **73**, 62-78.

Lancaster, Kelvin (1971), *Consumer Demand: A New Approach*, New York: Columbia University Press.

Lau, Man-lui and Henry Wan, Jr (1994), 'On the mechanism of catching-up', *European Economic Review*, **38**, 952-63.

Lucas, Robert E. Jr (1976), 'Econometric policy evaluation: a critique', *Journal of Monetary Economics* (supplement series), **1** (2), 19-46.

Lucas, Robert E. Jr (1988), 'On the mechanics of economic development', *Journal of Monetary Economics*, **22**, 3-42.

Morawetz, David (1981), *Why the Emperor's New Clothes are Not Made in Columbia: a Case Study of Latin American and East Asian Manufactured Exports*, New York, NY: Oxford University Press.

Solow, Robert M. (1966), 'Review of Capital and Growth', *American Economic Review,* **56**, 1257-60.

Stern, Joseph J., Kim, Ji-hong, Perkins, Dwight H. and Jung-ho Yoo (1995), *Industrialization and the State: The Korean Heavy and Chemical Industry Drive*, Cambridge, MA: Harvard University Press.

Stokey, Nancy L. (1991), 'Human capital, product quality and growth', *Quarterly Journal of Economics*, **106**, 587-616.

Van, Hoang Pham and Henry Y. Wan, Jr (1997), 'Interpreting East Asian growth', in Bjarne S. Jensen and Kar-yiu Wong (eds), *Dynamics, Economic Growth and International Trade*, Ann Arbor MI: Michigan University Press.

Wan, Henry Y., Jr and Jason Weisman (1999) 'Hong Kong: the fragile economy of middlemen', *Review of International Economics*, **7**, 410-30.

Young, Alwyn (1991), 'Learning-by-doing and the dynamic effects of international trade', *Quarterly Journal of Economics*, **106**, 369-405.

Young, Alwyn (1993), 'Invention and bounded learning-by-doing', *Journal of Political Economy*, **101**, 443-72.

Why Rapid Growth is Associated with Stagnant Total Productivity?

Review of "Total Factor Productivity and the Catching-up Process", jointly with Yeun Yeun Lim[*]

The total factor productivity growth (TFPG) puzzle Traditionally, the method of total factor productivity growth has been widely applied in economics without causing much comment. Also the four Asian Newly Industrialized Economies (NIEs) were regarded as models for sustained rapid development. But then Kim and Lau (1994) and also Young (1994, 1995) showed that the NIEs have very low scores in TFPG.

This Article argues that such conclusions are due to the inherent bias of the method in measuring TFPG, which becomes glaring when economies are at a stage of launching rapid growth. The reason is that much of the once-for-all capital charges are made at that stage. An example is the Korean automobile company, Hyundai Motors, which spent heavily for a dozen years to enter the American market. When researchers noticed the heavy capital spending, not accompanied by concurrent output gains, they placed no weight on any resultant advantages that might lie in the future, and concluded wrongly about low gain in productivity.

A penetrating observation was made by Professor Wan-Wen Chu. If we study the economies which ranked very high in terms of their TFPG scores, like Egypt and Pakistan, we will find that they never did well in terms of growth. Therefore, in evaluating economic development, the TFPG approach should not be accorded much importance.

Further discussion Wan (2004) distinguishes the criticism made against the biased methodology, from criticism against the data or statistical procedure used. In the latter case, errors may be distributed evenly, straddling the true phenomenon. Here, the true productivity gain is understated in a systematical manner.

---

[*]The article first appeared in *Human Capital, Trade and Public Policy in Rapidly Growing Economies: From Theory to Empirics*, Michele Boldrin, Been-Lon Chen and Ping Wang (eds.), pp. 129–152, 2004. The author is grateful to the publisher, Edward Elgar, for granting the permit to reprint in this volume.

The years in the new century have seen both the marked slowing down of growth and the threat of income polarization in all the Asian NIEs. Since the rapid growth of Japan ended when Japanese per capita real income was almost within 10% of the American level, the recent slowing down of the economic growth of Korea and Taiwan appear rather premature in comparison. This might lead some observers to return to the views of Kim and Lau, or Young, a decade ago. A more balanced view is likely to give more weight to the crowding out effect of China's rapid growth, with impact on the world's terms of trade, turning against the traditional export of East Asia. Further progress is possible, but takes far more effort. Moreover, the above discussion also highlights the fact that the axle-and-spokes model outlined in Article 13 is only a first approximation: there are interactions to be considered among the "spokes" (namely, the East Asian economies in their dealings with America, the technology leader).

Total Factor Productivity and the Catching-up Process

Yeun Yeun Lim and Henry Wan

1 INTRODUCTION

Growth accounting introduces four types of systematic bias that understate the efficiency gain in newly industrialized economies (NIEs) and cause a variety of unwarranted conclusions. For development studies, a better performance measure is the proportional rate of income gap reduction.

This chapter is part of a larger study. It serves three purposes: first, to reconsider the notion of total factor productivity growth (TFPG); second, to offer an alternative performance measure for economic development; and finally, to relate these two measures empirically. These issues are addressed in the next three sections. Some concluding remarks then follow.

2 ON TFPG

Today, TFPG is a ubiquitous empirical tool for economic growth and development. Debates raged in the early 1990s, when the measurement of the TFPG of the Asian NIEs led to four surprising conclusions, namely, these economies:

1. had insignificant and indifferent rates of technical progress,
2. gained merely a one-shot benefit from trade, at best,
3. owed their output growth only to increased input use (in particular, capital input), and
4. would suffer the same fate as that of the former Soviet economy (the 'Krugman hypothesis').[1]

According to Felipe (1999), these findings are supported by the 'fundamentalists' with additional estimates, but criticized by the 'assimilationists', because of contradicting measurements of TFPG and because growth accounting took no account of important facts from case studies, such as the assimilation of foreign technology. Yet, in the cited literature, almost no one had established any systematic bias in growth accounting,[2] or offered any alternative measurement for developmental performance.

These last two aspects are important from the historical perspective. TFPG was introduced by Solow (1957), using the aggregate production function. According to Solow (1966, 1257-60), the aggregate production function is not 'rigorously justifiable'. For him, it serves only as 'either an illuminating parable or a mere device to handle data, to be used so long as it gives good empirical results, and to be abandoned as soon as it doesn't, or as soon as something better comes along'. Under Solow's standard, the presence of either *systematic bias* or a *better alternative* would limit the application of TFPG. This will be so especially for the non-OECD economies, an application about which Solow (2000) has serious reservations.

Further digression is in order. The efficacy of growth accounting rests on three critical assumptions:

1. there is only one universal good,
2. the saving/income ratio is exogenously decided by behavioral factors, and
3. production technology is unaffected by influence outside the economy.

As we shall see later, the relaxation of these assumptions may invite systematic bias.

Solow (1957) was the first to apply growth accounting to a mature economy — America. As the leading industrial power at that time, America had little to learn from others. Thus, in his context, the third assumption is rather innocuous. Now, that growth accounting exercise was a complement to Solow (1956), which established the fact that given any substitutability between capital and labor, the Harrod–Domar model loses its 'knife-edge' property. To prove his point, Solow retained the first and second features. These came from the writings of Roy Harrod and John Maynard Keynes, where in the one-good economy, the saving behavior follows the 'Fundamental Psychological Law' and 'Animal Spirit' decides the investment. These assumptions were never the only consideration for Solow, for example, witness the theoretic investigation in Samuelson and Solow (1956), which offers a *many-good* version for the Ramsey model of *optimal saving*.

In this chapter, we take a different approach from the literature surveyed by Felipe. It may well be true that the 'Krugman hypothesis' makes no distinction between the former Soviet Union, an isolated victim of creative destruction, and Singapore, the host that benefited from the best high-tech multinational corporations (MNCs). It may well be true that the hypothesis stands on both the Kim and Lau (1994) study *and* the Young (1994) findings: the former concludes that statistically, the efficiency gain of Japan is significant and that of Korea is not; the latter ranks Korea higher than Japan in productivity gain. But our concern here is not how valid is a particular set of estimations, but, whether, as a method, growth accounting carries what kind of implicit, systematic bias about NIEs, wherever they are, in East Asia today, or in any other location at any other time.

By their nature, NIEs are in a process of becoming more industrialized, and they have only started doing so recently. This has systematic effects on individual, firm, sector and economy-wide levels.

2.1 Individual Level

At the *individual level*, agents with forethought usually save more to invest in the future, if industrialization presents more rewarding investment prospects. This causal chain is shown as the arrow with a question mark in Figure 6.1. It is not considered in growth accounting.

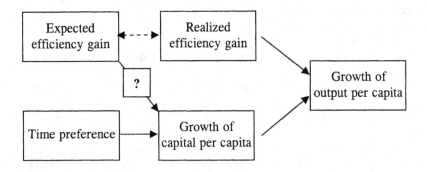

Figure 6.1 Causal chain in question: does efficiency gain matter to investment?

2.2 Firm Level

At the *firm level*, in an economy undergoing industrialization, enterprises more frequently make and implement long-term plans. For benefits in the long-haul they incur once-and-for-all investment in sunk cost. This situation is depicted in Figure 6.2.

One example is the well-documented entry of Hyundai Motors of Korea into the American market. This move was deemed crucial to Hyundai's viability (Stern et al., 1995). In preparation, for this move, Hyundai invested for years, and acquired the technology to meet the *American* standard for emission control. An allowance was made for a loss of $1,000 per car on its first American sales. Since both learning by exporting and the investment were indispensable to the whole project, clearly efficiency gain cannot be computed as a residual. Also trade must benefit growth. The project was planned in the 1970s, under President Park's Heavy-Chemical Industry

Drive. After a decade-long gestation period, the first American sales were made in 1986.

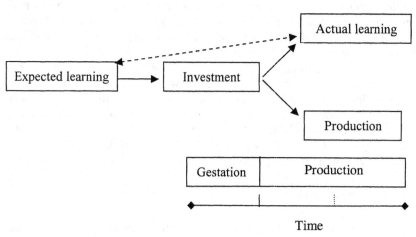

Figure 6.2   Phased production

The NIEs are, after all, economies that are *newly* industrialized. There tend to be proportionately more projects in the gestation phase. Because of such separation in time, growth accounting − based on the aggregate data from such economies − is likely to exaggerate the importance of increased capital spending during the early years.

Assuming that the production phase is twice as long as the gestation phase, a comparison between an NIE and a 'mature' industrialized economy is depicted in Figure 6.3 Proportionately speaking, the NIEs have fewer projects in the production phase but more in the gestation phase. According to traditional growth accounting, more capital spending means less efficiency gain, since the latter is regarded as a residual.

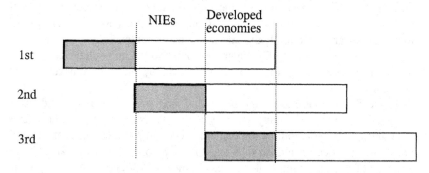

Figure 6.3   Economies and overlapping generations of projects

2.3 Sector Level

At the *sector level*, the first movers in a new industry make investments that provide information beneficial to the late-coming rivals. This discourages firms from being pioneers. In economic development, the justification for an industrial policy is its ability to remedy coordination failure. Whether due to government action (such as in Taiwan, Korea and Singapore) or a changing environment (such as in Hong Kong), new industries begin to emerge. Granted that for each firm, certain sunk cost is incurred in capital spending at the initial stage, and firms enter industries in all economies all the time, yet in a new industry, the firm making the first move must pay more in sunk cost. Proportionately there are more new industries in NIEs; therefore more capital spending is to be expected.

2.4 Economy Level

At the *economy level*, the process of industrialization provides valuable experience, both improving product-specific skills in those current operations and acquiring generic capability for more complex operations. The enhanced generic capability makes it profitable for firms to enter industries that use more valuable equipment per worker, that is, in industries with a higher capital/labor ratio.

For the sake of simplicity, consider an economy with a sequence of three sectors, light, heavy and high-tech, each operating under constant returns. Each industry is more complex than the last, which means a higher capital/labor ratio is used at any factor-price ratio. Entry into more complex industries is facilitated by the accumulation of generic industrial capability. The production process in any industry contributes to the accumulation of such competence. This is represented in Figure 6.4. The production process of each industry yields a threefold joint product: (i) the output, (ii) the specific skill that is useful in the same industry and (iii) the accumulation of generic industrial capability. The last one contributes to the operation of industries of greater complexity and hence capital intensity.

As in Van and Wan (1997), Figure 6.5 portrays the unit-value isoquants for the three industries, in both a developed economy and a 'pre-development' economy.

In the figure, there are three unit-value isoquants, shown as solid lines, labeled light industry, heavy industry and high-tech industry. Each shows the minimum labor–capital pairs that are needed to produce one unit value of output in the specific industry. Along the common tangent line ab (cd) for any pair of adjacent unit-value isoquants, the capital/labor ratio is higher in the heavy (high-tech) industry than in the light (heavy) industry. Points on

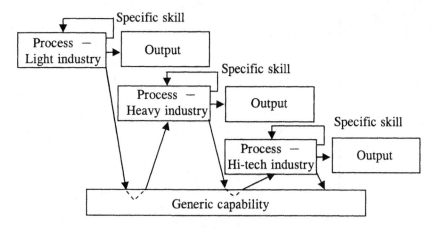

Figure 6.4   Specific and generic learning

any common tangent line represent the pairs of labor and capital inputs which can be so divided and allocated to the two adjacent industries, so that under constant returns, they will still produce one unit value of total output. The three isoquants together with the two common tangent lines become ee, the unit-value envelope for the pre-development economy. Only labor–capital pairs above or to the right of this envelope can produce one unit value of output. In contrast, in the developed economy, less input can still produce a unit value of output by using more advanced technology. This is depicted by

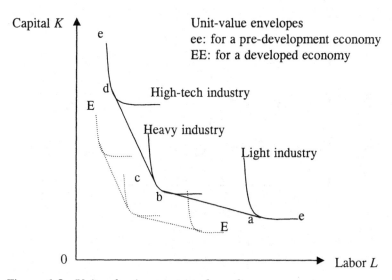

Figure 6.5   Unit-value isoquants and envelopes

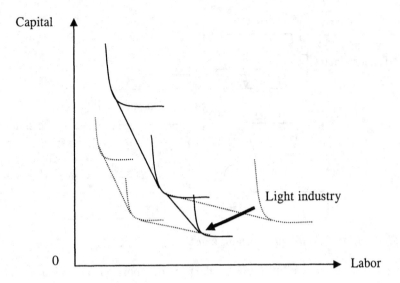

Figure 6.6   Early developing phase

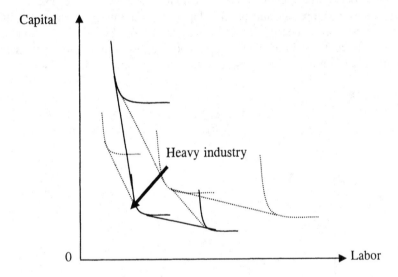

Figure 6.7   Late developing phase

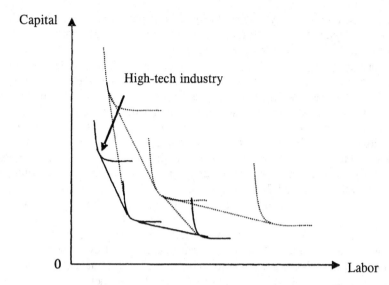

Figure 6.8 The developed economy

the unit-value industry-specific isoquants, their common tangent lines, as well as the envelope EE.

The development process allows the developing economy to assimilate foreign technology, but to do so for only one industry at a time. Moreover, progress will start from the simplest or the most labor-intensive sector, and move gradually into the more technically complex and the more capital intensive sectors. These are shown in Figures 6.6, 6.7 and 6.8. The envelope curve, shown as a solid line, joins the available unit-value isoquants with common tangent lines.

2.5 Summary

It is time now to take stock of the implications of the above analysis. Under the analysis described in Section 2.4, an economy enjoying rapid output growth would accumulate much generic capability, which will lead to a rapid shift of comparative advantage toward the capital-intensive industries. Under traditional growth accounting, capital accumulation would be regarded as the main source for growth, leaving little as the 'Solow residual'.[3] Now consider the analyses in Sections 2.2 and 2.3 together. Proportionately speaking, the NIEs are likely to have more industries that are new, with their firms paying the price of the first mover with heavier spending in sunk cost. There will also be more firms involved in the early phases of long-term plans, spending heavily during the gestation period of their plants. The 'pre-development' economies do not have to invest in such capital spending. Mature industrialized economies have already gone through this phase, and are presently enjoying the fruits of past endeavor. Thus, under the traditional growth accounting, the playing field is never level when one compares the NIEs against the other economies. Therefore, the actual productivity gain of the NIEs should be systematically larger than is found under growth accounting. This is true both in the relative sense, due to the analyses in Sections 2.2 and 2.3, and in the absolute sense as in Section 2.4. Although their productivity gain is less visible to the practitioners of growth accounting, it should be obvious to agents in those economies. According to the analysis in Section 2.1, such awareness will increase the rate at which they need to save in order to invest, in response to the encouraging prospects for growth. On the other hand, those drawing conclusions from their estimated TFPG would not look into what motivates investment, paying no heed to the Lucas critique (1976). In that sense, the role of efficiency gain (and what 'openness' has contributed to it) is systematically misrepresented, over and over again, all in the same direction of understatement.

3   AN ALTERNATIVE PERFORMANCE MEASURE

3.1   Motivation

Growth accounting was introduced to serve growth theory, which arose in the middle of the twentieth century. The growth theory has its focus on the *fully developed economies*; the premise is independent evolution, with influence from outside of the economy taken as given. By the end of the century, two trends become evident. First, the world economy has become increasingly integrated into a global system. As shown by data from the World Trade Organization, total trade has grown faster than total output, in almost all sectors, from agriculture to mining to manufacturing, and for all four post-Second World War subperiods, namely, 1950–63, 1963–73, 1973–90, and 1990–99.[4] Second, the growth literature, such as Lucas (1988, 1993), also cites the dramatic record of the NIEs[5] as evidence. Nowadays, growth theorists apply the same analytic approach to both the fully developed and other economies.

It is only natural that the new century will bring forth new research efforts, built upon the achievements of earlier theories, but also taking into account additional facts. The outline of such research is already predictable. It must capture a cardinal fact of this brave new world: the interdependence among the various economies, from the most advanced to the less developed. This, of course, is a theme already examined by Prebisch (1959) and Vernon (1966), and analyzed in the influential paper of Krugman (1979).

What has not been studied in depth is the fact that some economies of the developing South, like Japan, can reinvent themselves as members of the developed North. Logically, this process should be the most important matter in the field of development economics.

The new theory should also be empirically based. During the last dozen years or so, various types of endogenous growth model have arisen. Solow (2000) voiced his reservations, because each of these theories relies heavily upon highly specific assumptions. Now in all natural sciences, the presence of competing explanations of reality is commonplace. An example is whether global warming has already begun. In field after field, time after time, scientists eventually reach consensus by searching for testable implications and the observed evidence. There is every reason to believe that research in economics will proceed in a similar manner, rebuilding consensus on observations. Indeed, there is already a thriving literature on the convergence hypothesis. However, most such research is not based upon an overall conceptual framework. Consequently, the observed results often appear mutually contradictory, and defy interpretation. That is why we shall revisit such grounds anew.

3.2 The Technical Gap: The Concept and the Quantification

Having decided to study the interdependence of various economies empirically, we believe a good starting point is the series of per capita GNPs at international prices, as available in the data bank, namely, the World Development Index. There are 110 economies with uninterrupted data over those 24 years, 1975–98.[6] Set $N=110$, $T=24$. We shall call these $NT = 2,640$ entries the *basic array*. Invoking a theme that has long been studied, namely, the 'technology gap,' the next step is to search for evidence for a theory about the interactions between the advanced 'center' and the followers in the 'periphery'. Our objective is to find for any 'following economy' at any instant, a measurement for this technology gap.

In principle, the problem can be quite complex. In real life, the center for technical progress is likely to cut across national boundaries. It may include both Tokyo, Japan and Silicon Valley, California, USA, but not Hokkaido, Japan or West Virginia, USA. Given the statistics available to us, our task becomes much simplified if we can approximate the center with a single economy.

In searching for one particular economy as a proxy for the center, it is preferable to follow some formal criteria. This might be done in two steps. First, over the era studied,[7] look *first* for a class of economies, each of which has enjoyed the highest per capita real GDP for at least one period. Call this class (of economies) the *dominant set*, and refer to its size as 'n'.

This set is said to be *properly dominant*, if $n < N$. The presence of a proper dominant set presumably implies a differentiated world. Second, find out in per capita real GDP, whether any of these n economies in this set ranks within the top n places, for all the N periods. If so, call this a *leading economy*. An economy fulfilling this 'ranking condition' must have access to a broad range of 'best practices'. Hence it can serve as the source of technology transfer. Finally, ask whether such economic leadership is unique. if the answer is positive, the technology gap can be computed in a straightforward manner.

The above discussion is lengthy but necessary. When working with many economies over a sufficiently long era, it seems to be too much to expect that there is only a single leader, and that particular economy is also the sole member of the dominant set. (See Appendix 6A for the five examples that clarify such concepts.)

For once, economists are quite lucky. Data show that together with Luxembourg, Switzerland and the United Arab Emirates, America belongs to a four-economy properly dominant set. Further, among these four, America alone is the economic leader.[8]

Overtaking the economic leader is neither impossible by logic, nor unprecedented in history. Yet, over the two and half centuries after the Industrial Revolution, the only clear case of such an event is America overtaking Britain. In that case, America, as an emerging leader, had exhibited tremendous technological precocity for a long period. The observations within our basic array offers few clues about *whether*, *when* and *how* the American economic leadership will be displaced by *which* other economy. In the recent past, there is as yet no other economy, beside America, that has exhibited such extraordinary technical vigor.

The presence of a consistent economic leader is convenient for studying those 106 economies outside the proper, dominant set.[9] Using concepts going back to Alexander Gerschenkron and Simon Kuznets, we may study a few purely arithmetical relationships between q_{it}, the per capita real GDP of a specific economy i and Q_t, the same for the leading economy. The ratio, $r_{it} = q_{it} / Q_t$, is sometimes referred to as the relative per capita real output (or GDP) and R is defined as the steady-state value of r_{it}. R may be assumed to be either unity, which means an actual catching-up with the leader, or it may take some other positive value, on account of certain other immutable facts. For example, one may consider the advantage of Singapore, as both a natural harbor and a defensible island at the head of the Malacca Strait, or the challenge for Finland of having the short growth season of 'Arctic farming'. Thus, ultimately Singapore may be somewhat richer than America and Finland somewhat poorer. In the late twentieth century, the rising output per capita has been the norm rather than the exception for most economies. Therefore in development economics, *international inequality*, rather than *poverty*, poses the popular challenge.

From this perspective, what is relevant are the expressions, $Q_t - q_{it}$, and perhaps even more appropriately, $g_{it} = (Q_t - q_{it})/Q_t = 1 - r_{it}$. These are specifically, the absolute and relative (per capita, real) output gaps of economy i, relative to the economic leader. At the same time, due to the non-rival nature of knowledge, emulation (or imitation) is often easier than innovation. The presence of an output gap is both a challenge, with its closing as the goal for development, and an opportunity. The presence of the gap makes it easier to improve the current practice toward the 'best practice'. Thus we shall refer to g_{it} as the *technological backlog*.

To recapitulate, in the mid-twentieth century, growth theory arose in order to study the advanced economies under *independent* evolution. At the dawn of the new millennium, a catching-up theory should be developed in this increasingly *interdependent* world, for the sake of all the technologically less advanced, whether in Bombay, Singapore, Sydney or Paris. After all, from laser to optical fiber, from the production of sub-micron semiconductors to Internet communication via the globally-positioned satellite system, from containerized shipping to bio-engineered food, most of such progress becomes implemented, if not also initiated, in a single economy. This fact poses specific economic choices for that 95 percent of the world's population residing elsewhere.

Speaking generally from the economic point of view, there are three parts of the current world: the developed North, the less-developed South, and the evolving East. The North and the South may appear poles apart. But there is never any East Pole. The East is a metaphor for those regions emerging from the ranks of the South to converge toward the North. Those converging at a fast pace largely rely on their close economic relationship with America, that economy in the North which is the incumbent economic leader. The observed performance of East Asia represents a phase of transformation. This process of transformation is not automatic, or instantaneous, or accessible to all. By themselves, the poorest economies may not attempt the transformation at all, or even if they try as hard as possible, not all may succeed. For others, conscious government action may be needed to overcome market failure. In any case, a self-sustained transformation may take time to bear fruit.

What made Japan (and Korea and Hong Kong) economically successful is not all that different from some more recent development episodes in the periphery of Europe along the great arc, from Israel (in the Near East) to Cyprus, from Malta to the Iberian Peninsula and thence to Ireland. Their record reflects the same general process at work. In that sense, both the wrong and the right steps taken by these economies are useful at least to those 95 percent of humankind referred to above.

The empirical findings on such issues are the subject matter of the ongoing studies of Lau, Hong and Wan, and much of the historical and institutional analysis will be elaborated in the monograph of Wan (2004). In this chapter, we have two principal goals in mind: first, the catching-up rate, and second, the growth of total factor productivity (TFP), which serves as the workhorse in usual empirical macroeconomics.

We shall first present some analytic relationships between the catching-up rate, z_{it}, (which is the relative rate of change of g_{it}), and the growth rate, G_{it} (which is the relative rate of change of q_{it}), under some simple hypotheses. Next, we shall present some elementary findings by analyzing the evidence from the basic array. We find that the growth paths of several economies such as Japan and Singapore, as well as Malta, bear close resemblance to the predicted time paths for per capita product under one of our simple models. Furthermore, the findings in Lau and Wan (1994) imply that $R < 1$. In other words, the catching-up tends to be incomplete. This is in agreement with some of the simple models.

We then compare the rankings of 66 economies by Young (1994) with the average catching-up rates we have obtained from the basic array. The weak correlation between these two rates is related to the low TFP of the East Asian NIEs, as found by Kim and Lau (1994). Such paradoxical results can be explained by the nature of East Asian development, namely, the remedy of market failure during the launching of new industries. In this phase, massive investment is made prior to the initiation of industrial production. Due to the non-synchronized cost and benefit flows of such investment, the conventional procedure of growth accounting can easily lead to paradoxical results.

3.3   Some Basics about the Catching-up Models

We now focus attention on one economy at a time. Our purpose is to characterize the evolution of the income gap, for economies in the North (that is, among the developed economies), in the South (that is, among those in the pre-development phase) and in the East (that is, the 'emerging economies'). We shall provisionally assume that $R = 1$, so that every economy can exactly catch up with the leading economy. The notations can be greatly simplified by suppressing any subscripts for economy or time for the gap measure, $g = 1 - r$, which is always a positive fraction.

We then plot the gap $g(t)$ against time t in semilog scale and call it 'the economy curve' for convenience. Note that $\log g(t)$ always appears as negative magnitude, below the time axis. Our attention is on the proportional reduction rate of the gap,

$$(dg/dt)/g = d(\log g)/dt.$$

This is just the slope of the *economy curve*. The steeper the curve, the faster is the proportional rate of gap reduction. If the gap is eliminated for a particular period, the economy curve will diverge to negative infinity with a vertical slope. An exponential decay of the gap is represented as a negatively sloped straight line. A concave (convex) economy curve implies an increasing (decreasing) rate of proportional gap reduction. These concepts are illustrated below.

Figure 6.9(a) displays the economy curve for France, as an example of a developed economy. There is a very mild negative slope for the economy curve. By and large, the magnitude of the proportional income gap has not changed much at all for the quarter of a century being studied.

Figure 6.9(b) depicts the positively sloping economy curve for Côte d'Ivoire, which is falling behind relative to America, the leading economy. This is an example of a 'pre-development' economy. In spite of the gradual increase of the per capita real GDP, the income gap widened over the period of study.

Figure 6.9(c) shows four 'emerging economies', Korea and Singapore from Asia and Ireland and Malta from Europe. Over the period studied, all four have managed to narrow the income gap relative to America since each of these economy curves exhibits a general negative trend. For much of this period, up to the very end, the income gaps have been narrowed down at an increasing proportional rate. Only during the Asian financial crisis, do the economy curves of Korea and Singapore acquire a positive slope. Malta is steadily narrowing down the income gap between it and America, at an accelerating rate during the earlier years but at a decelerating rate at the very end. Among these four, Ireland alone maintains an increasing rate of gap reduction throughout the entire period.

To gain more perspective, we display the performance of Japan in Figure 6.9(d). The high growth period of Japan had passed by 1975. This figure shows the gap closing at a decreasing pace during the period shown. In the end, the gap between Japan and America remains at a certain magnitude, in spite of a sequence of seesaw movement. The broken line indicates the overall trend of catching-up. The third-degree polynomial trend line reveals the fact that there is a phase of accelerated growth for Japan, followed by deceleration, while the American growth rate is much more stable.

So far we have selected seven out of the 106 economies for display. From these, it is evident that the catching-up process is determined by three sets of factors: (a) the economy-specific factors; (b) the policy choices; and (c) the phase of the process.

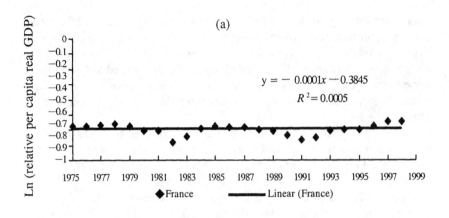

(a)

$$y = -0.0001x - 0.3845$$
$$R^2 = 0.0005$$

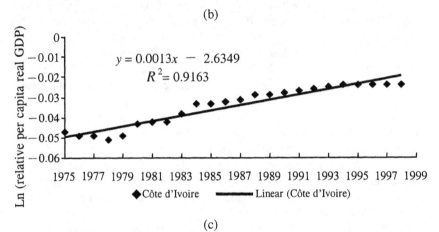

(b)

$$y = 0.0013x - 2.6349$$
$$R^2 = 0.9163$$

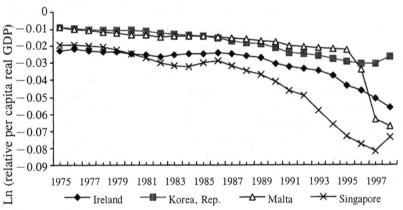

(c)

(d)

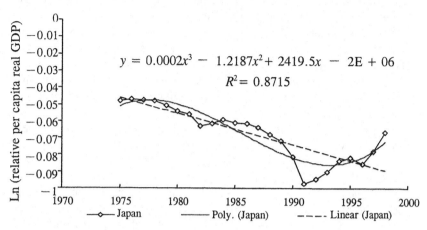

$$y = 0.0002x^3 - 1.2187x^2 + 2419.5x - 2\mathrm{E} + 06$$
$$R^2 = 0.8715$$

Figure 6.9   Gap in semilog

In this exploratory study, we have run 106 economy-specific linear equations regressing the logarithm of the gap against time. In such equations, the constant term is a measure of the average gap for an economy over the period of study, 1975–1998.

In Figure 6.10, we display a scatter diagram plotting the slope coefficients against the constants for those economy-specific equations. The figure requires some careful interpretation. For the 24 years in question, it shows that:

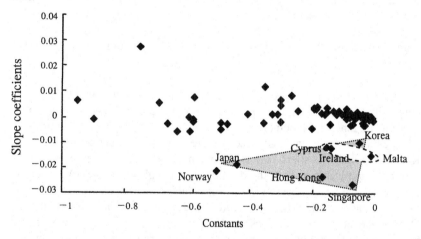

Figure 6.10   Scatter diagram for 106 economies

1. Of all the 106 economies, income gaps were widening (narrowing) for 64 (42) of them, over the period in question. Gap narrowing is not the usual pattern, let alone something automatic.

2. Those economies with the smallest initial gap (and therefore the most negative logarithmic values) correspond to observations near the left border of the figure. These economies are not associated with negative slopes that signify the trend for closing the gap further. This means that none of these 106 economies is catching up with America (the leader) in the near future.

3. Those 64 economies that are falling behind (that is, with positive slopes) have observations above the horizontal axis. The 'center of gravity' of this subset is near the right border. That is to say, their initial gap is very large so that the logarithmic values are negative, also close to 0. In other words, the typical economy that is falling behind is one with an initial gap approaching 1. That is to say, in purchasing power parity (PPP) terms, the values of their per capita GDPs are exceedingly small fractions relative to the American value.

4. In contrast, those 42 economies that are catching up with America have observations below the horizontal axis. Their 'center of gravity' is somewhat away from the right border. That is to say, the typical economy that is catching up is not among those with extremely low real GDP per capita relative to America.

5. In terms of the catching-up performance, the observations on the four East Asian economies have spanned a dotted triangle, and the observation on the three economies at the fringe of European Union (Ireland, Malta and Cyprus) are enclosed in an oval shape in dashed lines. The oval fits into the triangle like a hand into a glove. That is to say, for those who are successful in the catching-up process, similar economic forces seem to outdistance whatever differences might exist in cultural and historical spheres.

The last point is important. The scatter diagram seems to be almost a cloud, justifying the caution of Solow (2000) against cross-country comparisons in general. Nonetheless, for those that are successful in the process of catching-up, one can still describe the process in the manner used by Kuznets (1982). In short, a pattern amenable to research emerges. This pattern is applicable to both the developed economies (the North) and those economies that have somehow 'joined the club' (the East) in distinction to all the rest (the South). After all, Korea is the most recent member of the OECD, the group Solow focuses attention on. The result is an expanding horizon, with some hopeful regularity in the pattern of 'club' expansion.

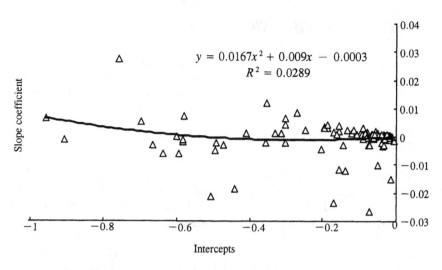

Figure 6.11   Scatter diagram with quadratic trend

With an added parabolic trend line, Figure 6.11 crystalizes points 3 and 4 above. The parabola is convex, with its apex below the horizontal axis. As observed by Lucas (1988) and discussed in Lau and Wan (1994), the poor economies have the least growth. This is presumably because of their limited capacity to exploit the available technological backlog. Rich economies have the greatest ability to learn from others, yet the amount of available technological backlog is minimal. The result is that the mid-income economies have the most impressive record in catching-up.

As a matter of fact, some more may be said. First, the leading economy has the most ability to imitate any near competitor, should the latter establish some local advantage over any limited range of the commodity spectrum. The revival of the American competitiveness against Japan in the last decade in areas such as quality control in auto making is a clear example. Second, as emphasized in Lau and Wan, catching-up is far from a free lunch. Resources must be committed even in the process of emulation. As Kuznets (1982) emphasized, poor economies cannot utilize the huge technological backlog, because there are various constraints blocking their progress. In market economies, investment decisions are usually made by private agents. Among these constraints, coordination failure is a crucial cause. The NIEs manage to have some success, often as a result of fortunate or judicious government action. In this process, long-term, massive investment has been made by either the government or the private sector, in the launching of new industries. See Itoh et al. (1991) and Miyajina et al. (1999).

4   RELATING THE TWO INDICES

We have now shown that the catching-up rate is an intuitive concept with some descriptive power over the empirical data. The concept of TFP has received wide attention in the recent literature, yet its use has also led to rather paradoxical conclusions. The question is, do economies showing strong growth in TFP also have outstanding records in catching up? From the 53 economies that appear in both the study of Young (1994) and our data for the catching-up ratio, we obtain Figure 6.12. Given the staggered period of coverage, one may ask whether the rate of TFP growth during 1970−85 can be a basis for predicting the ability of an economy to catch up for the 1975−98 period. Based upon the scatter diagram of Figure 6.12, the answer is clearly no. In fact, as highlighted by the twin blips in the figure, economies with low TFP growth, like Singapore, Japan and Korea, have reduced their income gap at proportional rates no slower than any other economy. Likewise, three of the four economies with the highest scores in TFPG − Egypt, Pakistan and Congo − have seen their income gap widened rather than reduced.[10]

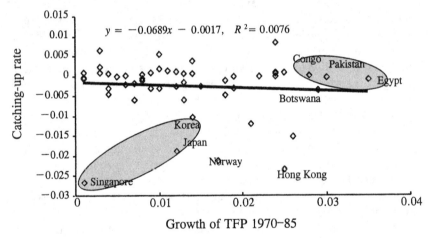

Source: Young (1994).

Figure 6.12   Relating two indices

5   CONCLUDING REMARKS

Economists are presumably interested in the *future* levels of per capita GDP, in real terms, rather than in the *current* figures of per capita GDP, or TFPG, or the rate of proportional gap reduction. *Current* rates of output growth are not heavily relied upon, because such growth rates are expected to vary from time to time. Solow (2000) explained the stand of the neoclassical growth theorists. For a country like America, one should first of all calculate the time path of TFP, and determine the implication of such an estimate for the economy. A separate 'theory of technology' can then be used to forecast the future trend of TFPG. The practitioners of growth accounting usually omit the formal forecasting of the future value of TFPG, as if its current value is assumed to last into the future. When the economy in question is a developing economy, enjoying the fruits of new-found mineral wealth, such an extrapolation is obviously prone to error.

The computation of the current relative rate of income gap reduction is certainly not an end in itself either, because as the past record shows us, this rate can also vary over time. On the other hand, it appears a much more useful intermediate step for research than TFPG. It helps to focus attention on the process of assimilating technology from abroad. This is both a principal link in the causal chain of growth, and is dependent upon policy regimes. For example, the effect of 'openness' should be explored in full. In all these, further study is needed.[11]

According to Young, East Asian high growth is based upon high investment; according to Krugman (1994), the high rate of investment that East Asian economies are engaging in may not be sustainable. Yet ten to 15 years after their period of study, the high performance of East Asian economies remains relatively strong, when the criterion of performance is 'catching-up' rather than the rate of growth, *per se*. The change in performance criterion here carries some importance. In particular, by using the catching-up criterion, it is not expected that any economy (say, Singapore), which is technologically no better than the 'leading economy', can maintain a higher rate of growth than the technological leader, when the gap is largely erased. Incidentally, on this catching-up basis, Japan has performed a good deal better than Korea. Their growth slowing down owes much to the exhaustion of the technological backlog rather than the saturation of capital investment.

APPENDIX 6A

Five Examples of the Search for the Leading Economy

Consider the case with three economies ($N = 3$) over three periods ($T = 3$). The values of per capita real GDP are tabulated below for Example 1. The highest value for any period is marked by an asterisk. In this case, each economy is the one with the highest per capita GDP in a different period. The dominant set is the same as the population of all economies, so that $n = 3 = N$. There is no proper, dominant set.

Example 1	No proper dominant set		
q_{it}	$t = 1$	$t = 2$	$t = 3$
$i = 1$	1	5	9*
$i = 2$	3*	4	7
$i = 3$	2	6*	8

Next, we consider Example 2, with the relevant data tabulated below. In all three periods, the peak value is associated with either economy 1 or economy 2. Again the highest value for any period is marked by an asterisk. In this case, the dominant set is $\{1, 2\}$, with two members, so that $n = 2 < N = 3$. This is a proper subset of the population of all economies. Therefore, we call $\{1, 2\}$ a proper dominant set. However, each member of the proper dominant set fails in some period to rank within the first $n = 2$ places. specifically, economy 1 fails in period 1 and economy 2 fails in periods 2 and 3. In each case, a failure marked by a hash, #. Therefore there is no 'leader' in the population of is economies.

Example 2	No leader in the proper dominant set		
q_{it}	$t = 1$	$t = 2$	$t = 3$
$i = 1$	1#	6*	9*
$i = 2$	3*	4#	7#
$i = 3$	2	5	8

We next consider Example 3, where again the economies 1 and 2 form a proper dominant set, $\{1, 2\}$ with two members. Only economy 3 fails to rank within the first $n = 2$ places. The use of * and # are the same as before. Now economies 1 and 2 rank within $n = 2$ places in every period. A 'leader economy' is marked by a dagger,[†].

Example 3	No single leader		
q_{it}	$t = 1$	$t = 2$	$t = 3$
$i = 1$ [†]	2	5	9*
$i = 2$ [†]	3*	6*	8
$i = 3$	1#	4#	7#

In the next example, again both economies 1 and 2 form a proper dominant set, so that $n = 2 < 3$, but only economy 1 ranks within the first two places every period, so that there is a unique 'leader economy'.

Example 4	Existence of a single leader		
q_{it}	$t = 1$	$t = 2$	$t = 3$
$i = 1$ †	2	5	9*
$i = 2$	3*	6*	7#
$i = 3$	1#	4#	8

Finally in the last of our five examples, we consider the case where the dominant set is a singleton, that is identical to the unique leader economy, namely economy 1.

Example 5	A single leader is the dominant set		
q_{it}	$t = 1$	$t = 2$	$t = 3$
$i = 1$ †	3*	6*	9*
$i = 2$	1#	4#	8#
$i = 3$	2#	5#	7#

ACKNOWLEDGMENTS

The second author is most grateful for the comments of Dr. Simone Clemhout and the helpful assistance from Ms. Andrea Williams-Wan. All remaining errors are the responsibility of the authors.

NOTES

1. See Wan (2001) for more details.
2. An exception is Pack (2001).
3. It is also not clear how an aggregate production will be estimated under growth accounting as the observations come from a sequence generated by a mechanism depicted in Figures 6.5, 6.6, 6.7 and 6.8.
4. The exception is mineral products between 1973 and 1990.
5. These are not yet fully developed.
6. For political reasons, Russia, Germany and Taiwan do not have an unbroken data series over the 24 years. Both Hong Kong and the rest of China are represented.
7. Here an era covers more than one period, as is the usage in geology.
8. Simple logical examples can be constructed to show that the existence of neither the *properly dominant set,* nor an economic *leader* can be guaranteed in all possible worlds. Moreover, the *economic leadership* need not always be unique.

9. What can be said about the United Arab Emirates, Luxembourg and Switzerland will be dealt with later.
10. One might say that ten or 15 years do not represent the long run. How about another ten or 15 years? With due respect, the wait for a 'Congo Miracle' seems increasingly to look like the wait for Godot.
11. The ongoing work of Hong, Lau and Wan explores the effect of exports. For an empirical verification of the bias of the TFPG, see Park and Van (2001).

REFERENCES

Felipe, Jesus (1999), 'Total factor productivity growth in East Asia: a critical survey', *Journal of Development Studies*, **35**, 1–41.

Itoh, Motoshige, Kazuharu Kiyono, Masahiro Okuno-Fujiwara and Kotaro Suzumura (1991), *Economic Analysis of Industrial Policy*, San Diego, CA: Academic Press.

Kim, Jong-Il and Lawrence J. Lau (1994), 'The source of economic growth of the East Asian newly industrialized countries', *Journal of Japanese and International Economics*, **8** (3), 235–71.

Krugman, P. (1979), 'A model of innovation, technology transfer and the world distribution of income', *Journal of Political Economy*, **87** (2), 253–66.

Krugman, P. (1994), 'The myth of Asia's miracle', *Foreign Affairs*, **73** (6), 62–78.

Kuznets, S. (1982), 'Modern economic growth and the less developed countries', in Kwoh-ting Li and Tzong-shian Yu (eds), *Experience and Lessons of Economic Development in Taiwan*, Taipei: Academia Sinica.

Lau, Man-lui and Henry Y. Wan, Jr. (1994), 'On the mechanism of catching-up', *European Economic Review*, **38**, 952–63.

Lucas, Robert E., Jr. (1976), 'Econometric policy evaluation: a critique', *Journal of Monetary Economics*, **2**, Supplement, 19–46.

Lucas, Robert E., Jr. (1988), 'On the mechanics of economic development', *Journal of Monetary Economics*, **22** (1), 3–42.

Lucas, Robert E., Jr. (1993), 'Making a miracle', *Econometrica*, **61**, 257–72.

Miyajima, Hideaki, Takeo Kikkawa and Takashi Hikino (eds) (1999), *Policies for Competition*, New York: Oxford University Press.

Pack, Howard (2001), 'Technological change and growth in East Asia: macro versus micro perspectives', in Joseph E. Stiglitz and Shahid Yusuf (eds), *Rethinking the East Asian Miracle*, New York: Oxford University Press, 95–142.

Park, Ghunsu and Pham Hoang Van (2001), *Technological Change as a Series of Localized Technical Gains: Evidence from Korea, Singapore, and Taiwan*, Working Paper #01–06, University of Missouri, Columbia, MO.

Prebisch, Raul (1959), 'Commercial policy in underdeveloped countries', *American Economic Review, Papers and Proceedings*, **49**, 252–73.

Samuelson, Paul A. and Robert M. Solow (1956), 'A complete capital good model involving heterogeneous capital goods', *Quarterly Journal of Economics*, **70**, 537–62.

Solow, Robert M. (1956), 'A contribution to the theory of economic growth', *Quarterly Journal of Economics*, **70**, 5–94.

Solow, Robert M. (1957), 'Technical change and the aggregate production function', *Review of Economics and Statistics*, **39**, 312–20.

Solow, Robert M. (1966), 'Review of John R. Hicks, Jr., *Capital and Growth*',

American Economic Review, **56,** 1257–60.

Solow, Robert M. (2000), *Growth Theory, An Exposition*, 2nd edn, Oxford: Oxford University Press.

Stern, Joseph J., Ji-hong Kim, Dwight H. Perkins and Jung-ho Yoo (eds) (1995), *Industrialization and the State: The Korean Heavy and Chemical Industry Drive*, Cambridge, MA: Harvard University Press.

Van, Pham, H. and Henry Y. Wan, Jr. (1997), 'Interpreting East Asian growth', in B.S. Jenssen and K.Y. Wong (eds), *Dynamics, Economic Growth and International Trade*, Ann Arbor, MI Michigan University Press, 286–86.

Vernon, Raymond (1966), 'International investment and international trade in the product cycle', *Quarterly Journal of Economics*, **80,** 190–207.

Wan, Henry Y., Jr. (2004), *Economic development in a globalized environment: East Asian evidences*, Norwell MA: Kluwer Academic Publishers.

Young, Alwyn (1994), 'Lessons from the East Asian NICs: a contrarian view', *European Economic Review*, **38** (3–4), 964–73.

References (in Brief Notes)

Aghion, P. and P. Howitt (1998). *Endogenous Growth Theory*. Cambridge, MA M.I.T. Press.

Aw, B.Y., S. Chung and M.J. Roberts (2003). "Productivity, output, and failure: A comparison of Taiwanese and Korean manufacturers", *Economic Journal,* 113(491), F485–510.

Barro, R. and X. Sala-i-Martin (1995). *Economic Growth.* New York: McGrawHill.

Baumol, W.J. (1986) "Productivity growth, convergence and welfare: What the long-run data show", *American Economic Review,* 76, 1072–1085.

Bhagwati, J.N. (2004). *In Defense of Globalization.* New York: Oxford University Press.

Cheng, L.-L. (2001). "Sources of success in uncertain markets: The Taiwanese footwear industry", in Deyo, F. C., R. Doner and E. Hershberg (eds.), *Economic Governance and the Challenge of Flexibillity in East Asia.* New York: Rowman and Littlefield.

Diamond, J.M. (2005). *Collapse: How Societies Choose to Fail or Succeed.* New York: Viking.

Fuller, D.B., A. Akinwande and C.G. Sodini (2005). "Leading, following and cooked goose? Explaining innovation successes and failures in Taiwan's electronics industry", in Berger, S. and R.K. Lester (eds.), *Global Taiwan, Building Competitive Strengths in a New International Economy.* Armonk, NY: ME Sharpe Inc.

Fung, K.C., A. Garcia-Herrero, H. Iizaka and A. Siu (2005). "Hard or soft? Institutional reforms and infrastructure spending as determinants of foreign direct investment in China", *Japanese Economic Review,* 56(4), 408–416.

Hong, W. (2002). *Catch-up and Crisis in Korea.* Cheltenham, UK: Edward Elgar.

Hsing, Y.T. (1998). *Making capitalism in China: The Taiwan Connection.* New York: Oxford University Press.

Jones, L.P. and I. Sakong (1980). *Government, Business and Entrepreneurship: The Korean Case.* Cambridge, MA: Harvard University Press.

Kim, J.I. and L.J. Lau (1994). "The source of economic growth of the East Asian newly industrialized countries", *Journal of the Japanese and International Economies,* 8(3), 235–271.

Kim, L.S. (2000). "Korea's national innovation system in transition", in Kim, L.S. and R.R. Nelson (eds.), *Technology, Learning and Innovation.* Cambridge, UK: Cambridge University Press.

Kojima, K. (1978). *Direct Foreign Investment: A Japanese Model, Multinational Business Operation*. London: Croom Helm.

Komiya, R. (1988). "Introduction", in Komiya, R., M. Okuno and K. Suzumura (eds.), *Industrial Policy of Japan,* translated under the supervision of K. Sato. San Diego, CA: Academic Press.

Kuo, S.W.Y. (1999). "Government policy in the Taiwanese development process: The past 50 years", in Thorbecke, E. and H.Y. Wan, Jr. (eds.), *Taiwan's Development Experience: Roles of Government and Market*. Boston, MA: Kluwer Academic Publishers.

Kuo, W.J. and J.C. Wang (2001). "The dynamics of Taiwan's SMEs: The case of electronics", in Guerrieri, P., S. Iammarino and C. Pietrobelli, (eds.), *The Global Challenge to Industrial Districts: Small and Medium-sized Enterprises in Italy and Taiwan*. Cheltenham, UK: Edward Elgar.

Lee, K.Y. (2000). *From Third World to First: The Singapore Story, 1965–2000*. New York: HarperCollins.

Lin, J.Y. (1995). "The Needham puzzle: Why the industrial revolution did not originate in China", *Economic Development and Cultural Change,* 43(2), 269–292.

Lin, J.Y. (2005). "Viability, economic transition and reflection on neoclassical economics", *Kyklos,* 58(2), 239–264.

McKinnon, R.I. (2004). "Comment" (on "The Korean Economy before and after the Crisis" and "What Caused the Crisis? A post mortem"), in Chung, D.K. and B. Eichengreen (eds.), *The Korean Economy beyond the Crisis*. Cheltenham, UK: Edward Elgar.

Miwa, Y. (1996). *Firms and Industrial Organization in Japan*. New York: New York University Press.

Miyajima, H. (1999) "Regulatory framework in post-war Japan", in Miyajima, H. et al. (eds.), *Policies for Competition*. New York: Oxford University Press.

Mody, A. (1990). "Institutions and dynamic comparative advantage: The electronics industry in South Korea and Taiwan", *Cambridge Journal of Economics,* 14(3), 291–314.

Mokyr, J. (2000). "The industrial revolution and the Netherlands: Why did it not happen?" *De Economist,* 148(4), 503–520.

Morishima, M. (2000). *Japan at a Deadlock*. New York: St. Martin's Press.

Quah, D.T. (1996). "Twin peaks: Growth and convergence in models of distribution dynamics", *Economic Journal,* 106(437), 1045–1055.

Ruttan, V.W. (2001). *Technology, Growth, and Development: An Induced Innovation Perspective*. Oxford: Oxford University Press.

Sachs, J.D. and A. Warner (1995). "Economic reform and the process of global integration", *Brookings Papers on Economic Activity,* 1–118.

Smith, A. (1776). *An Inquiry into the Nature and Causes of the Wealth of Nations.* London: Strahan and Cadell.

Stern, J.J., J.H. Kim, D.H. Perkins and J.H. Yoo (1995). *Industrialization and the State: The Korean Heavy and Chemical Industry Drive.* Cambridge, MA: Harvard University Press.

Sturgeon, T.J. and J.R. Lee (2005). "Industry co-evolution: A comparison of Taiwan and North American electronics contract manufacturers", in Berger, S. and R.K. Lester (eds.), *Global Taiwan, Building Competitive Strengths in a New International Economy.* Armonk, NY: ME Sharpe Inc.

Thorbecke, E. and H.Y. Wan, Jr. (1999a). "Some further thoughts on Taiwan's development prior to the Asian financial crisis and concluding remarks", in Thorbecke, E. and H.Y. Wan, Jr. (eds.), *Taiwan's Development Experience: Roles of Government and Market.* Boston, MA: Kluwer Academic Publishers.

Thorbecke, E. and H.Y. Wan, Jr. (1999b). "Epilogue: How did Taiwan withstand the Asian financial crisis?", in Thorbecke, E. and H.Y. Wan, Jr. (eds.), *Taiwan's Development Experience: Roles of Government and Market.* Boston, MA: Kluwer Academic Publishers.

Wan, H.Y., Jr. (2004). *Economic Development in a Globalized Environment: East Asian Evidences.* Norwell, MA: Kluwer Academic Publishers.

Young, A. (1994). "Lessons from the East Asian NICs: A contrarian view", *European Economic Review*, 38, 964–973.

Young, A. (1995). "The tyranny of numbers: Confronting the statistical realities of the East Asian growth experience", *Quarterly Journal of Economics,* 110(3), 641–680.

Content Index

271

Printed in the United States
By Bookmasters